THE MILITARY IN YOUR BACKYARD

How to Determine the Impact Of Military Spending In Your Community

by Randy Schutt

May 1984

Center for Economic Conversion (CEC)
222 View Street, Suite C
Mountain View, CA 94041
(415) 968–8798

Abstract

This workbook explains in detail how to find out how much military money comes into a community, which companies or bases receive this money, what products or services are purchased, and the effects on the local community. It shows how to determine the number of people who work directly or indirectly for the military and how dependent a community is on military spending. It explains the effects of buildups and cutbacks in the defense budget and how to plan for conversion of military bases and factories to alternative, socially-useful purposes. The workbook has a 20-page annotated bibliography and a 15-page description of peace and social action resource centers which can provide additional information. It contains over forty figures with samples of resource documents, worksheets, and examples of research results.

Copies of this workbook are available from the Center for Economic Conversion (CEC), 222 View Street, Suite C, Mountain View, CA 94041, (415) 968-8798 for $13.00 plus $0.80 tax for California residents plus $1.20 for postage and handling. For a description of the Center for Economic Conversion, see page 153.

About the Principal Author

Randy Schutt has BS and MS degrees in Mechanical Engineering from Stanford University (1977). He has worked as a thermodynamics engineer, policy analyst, systems analyst, programmer, technical writer, and carpenter. He has designed a bread-baking solar oven and has helped construct a solar greenhouse and solar house. For the past seven years, Randy has also been politically active, working with peace, anti-nuclear, and social justice groups and teaching the theory and practice of non-violent direct action and the consensus decision-making process. He is 29 years old and lives in a co-operative house in Menlo Park, California.

Acknowledgements

When we first started working on this workbook, we knew there was a great need for this kind of information because many people had asked us for it over the years. However, we didn't anticipate that several other groups around the country had also recognized the need and had begun to prepare similar materials. As we worked to develop new ways of researching the military industry, we kept discovering these other efforts. None of them had exactly the same focus and as the workbook we hoped to write, but all of them had invaluable information on one or more of the topics we planned to cover.

Fortunately, we have been able to include much of the material generated by these other groups in this workbook, saving us months of researching and writing and enabling us to write a more comprehensive manual. Our thanks go to New York Public Interest Research Center (NYPIRC), Highlander Research and Education Center, Mendocino County Jobs with Peace Coalition, Bay State Center for Economic Conversion (BAYCforEC), National Action for Research on the Military/Industrial Complex (NARMIC), Connecticut Freeze Campaign Economic Conversion Task Force, SANE, Coastsiders for a Nuclear Free Future, and Mobilization for Survival (MfS), for letting us use their materials.

Many individuals helped write, edit, and review the text, provided valuable information on military spending and its local effects, told us of good resources, provided us with access to microcomputer wordprocessors and printers, or provided us with guidance and moral support:

The CEC staff: Michael Closson, Tim Stroshane, and Joel Yudken. Joel originally conceived the idea of the workbook and he and Michael wrote several sections.
CEC consultant: Dave McFadden

Kenneth Bertsch, Bill Bothamley, Louise Bruyn, Tom Conrad, Greg Cross, Beth Cohen DeGrasse, Anne Fitzmaurice, Rebecca Gebhardt, Ed Glennon, Lenny Goldberg, Craig Gordon, Ellen Green, Bill Hartung, Steve Johnson, Marilyn Kjellen-Rogers, Jeff Levin, Don Lipmanson, Ann Markusen and her urban planning class, John Markoff, Diarmuid McGuire, Corwin Nichols, John Raess, Rainbow, John Reuyl, Tom Schlesinger, Eric Segal, Linda Shaw, Lenny Siegel, Clao Styron, Ted Syrett, Bill Vitale, Tom Webster, and Scott Weikart.

We would especially like to thank Sara Boore for the cover graphic and help with paste up and Carol Manahan for the cover and book design.

This book was supported by grants from the Eastman Fund; Tides Foundation; First Presbyterian Church, Palo Alto, CA; California Project; Olive and Henry Mayer; and several individuals who wished to remain anonymous. Special thanks to Joy Marcus and Kit Bricca for their invaluable fundraising efforts. Our gratitude goes to the United Farmworkers of America, AFL-CIO for printing this workbook.

To anyone we may have neglected to mention, our apologies.

iv

Table of Contents

List of Figures

Chapter 1   Introduction

The economic impacts of military spending have a direct effect on the quality of our lives and the health of our communities. Yet very little systematic research has been done on this over the last few decades. We have put together this workbook to provide easy-to-use guidelines and research techniques to help you determine the impact of military spending on your community. It includes step-by-step instructions, information sources, and a list of peace and social action resource centers that can assist you.

Knowledge is power: learning about the military contractors in your area is a way to begin to exert some control over the military industrial complex. This book will enable you to easily and cheaply obtain information on military spending in your community and put it in a useful form. The results can then be used as background information when you:

-- Place an arms control initiative on your local ballot;

-- Request local government support for arms reduction policies in the form of resolutions, etc.;

-- Fight against reductions in vital human services that accompany shifts in the federal budget towards military spending;

-- Fight against specific weapon systems which are produced in your community;

-- Target a specific company in your community for its military work, or its poor environmental, employment, or safety practices;

-- Counter the "job hostage" arguments used to defend continued military spending;

-- Design practical plans for conversion of military industry to socially-useful production;

-- Analyze the local economy for other reasons.

Such research need not wait for an expert. You can do this work by yourself or with other concerned people. Please don't be discouraged by the girth of this book; the results you can obtain by following the fairly simple procedures just in Chapter 2 can be of immediate use to you even if what follows may seem overwhelming.

Finding Information

At first it might seem difficult to get information on military activities in your community. The government classifies immense amounts of information, companies are quite protective of proprietary developments, and employees at defense plants and military bases tend to be conservative and close-mouthed. But it is surprisingly easy to get a good sense of the activities and production in your area.

Military production is a multi-billion dollar industry and, like any large industry, the industrial managers and government contracting agencies must have up-to-date information on what kinds of weapons the government wants, what new research has been done, what new products exist, where it is produced, how much it costs, and how to go about ordering it. Information on all these topics is prepared and disseminated constantly by many groups. The government has information on corporations, occupations, and industries to help in economic planning and forecasting and to regulate business. Specialized trade magazines and marketing services collect this same information to help companies in their marketing and procurement. Much of this information is easily accessible in libraries and from other public sources.

Military bases are like small cities with thousands of residents who all work for the same company. Bases must provide services just like any other city and monitor the activities of their "employees" just like any company. Since they are public facilities, information on their activities is usually available to the public upon request.

Often the difficulty is not in getting information but in sifting through large quantities of it and figuring out how to interpret it. Getting information for a single community (versus for the nation or for a state as a whole) is also usually difficult.

The purpose of this workbook is to help you locate and order the information you need and provide an easy-to-follow methodology to help you interpret it. Some of the techniques used in this book have been developed by researchers at the Center for Economic Conversion (CEC) (formerly the Mid-Peninsula Conversion Project) over the nine years of its existence. Other techniques we have developed in the course of researching this workbook. Still others have been developed by other organizations and individuals around the country.

A Note on Semantics

When talking about the production of military equipment in the United States, the euphemism "defense industry" generally is used. This terminology is widely accepted and almost any other term is confusing. However, "defense" is a misnomer since this equipment is used both for offensive and defensive purposes. It is, however, all "military" equipment, so we prefer this term. But when we talk with librarians and other researchers, we are forced to use "defense industry" so they can understand us. In this manual we have used both the terms "defense industry" and "military production industry" to mean the same thing.

1.A. An Overview of the Workbook

This workbook is intended for use by non-technical people interested in determining the extent and effects of military spending in their community. It should be particularly useful for people living in an area with large amounts of military contracting, like the "Silicon Valley" where we live. But it should also be useful for those in other areas of the country. We have included methods for finding out about military bases and for determining the net tax drain of the military on communities with little or no military contracting.

After researching your community using this workbook, you will know what military activity there is and what products are being made. You should have a good estimate of the percentage of the workforce that makes military products. You may be able to determine the percentage of total wages paid to these workers, the percentage of total sales that goes to military purposes, the number of technical people working for the military, the profits of the companies working on military products compared to those working on civilian products, and other information.

You may learn just how dependent your community is on the military for its economy and employment, that is, its **military dependence.** This information, coupled with the desire of many people to work on socially-useful products instead of military equipment, may spur them to push for conversion to civilian production or at least to make plans for conversion.

Each chapter begins with a description of the kind of information you can obtain with the procedures and resources shown in that chapter. This is followed by the detailed procedure and a detailed description of the various resources you need and their limitations. The figures are collected at the end of each chapter.

Since the descriptions of the resources are sometimes quite long, you may wish to skim quickly over such sections or skip them altogether on your first reading. Then when you decide to order the reports, you can read the descriptions in detail to see which ones are the most useful for you.

Chapter 2 describes various sources of information on the total amount of prime military contracts from the Department of Defense (DoD), the Department of Energy (DoE), and other federal government agencies. With this information you can determine the largest contractors in your area.

Chapter 3 describes how to find out what military products these contractors make.

Chapter 4 tells how to track down information on a particular company and prepare a company profile. This is especially useful for discussion with the employees of the company. This chapter also tells how to research a military base.

Chapter 5 describes how to determine the extent of military employment in your community. This includes employment at military bases and both direct and indirect employment in the military industry. This chapter also discusses the types of occupations in military industry.

Chapter 6 tells you how to determine the impact of military spending on the local economy and local government budgets.

Chapter 7 discusses several measures of military dependency and tells you how to determine how militarily dependent your community is.

Chapter 8 describes some of the effects of military buildups and cutbacks upon your community.

Chapter 9 describes the kind of information you need to plan for conversion of military industry to socially-useful production and how to go about getting it.

Chapter 10 discusses how you can take the research you have done and use it most effectively.

The Reference section lists the references used in this workbook and how to order them as well as additional sources of information. The section called Peace and Social Action Resource Centers and their Publications lists organizations that can help you in your work. There is a List of Abbreviations and three Appendices with information on standard reference books for researching a company, why companies like military contracts, and how to order Congressional Hearing transcripts.

Final note: whenever we introduce a new word or concept we have printed it in **bold** and tried to define it.

1.B. How to Use This Workbook

First, skim through the whole book just to see what it covers and the types of results you might obtain. Note especially the listing of Resource Centers with people who might be able to help you.

If your community has only a few local companies with military contracts, you will be particularly interested in Chapters 4, 6, 8, 9, and 10. If you have a large military base then you'll be interested in Sections 4.F. and 5.A. If there is no military contracting in your community, then Chapter 6 will be of interest.

As you read through each section, examine the samples of references and the examples of data derived from these references. Consider what information would be most useful for your community. You may want to read through Chapter 10: Using the Results of Your Work. Other groups around the country have researched their communities; you may want to order copies of their reports to give you ideas for your own work (see the Resource Center section).

We have tried to make this workbook as easy to understand and use as possible. If the going gets rough, call the people at the various Resource Centers for help. Seek out sympathetic industry insiders to give you detailed briefings on what is going on in your area. Talk to friends, neighbors, and news reporters and before long you will be discussing P-3 Orions and AN-GLK-3As just like the people who build them (oh no!). But please, dear reader, don't give up.

1.C. How to Order Materials

Various resource documents are listed in the References section and the Resource Centers section. The listings include the cost of the reports as of late 1983 or early 1984 and the address for ordering. It is always courteous to include a small donation to cover the cost of documents you get free from peace groups.

Most government documents are available in a Federal Government Depository (library). Ask your local librarian for the nearest one. There are also federal government bookstores located in major cities where you can purchase the more common books and order others. A large public or college library will have many of the other resources including some of the military trade magazines. Resources are easier to find than you might think.

1.D. Who We Are and Our Backyard

The Center for Economic Conversion (CEC) is located in the heart of "Silicon Valley," the Santa Clara Valley located on the peninsula south of San Francisco between the Santa Cruz mountains and San Francisco Bay. Extending from Stanford University (near Palo Alto) south through Mountain View, Sunnyvale, Santa Clara, San Jose, and Gilroy (all in Santa Clara County) and north into Menlo Park, Redwood City, San Carlos, San Mateo, and South San Francisco (in San Mateo County), a large industrial area has developed producing military equipment ranging from guided missiles to electronic warfare devices as well as commercial electronics, computers, and (still some) agriculture.

Because the military industry in the Valley comprises mostly aerospace, tanks, and electronics production, we have found it easiest to locate information in these areas. We may have overlooked some of the better sources on shipbuilding, ammunition production, and other industries outside our direct experience. We would like to learn of any good sources you know or find.

Many of the examples used in this workbook are for the Santa Clara Valley. Generally when we use the term "Santa Clara Valley" we mean the entire area in Santa Clara and San Mateo Counties. This includes a lot of land in the rural areas outside of the valley proper. But since most data is recorded for the counties as a whole, it makes sense for us to look at this entire area.

When we refer to "your community" we mean whatever area you investigate. It might be whole states like New York, a couple of counties like Santa Clara Valley, a particular Congressional District, or a particular city like Amarillo, Texas. The Santa Clara Valley receives a very large injection of prime military contracts -- $ 4 billion in Fiscal Year 1983. If your area (like most) has much smaller amounts, it may make sense for you to focus on a whole state or region.

Standard Metropolitan Statistical Areas (SMSAs)

Information is frequently collected by state and Federal agencies according to counties or Standard Metropolitan Statistical Areas (SMSAs) -- metropolitan areas defined by the Census Bureau (see Figure 1.1). About 170 million people live in the 318 SMSAs in the U.S., or about 75% of the total population [Statistical Abstract of the United States, 1982-83, Table 15]. You can find a list of the SMSAs and their component counties in two Census Bureau reports: Statistical Abstract of the United States and Shipments to Federal Government Agencies.

Santa Clara County comprises one SMSA. This is fortunate since it allows us to compare data compiled in these two ways. San Mateo County is, unfortunately, just a small part of the San Francisco-Oakland SMSA.

Information by city is often useful for talking to city councils or local newspapers (e.g., the Palo Alto Weekly) which have a very local focus. Collecting data by Congressional District (CD) is usually difficult, particularly if the districts have been gerrymandered. You often must get the information for each city and then allocate it to the particular CD. Sometimes even this doesn't work because cities are split into different CDs. In some areas (like Silicon Valley), voters in several Congressional Districts commute each day into other CDs where they work on military products. So a community-wide analysis makes the most sense anyway.

Figure 1.1 A Map of Standard Metropolitan Statistical Areas (SMSAs)

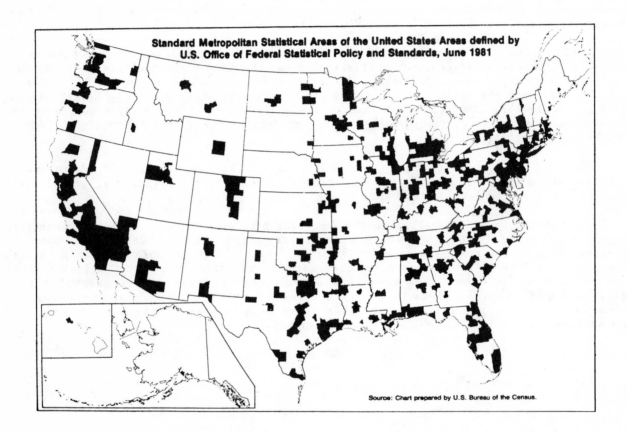

Standard Metropolitan Statistical Areas of the United States Areas defined by
U.S. Office of Federal Statistical Policy and Standards, June 1981

Source: Chart prepared by U.S. Bureau of the Census.

Chapter 2   Miltary Contracts

Most people have no idea how much money is spent to produce military products in their community. We have found that compiling this information and disseminating it has been very useful. This chapter shows you how to find and present this information in a productive way.

Each year the Department of Defense (DoD) contracts with companies around the world to build the equipment and facilities and provide the services necessary for its work. **Prime contractors** are companies that receive money directly from the DoD to perform a specific task. These prime contractors often pay other companies, called **subcontractors**, to do a part of the work. Prime contractors also use part of the money to buy materials and supplies, contract for services (janitorial services for example), and hire consultants. When companies contract with the DoD for a project, they include in their proposal all these costs and a profit.

Sometimes there is confusion about subcontracts. Even though a company only works on a piece of a weapon, it may be working under a <u>prime</u> military contract. A major weapon like the B-1 bomber has many prime contractors, each of which works on some significant piece of the weapon. When these pieces are completed, rather than being sent to the DoD, they are instead sent to one company (Rockwell International in this case) to be assembled into the final product. Rockwell is called the "main" or "principal contractor or the "system manager." Sometimes they are called the "prime" contractor, which is very confusing. We use **"prime contractors"** to mean all the contractors with contracts directly from the DoD.

Each of these prime contractors may subcontract out part of the work on their piece. The DoD keeps track of all the contracts they award, but the subcontracts from these prime contractors are usually only known by the prime and subcontractor.

Note: The figures given in the documents described below are for **contract awards**. When a new weapon system is first conceived, one or more contractors bid for the work. One contractor is then chosen to produce each piece of the weapon and awarded a contract (sometimes more than one contract with different contract numbers). The **contract** is simply an agreement that the contractor will do the work and be paid for it. However, the company does not immediately receive all the money for the contract nor does it have to wait until all the work for the contract has been completed. Rather, the company is paid as each major task is completed (**progress payments**). Each of these payments is called a **contract award**. The contract may extend over many years, but there will usually be several <u>contract</u> <u>awards</u> made each year for a given contract. Also, tasks are typically added, deleted, and changed as the work progresses and the contract is re-written to reflect these changes.

Sections 2.A. through 2.D. below describe how to determine the amount of money the companies in your community and state received in <u>prime</u> contracts from the DoD. Section 2.E. discusses subcontracts. Section 2.F. describes how to determine the amount of money companies received in prime contracts from the Department of Energy (DoE) and NASA.

Section 2.G. discusses how to determine the total amount of military money of all kinds that comes into your community. And Section 2.H. describes some of the sources of the information you need for these calculations.

2.A.   Determining State and County Totals for DoD Prime Contract Awards

The Pentagon prepares a report each year called <u>Prime Contract Awards Over $25,000 by State, County, Contractor, and Place (ST25)</u>. This report comes on microfiche, contains about 1,300 pages worth of data, and costs $60.00. (See Chapter 11 for ordering information. Also see Section 2.H. for more information on the DAMDS system from which this data is derived.) The report lists the prime contractors which received <u>awards</u> over $25,000 during the fiscal year (October 1 to September 30). Note that in fiscal year (FY) 1982, the lower cut-off amount was only $10,000.

The Pentagon report is divided by county with contractors listed alphabetically (see Figure 2.1). The listings for each contractor are then further broken down by each city in which it has a facility that received a prime contract. The total amount of contract awards for each company/city is listed and this amount is itemized by the contracting service (Army, Navy, Air Force, Defense Logistics Agency, and Corps of Engineers). Usually only the total aggregate amount for each company/city is of interest. The total amount awarded in each county is recorded at the end of the listings for the county.

Recording the county and state totals is simple since these numbers are listed. All that is required is to put them in order according to amount and calculate such figures as percentage of state total, percent growth over last year, last year's rank, etc. (see Figure 2.2). Our preparation time for California (58 counties) is about 2 hours.

Note: Microfiche are not quite as easy to use as paper copies, but this should not present much of a problem. Most libraries have microfiche readers and many also have copiers which will print out one page of the microfiche for a dime or so. You might also be able to buy a used reader for $5-10.

2.B.   Determining City Totals for DoD Prime Contract Awards

The DoD lists the same contract information by city in a report called <u>Prime Contract Awards Over $25,000 By State, Place, and Contractor (ST24)</u>. This report also costs $60. The contractors are listed alphabetically under the city (place) in which the facility that will perform the contract is located (see Figure 2.3). With this report you can easily get the total amount of prime contracts by city. [Note that for companies located in unincorporated areas (non-cities), the contracts are listed by the community name for that area. It helps to skim the listings in the <u>by County (ST25)</u> report to find all these community names so you don't overlook any.]

Record the names of all the big contractors (greater than, say, $5 million total). Order the cities and contractors by size of contract (see Figure 2.4). You may also want to count the number of contractors in each city.

With the <u>by Place (ST24)</u> Pentagon report, it is also fairly easy to prepare a list of the prime contract awards for all the cities in the state (see Figure 2.5). For California, this only takes about 2 hours.

If you do not want to spend the money for this additional report, you can use the <u>by County (ST25)</u> report and follow this procedure:

1.   Write the name of each city in the county at the top of a separate piece of paper.

2.   Carefully go through the Pentagon report and record the amounts on the

appropriate city sheet. Record the names of all the big contractors (greater than $5 million total, for example) for future use. To minimize addition errors, leave a space for subtotals at the end of each page's worth of listings (see Figure 2.6).

3. Sum the amounts for each city. Also count the number of contractors for each city. The total for all the cities in the county will invariably be a little different than the county total listed because of recording and addition errors. Don't worry about small differences (less than 0.1% of the total, for example).

4. Put the cities in order by total contract amounts (see Figure 2.4). Order the major contractors in each city by size of contract and list them separately.

Figuring the amounts using this procedure for Santa Clara and San Mateo Counties (730 contractors in 30 cities) takes about 4 hours. Determining the amounts for all the major cities in a big state like California, though, would take a considerable amount of time.

2.C. Determining Your Community's Top DoD Prime Contractors

There is usually great interest in the biggest prime defense contractors. Each year we calculate the Top 100 companies in Santa Clara and San Mateo Counties and publish the Top ?0 in our newspaper, the Plowshare Press. [Note again though, that these are only the companies with the largest amount of prime contract awards -- suppliers of materials and production equipment and companies which work mostly under subcontracts are not considered at all in these reports. Also these are only the awards over $25,000.]

1. Scan through the listings (ST25 or ST24) to get a sense of what kind of companies you have in your area and the size of the contracts they have received. You'll need to decide how many companies to analyze. Those with small amounts of prime contract awards are probably not very important (although a few may have contracts for weapons you want to follow). Choose a cutoff amount that will include a selected number of companies. For the Santa Clara Valley, this amount was about $85,000,000 for the Top 20 and about $650,000 for the Top 100 in FY 1982. Total contracts were $4 billion.

2. For each company on the list with contracts greater than your cutoff amount, prepare a file card. We use 5" by 8" cards (see Figure 2.7). List the parent company name, the division names and the city in which they are listed, the amount of contract awards for each city in the fiscal year, and the total amount for the company. Leave a space for its rank in the community.

3. Now order the cards by total amount. Go through the cards and list the rank in the space you left. Note those companies that garnered a larger or smaller amount of military contracts than last year for further investigation. The information may be displayed in several ways (see Figure 2.8 for one example) depending on how you will use it.

4. Each year, create new cards for companies with large amounts of military contract awards and save the cards for companies that received much less contract dollars than in previous years (they'll probably be back in some later year).

Note: Because of mergers and acquisitions, some companies listed in the Pentagon report are actually owned by other companies. On the other hand, because of divestments or sales to other corporations, some divisions with names that sound like they should be owned by one company are actually independent or owned by another company. This phenomenon is particularly common in the fast-changing electronics industry. Determining who owns whom may be difficult (see Section 4.B. for a suggested methodology). For your first analysis don't worry too much about this -- it is impossible to keep up. As you learn more about these companies and get better sources of information it will be easier. When you do learn which companies are owned by other companies, you can paper-clip the cards of the subsidiaries together and list them along with the parent company.

Preparation time for the Top 20 and Top 100 rankings for the Santa Clara Valley takes about 14 hours. Making up the cards initially for all the companies probably requires another 3-5 hours.

By analyzing the companies in your area each year for several years, you can observe increasing or decreasing dependence on the military. For example, FMC Corporation (formerly Food Machinery Corporation) has undergone a "reverse conversion" in its San Jose facility. Its civilian production of farm machinery has, over the years, been replaced by production of armored military vehicles. This is reflected in FMC's DoD prime contract award amounts (see Figure 2.7).

Be careful though, because a single prime contract award made at the end of one year may carry over into the next year. And military subcontracts (which aren't recorded) may replace prime contracts (which are), making it appear the company is getting less militarily dependent when it is not.

2.D. Determining Your State's Top DoD Prime Contractors

A list of the prime military contractors in your state is particularly useful in talking with state legislators about the need for conversion legislation. Also, most people are interested in how their state fares and who are the major prime contractors. It is often shocking how much money the contractors actually get in prime military contracts. It is also of interest that military contracts are extremely concentrated both geographically and in terms of the number of companies which receive them.

For fiscal year 1982, we calculated the amount of contracts for the Top 32 corporations in California and printed the results for the Top 12. The Top 32 had total contracts greater than $100,000,000 each and the Top 12 had more than $350,000,000. Twelve seemed like a good cutoff because numbers 13 through 15 had significantly lower totals and all three had about the same amount ($270,000,000). The New York Public Interest Research Center (NYPIRC) analyzed and published the Top 25 contractors in Fiscal Year 1981 in New York State. Number 25 had $31 million in prime contracts.

The procedure for calculating the largest prime military contractors for the state is almost exactly the same as for determining the largest county contractors.

1. Scan through the by County (ST25) report and write down a list of who you think are the largest contractors. This way, you can reduce the number of companies that you will research further. This task is usually easy since everyone knows the names of these companies, thousands of people work for them, and their classified ads are some of the largest. But some of the groups of companies owned by conglomerates may slip past you. See the discussion in Section 4.B. about ways to find the more obscure ones. The top contractors usually don't change much from year to year.

2. Prepare a separate sheet of paper for each company with its name at the top (see Figure 2.9). Since all company divisions that start with the same parent name (for example "Hughes") will be listed together in the Pentagon report, you only need one sheet of paper for each. But for divisions of the same conglomerate that have different names, you should prepare a separate page for each. Be sure to make a sheet for every subsidiary of a major company that might be among the top contractors.

3. Alphabetize the papers by company names. This will make it easier to go through the Pentagon report and find the appropriate names.

4. Now go through the by County (ST25) county by county and check for each name you have on a page. List the county name, the name of the company and division as listed, the city, and the total amount of the contracts.

An easier way to find the contract totals for each contractor in the state is possible if you have the Pentagon report <u>Alphabetical</u> <u>Detail</u> <u>of</u> <u>DoD</u> <u>Prime</u> <u>Contractors</u> <u>over</u> <u>$25,000</u> <u>(ST18)</u> printed on 33 separate microfiche (see the detailed description in Section 3.B.). For each contractor this report lists the total contract amount for each city. You can simply look up each contractor, scan down the listings until you find your state, then record the total amount shown under each city (called the "Location Total").

5. Next, combine all the pages of the same conglomerate and add up the totals for the entire corporation. Put these in order and pick out the top ones. Prepare a listing of the top contractors showing the total dollar amount of contracts, the number of facilities, and the major facilities with their location and total amount of contracts (see Figure 2.10).

Determining the Top 32 contractors in California for FY 1982 with the <u>by</u> <u>County</u> <u>(ST25)</u> report took about 20 hours. For other states with fewer counties and less total prime contracts, this task should be much less onerous. California garners about 20% of the total prime military contracts in the country and has 58 counties, many of them with hundreds of contractors. It is easy to make mistakes -- we found that it was best to take it easy, go slowly, check everything twice, and count on re-doing part of the work.

2.E. DoD Subcontracts

All the information available from the DoD is for prime military contracts. However, when a company receives a large prime contract, it frequently farms out **subcontracts** to other companies to do part of the work. Information on subcontractors is generally very difficult to track down.

In 1979 (and only in this year), the DoD required all large contractors (over $500,000) to report their subcontractors. A summary of the state to state flow of money due to subcontracts was published in <u>Geographic</u> <u>Distribution</u> <u>of</u> <u>Subcontract</u> <u>Awards,</u> <u>Fiscal</u> <u>Year</u> <u>1979.</u> For each state the report lists how much money was subcontracted to firms in other states and how much was subcontracted from firms in other states to firms in the state. This report shows, for example, that California prime contractors (with more than $500,000 in total contracts) awarded $881 million to subcontractors in California and $739 million to subcontractors in other states. California subcontractors received $1,276 million from prime contractors in other states. Because it was the first year firms were required to report this information, only about 36.5% of the total amount of subcontracts was actually reported. Since the information is fairly old and incomplete, you should not read too much into these figures.

Subcontracts Awarded by a Prime Contractor

The prime contractor may be willing to give you information about its subcontractors, at least in general terms. If you are interested in a specific contract, you can request a list of subcontracts from the DoD Purchasing Office that granted the contract and oversees the work (see Section 3.C.). You may have to make a request under the provisions of the Freedom of Information Act (see Section 3.B.). Your local Congressional Representative or a sympathetic news reporter might be able to get this information more easily from the prime contractor.

Subcontractors for Specific Weapons

If you are interested in subcontractors for a particular weapon system, you may be able to get the information by writing to the DoD Purchasing Office that oversees that weapon (see Section 3.C.). NARMIC and the Council on Economic Priorities (CEP) have some information on subcontractors for some major weapon systems in their files (see the Resource Center section for the address of these organizations). CEP filed a Freedom of

Information Act (FOIA) request to the Pentagon for information on subcontractors for major weapon systems, but got very little new information.

Aviation Week and Space Technology magazine lists the major contractors for most aerospace equipment in one of its issues each year (see the References section). The advertisements in Aviation Week are also a good source. For example, the November 28, 1983 issue had a special 60-page B-1 bomber advertising supplement with a different prime contractor or subcontractor on each page.

The Wall Street Journal lists many of the larger contracts awarded each day based on DoD press releases. These listings are indexed in the Journal Index available in most libraries. These announcements sometimes include large subcontracts. Electronic News also carries large awards for electronic equipment.

If the weapon system has been criticized and may be deleted from the DoD budget (like the B-1 bomber in 1977 and the MX in 1983), Pentagon officials and prime contractors may compile a list of all the subcontractors and their locations to present to Congressmembers to convince them that this project will create jobs in their Congressional district. For example, since 1970, there have been numerous articles in Aviation Week listing all the major subcontractors, their locations, and the part of the bomber they were scheduled to build.

An Individual Subcontractor Company

When you focus on one subcontractor, it is much more difficult to learn which companies award it subcontracts and the work it performs. We learned from an ex-employee at Raychem Corporation in Menlo Park, California that much of its work is military subcontracting of mil-spec (meets military specifications) wiring. It is a major prime contractor, but apparently prime contracts only represent a fraction of its military work. Raychem's annual report and 10-K report hardly mention this work. (See Section 4.D. for more on these company reports.)

If the company won't tell you what or how much they produce, sympathetic employees or reporters may be the only good sources of information. But they may know a lot.

Researchers at the Council on Economic Priorities filed a Freedom of Information request and received the detailed breakdown of subcontract awards by the 13 largest prime contractors in 1979. Unfortunately, this was the only year in which this data was available. CEP analyzed this information for Hewlett-Packard Corporation and discovered that these 13 contractors gave $7.6 million in subcontracts to H-P nationwide ($3.3 million in the Santa Clara Valley). H-P received only $85.8 million in prime contracts in 1979 nationwide ($33.8 million in Santa Clara Valley). Subcontracts from these 13 prime contractors thus represented a sizeable amount of the military money H-P received that year.

Recommendations

Ferreting out subcontracts is a very difficult task. We recommend that you first try calling the prime or subcontractor. Then, if this fails, ask your Congressional Representative to request the information from the company or the DoD. Point out that the DoD did collect this information in 1979, but stopped. Encourage your Congressmember to pressure the DoD to collect it again.

2.F. Prime Military Contracts from DoE and NASA

Department of Energy (DoE)

The Department of Energy (DoE) is responsible for the research, development, testing, and production of all the United States' nuclear warheads, the production of all the nuclear material (uranium, plutonium, heavy water, etc.) necessary for these warheads, and disposal of all the nuclear waste from this production. The table below shows that more than half of the FY 1985 DoE budget goes to "defense activities" (as defined by the DoE). Half of the budget seems like a lot, but this category of "defense activities" doesn't even cover all the military spending: it doesn't include the weapons-related activities in such categories as Nuclear Waste Disposal Activities, Direct Energy Production, General Science, Support Activities, and Research and Development of Magnetic Fusion.

DoE Expenditures for "Defense Activities"

(Thousands of Dollars)

Fiscal Year	Total Budget	Defense Activities	Percent Defense Activities
1980	$ 11,375,000	$ 3,008,000	26%
1981	12,208,000	3,673,000	30
1982	13,809,000	4,905,000	36
1983	12,835,000	5,704,000	44
1984 (estimate)	12,633,000	6,718,000	53
1985 (request)	15,095,000	7,806,000	52

[Quoted in The Economic Consequences of a Nuclear Weapons Freeze (Council on Economic Priorities) based on the Department of Energy Congressional Budget Request FY 1985.]

The bulk of this money goes to a few government-owned contractor-operated (GOCO) facilities. A list of these research and production sites for nuclear warheads can be found in The Nuclear Weapons Book [p. 56, Investor Responsibility Research Center]. The list includes the private contractor that operates the facility and the number of employees. A summary listing of these facilities is shown in The Freeze Economy [Mid-Peninsula Conversion Project].

You can get a free computer printout of all the DoE contracts for your state from:

Robert F. Warren, Director
Procurement Management Systems and Analysis Division
Procurement and Assistance Management Directorate
Department of Energy
Washington, DC 20585

For further information on the data, contact Rosemary Goldberg in that office at (202) 252-4105.

Figure 2.11 shows an example of a DoE contract listing for FY 1983 for California (approximately 500 contracts total). Contractors are listed alphabetically. If the two letters in the middle of the contract number (AWARD BIN) are DP then the contract is for a Defense Program. NE stands for Nuclear Energy.

NASA

Since the end of the manned space projects (Mercury, Gemini, and Apollo) and cutbacks in the planetary exploration programs, the National Aeronautics and Space Administration (NASA) has spent more of its resources on military satellites and other military-related work.

A General Accounting Office (GAO) report, "Analysis of NASA's FY 1983 Budget Request for Research and Development to Determine the Amount that Supports DoD's Programs," (MASAD-82-33, Apr. 26, 1982) found that 20.5% of NASA's R&D budget is for military work in support of DoD programs. Another 7.7% of the R&D budget supported both DoD and civil programs. The amount of the total $6.613 billion NASA budget they found went for support of the DoD was 16.5%.

The report also showed that 31% of the FY 1983 NASA budget for the space shuttle is in direct support of DoD requirements. Of the first 44 operational shuttle flights through 1986, 13 will be flown solely for the U.S. armed forces. Through 1994, nearly half the 234 shuttle missions will be flown exclusively for the military. And some of the cargo carried by the space shuttle on the "commercial" flights is also military-related.

A good source of information on military space programs is Aerospace Facts and Figures ($10) published by the Aerospace Industries Association of America, Inc. This report includes a listing of the 60 largest NASA contractors, the total amount of their contract awards, and other general information on the aerospace industry. The NASA Annual Procurement Report is free and has much of the same information.

The DMS and GDP contract listings (see Section 3.B.) include NASA military contracts.

2.G. Total "National Defense" Spending in a County or City in FY 1980

This section describes how to determine the total amount of money that came into a County or City in FY 1980 for "national defense" (defined below). Unfortunately, no easy source of equivalent data is available for any year after 1980. But the 1980 figures should give you some idea of all the different agencies that spend military money in your area.

Military spending for a county or city can be easily determined using the Geographic Distribution of Federal Funds (GDFF). This publication has one volume for each state and lists federal spending by category in each county. Unfortunately, its publication was discontinued by the Reagan Administration (which raised a controversy in itself), so Fiscal Year 1980 is the last year for which it is available. FY 1980 ran from October 1, 1979 to September 30, 1980.

"National defense" spending according to GDFF consists of the Department of Defense (DoD), defense atomic energy activities in the Department of Energy (DoE), plus three small defense-related activities: Selective Service (in 1980, the remnants of the draft), the Federal Emergency Management Agency's (FEMA) work on civil defense plans, and the stockpiling of strategic materials by the General Services Administration. In 1980, the budget for national defense was $135.9 billion, $132.8 billion for the DoD, $2.9 billion for defense atomic energy activities, and over $100 million for defense related activities.

To determine national defense spending in your county or city:

(1) DoD Spending: Turn to the section in GDFF for your state covering the county or city you want to study. Spending is given for each federal department followed by other federal agencies. Spending for the Department of Defense is broken down into at most 11 categories (if no spending exists for a category in a county or city it won't appear). Figure 2.12 shows part of the listings for Santa Clara County, California including the DoD (and DoE) categories. Add the categories together into subtotals for personnel and prime contracts:

Subtotal	Category
Personnel	Civilian Pay
	Military Active Duty Pay
	Military Reserve and National Guard Pay
	Military Retired Pay
Prime contracts	Civil Functions Prime Contracts
	Military Prime Construction Contracts
	Military Prime RDTE Contracts
	Military Prime Service Contracts
	Military Prime Supply Contracts
	Prime Contracts less than $10,000
	Military Construction, Army National Guard
	(usually negligible)

Personnel and contracts are the two basic categories of DoD spending. They tell you if military bases or military procurement (of weapons, other products, and services) are more important in your county or city.

(2) Defense Atomic Energy: Defense atomic energy activities funds the development and production of nuclear weapons and materials, and reactors for nuclear-powered ships. Examine DoE spending in your county for any of the following programs:

Defense Nuclear Waste -- Energy Technology
Inertial Confinement Fusion -- Defense Programs
Naval Reactors -- Energy Technology
Nuclear Materials Production -- Defense Program
Nuclear Materials Security and Safeguards -- Defense Programs
Security Investigations -- Defense Programs
Verification and Control Technology -- Defense Programs
Weapons Activities -- Defense Programs

(3) Defense-Related Activities: There will probably be no spending for defense-related activities in your county. The GDFF lists only Selective Service and all of its spending was probably in Washington, D.C. in 1980. This can be checked by looking for the agency after spending for departments of the government is listed.

(4) Total: Add up the spending in the three categories. This is the national defense spending in your county for FY 1980.

Example: Monroe County, NY -- 1980 National Defense Spending

DoD Personnel	$ 22 million
DoD Contracts	78 million
DoD Total	100 million
Defense atomic energy	7 million
Defense related activities	--
TOTAL	$ 107 million

2.H. Sources of Information

The Defense Acquisition Management Data System (DAMDS)

Most of the reports used in this chapter are based on the DoD's Defense Acquisition Management Data System (DAMDS). This computer database file contains a coded entry for every DoD procurement (contract award) over $25,000. These files are available on microfiche and paper. (See the Reference Section on Prime Contract Data for a list of the most useful ones. Also see the discussion in Section 3.B. and Figure 3.3). The entries have information similar to that recorded in the FPDS system (see below), but also include a code for the weapon system on which the work will be performed.

Approximately 2% of the total amount of procurements are represented by contract awards between $10,000 and $25,000 and probably a comparable percentage are represented by awards under $10,000. The 400,000 awards listed in DAMDS thus represent the bulk of the total award amount.

The Federal Procurement Data System (FPDS)

The Federal Procurement Data System (FPDS), maintained by the Office of Management and Budget (OMB), has government-wide procurement information for fiscal years 1979 through the present. The FPDS master computer file contains detailed data regarding the procurement actions of 60 Federal agencies.

The system can provide a wide variety of information about Federal procurements in a format similar to DAMDS (the DoD originally set up FPDS too). It contains 24 data elements, including the name of the agency that awarded the contract, the contract number including order and/or modification number, the purchasing office and address, the date of the award, the principal place of performance, the dollars obligated, the principal product or service, and the name and address of the contractor.

A report is published each quarter (Federal Procurement Data System Standard Report) that examines the data from a variety of perspectives. This report is free if you request it in writing. Unfortunately, the data is summarized only for the nation as a whole and for all programs by state.

The FPDC also produces reports specifically tailored to individual information requirements. These are available for the cost of writing the computer programs to print out the data. A typical special report covering one year's worth of data costs between $150 and $250. This is available either on computer magnetic tape or paper.

For more information on this system, contact:

Federal Procurement Data Center
4040 N. Fairfax Drive
Suite 900
Arlington, VA 22003
(703) 235-1326

Figure 2.1 A Sample Page from Prime Contract Awards by State, County, Contractor, and Place (ST25) (Fiscal Year 1982)

PRIME-CONTRACTS BY STATE, COUNTY, CONTRACTOR, AND CITY - FY 1982

STATE	COUNTY	CONTRACTOR	CITY	AGGREGATE	ARMY	NAVY	AIR FORCE
						(DOLLARS IN THOUSANDS)	
CALIF	SANTA CLARA	VARIAN ASSOCIATES	LOS ALTOS	21			21
CALIF	SANTA CLARA	VARIAN ASSOCIATES	MOUNTAIN VIEW	13			13
CALIF	SANTA CLARA	VARIAN ASSOCIATES	PALO ALTO	89,090	17,475	20,355	47,507
CALIF	SANTA CLARA	VARIAN ASSOCIATES	SANTA CLARA	4,206	2,210	1,399	450
CALIF	SANTA CLARA	VARIAN ASSOCIATES	SUNNYVALE	33		33	
CALIF	SANTA CLARA	VARIAN DATA MACHINES	PALO ALTO	74		18	56
CALIF	SANTA CLARA	VARIAN GRAPHICS	PALO ALTO	47	47		
CALIF	SANTA CLARA	VECTEL CORP	PALO ALTO	21		21	
CALIF	SANTA CLARA	VELCON FILTERS INC	SAN JOSE	111			
CALIF	SANTA CLARA	VELONEX	SANTA CLARA	23		23	
CALIF	SANTA CLARA	VEN TEL INC	SANTA CLARA	106			106
CALIF	SANTA CLARA	VENATOR SYSTEMS INC	SAN JOSE	20	20		
CALIF	SANTA CLARA	VERSATEC INC	CUPERTINO	13	13		
CALIF	SANTA CLARA	VERSATEC INC	SANTA CLARA	797	321	340	136
CALIF	SANTA CLARA	VICOM SYSTEMS INC	SAN JOSE	205	140	65	
CALIF	SANTA CLARA	VIDEOMEDIA SED	SUNNYVALE	295	295		
CALIF	SANTA CLARA	VINDICATOR CORP	SUNNYVALE	2,150		2,081	69
CALIF	SANTA CLARA	VISUAL INSTRUMENTATION CORP	CAMPBELL	62			62
CALIF	SANTA CLARA	VITALOG CORP	PALO ALTO	17	17		
CALIF	SANTA CLARA	VOLT TECHNICAL CO	MOUNTAIN VIEW	17		17	
CALIF	SANTA CLARA	WANG LABORATORIES INC	SANTA CLARA	32			32
CALIF	SANTA CLARA	WANG LABORATORIES INC	SUNNYVALE	87			87
CALIF	SANTA CLARA	WARREN COUNTY ELECTRIC SUPPL	MOUNTAIN VIEW	21			
CALIF	SANTA CLARA	WARREN COUNTY ELECTRIC SUPPL	SANTA CLARA	24			
CALIF	SANTA CLARA	WATKINS JOHNSON CO	PALO ALTO	6,793	188	3,710	2,435
CALIF	SANTA CLARA	WATKINS JOHNSON CO	SAN JOSE	16,766	1,718	9,209	5,839
CALIF	SANTA CLARA	WESS DEL MACHINE & ENGINEERI	SANTA CLARA	19			
CALIF	SANTA CLARA	WESTERN MICROWAVE LAB INC	SUNNYVALE	76	31		45
CALIF	SANTA CLARA	WESTINGHOUSE ELECTRIC CORP	SUNNYVALE	95,135	487	71,119	23,529
CALIF	SANTA CLARA	WILLIAMS ELECTRIC CO	MOFFETT FIELD	962		962	
CALIF	SANTA CLARA	WILTRON CO	MOUNTAIN VIEW	486	108	248	130
CALIF	SANTA CLARA	WORLD WIDE ADHESIVE TAPES	MILPITAS	17		17	
CALIF	SANTA CLARA	WYLE DISTRIBUTION GROUP	SANTA CLARA	44	20	24	
CALIF	SANTA CLARA	XEBEC SYSTEMS INC	SUNNYVALE	32		32	
CALIF	SANTA CLARA	XEROX CORP	PALO ALTO	361		313	
CALIF	SANTA CLARA	XEROX CORP	SANTA CLARA	56			56
CALIF	SANTA CLARA	XERTEX CORP	SANTA CLARA	16			16
CALIF	SANTA CLARA	XIDEX CORP	SUNNYVALE	492	98	190	84
CALIF	SANTA CLARA	XONICS INC	SUNNYVALE	23			
CALIF	SANTA CLARA	XYNETICS INC	SANTA CLARA	73	49		24
CALIF	SANTA CLARA	YICK ELECTRIC CO INC	MOFFETT FIELD	430		430	
CALIF	SANTA CLARA	YIG & TEK CORP	SUNNYVALE	102		102	
CALIF	SANTA CLARA	ZAMBRE CO INC	MOUNTAIN VIEW	18			
CALIF	SANTA CLARA	ZENTEC CORP	SANTA CLARA	97	97		
CALIF	SANTA CLARA	ZETA LABORATORIES INC	SANTA CLARA	717	199	211	307
CALIF	SANTA CLARA	ZEUS COMPONENTS INC	MOUNTAIN VIEW	96			
CALIF	SANTA CLARA	ZINCO GENERAL CONTRACTOR INC	SAN JOSE	36			
		TOTAL COUNTY		3,888,160	1,331,279	1,821,032	697,089
CALIF	SANTA CRUZ	A S I DRAPERIES	SANTA CRUZ	72			72
CALIF	SANTA CRUZ	ALLIED ELECTRONICS CORP	SANTA CRUZ	18		18	

Page 18

Figure 2.2   Department of Defense Prime Contract Awards in California by County -- FY 1982

Total United States = $ 110,660,000,000

Total California   =   22,684,547,000 = 20.5% of the U.S. total

COUNTY	AMOUNT	% of Total	Growth Over Last Year
Los Angeles	$ 10,632,081,000	46.9%	42.2%
Santa Clara	3,888,160,000	17.1	32.0
Orange	2,692,088,000	11.9	32.1
San Diego	1,583,599,000	7.0	30.4
Santa Barbara	764,282,000	3.4	21.1
Alameda	449,766,000	2.0	21.3
Ventura	434,070,000	1.9	61.0
San Bernardino	413,285,000	1.8	44.6
Sacramento	328,987,000	1.3	32.7
San Francisco	293,639,000	1.3	21.8
Solano	281,974,000	1.2	30.5
San Mateo	185,036,000	0.8	8.4
Kern	128,335,000	0.6	-0.1
Rest of State	609,245,000	2.7	34.8
TOTAL STATE	$ 22,684,547,000	100.1%	35.8%

Figure 2.3 A Sample Page from Prime Contract Awards by State, Place, and Contractor (ST24) (Fiscal Year 1982)"

PRIME-CONTRACTS BY STATE, CITY, AND CONTRACTOR - (SEP 81 - SEP 82)

CONTRACTOR	CITY	STATE	AGGREGATE ($000)	ARMY	NAVY	AIR FORCE
					(DOLLARS IN THOUSANDS)	
PIONEER STANDARD ELECTRONICS	MOUNTAIN VIEW	CALIFORNIA	15			
PRECISION DATA INC	MOUNTAIN VIEW	CALIFORNIA	3,219		3,082	42
QUANTA RAY INC	MOUNTAIN VIEW	CALIFORNIA	928	441	221	266
R C A CORP	MOUNTAIN VIEW	CALIFORNIA	19	19		
RAYTHEON CO	MOUNTAIN VIEW	CALIFORNIA	624		25	
RECORTEC INC	MOUNTAIN VIEW	CALIFORNIA	46	23		23
ROBIN MATERIALS INC	MOUNTAIN VIEW	CALIFORNIA	77		77	
ROHR INDUSTRIES INC	MOUNTAIN VIEW	CALIFORNIA	13			13
SCHONBERG RADIATION CORP	MOUNTAIN VIEW	CALIFORNIA	40		40	
SCIENTIFIC MICRO SYSTEMS INC	MOUNTAIN VIEW	CALIFORNIA	34	34		
SEMTEX INDUSTRIAL CORP	MOUNTAIN VIEW	CALIFORNIA	41			
SMITHKLINE BECKMAN CORP	MOUNTAIN VIEW	CALIFORNIA	207	66		141
SPACE DESIGN INC	MOUNTAIN VIEW	CALIFORNIA	25			25
SPECTRA PHYSICS INC	MOUNTAIN VIEW	CALIFORNIA	438	139	157	142
SPERRY CORP	MOUNTAIN VIEW	CALIFORNIA	37	37		
STOESSER TOOL & DIE CO	MOUNTAIN VIEW	CALIFORNIA	17		17	
SUMMIT INDUSTRIES INC	MOUNTAIN VIEW	CALIFORNIA	58	22		
T R W INC	MOUNTAIN VIEW	CALIFORNIA	1,132		1,132	
TECHNOLOGY FOR COMMUNICATIONS INT	MOUNTAIN VIEW	CALIFORNIA	607	74		453
TELEDYNE INC	MOUNTAIN VIEW	CALIFORNIA	34			
TELEDYNE MICROWAVE	MOUNTAIN VIEW	CALIFORNIA	3,286	45	69	3,173
TELEDYNE SEMICONDUCTOR	MOUNTAIN VIEW	CALIFORNIA	11			
TELEVISION ASSOCIATES INC	MOUNTAIN VIEW	CALIFORNIA	76	76		
VALLEY OIL CO	MOUNTAIN VIEW	CALIFORNIA	40			
VARIAN ASSOCIATES	MOUNTAIN VIEW	CALIFORNIA	13			13
VOLT TECHNICAL CO	MOUNTAIN VIEW	CALIFORNIA	17		17	
WARREN COUNTY ELECTRIC SUPPLY INC	MOUNTAIN VIEW	CALIFORNIA	21			
WILTRON CO	MOUNTAIN VIEW	CALIFORNIA	486	108	248	130
ZAMBRE CO INC	MOUNTAIN VIEW	CALIFORNIA	18			
ZEUS COMPONENTS INC	MOUNTAIN VIEW	CALIFORNIA	96			
			254,438	51,791	164,120	34,044
ECONOSPECT CORP	NAPA	CALIFORNIA	11		11	
NOVA PIPING SYSTEMS INC	NAPA	CALIFORNIA	12		12	
SEELER ENTERPRISE INC	NAPA	CALIFORNIA	11		11	
			34		34	
A & E INDUSTRIES INC	NATIONAL CITY	CALIFORNIA	4,828		4,828	
A S W CORP	NATIONAL CITY	CALIFORNIA	73		73	
AABLE MACHINE TOOL REBUILDING CO	NATIONAL CITY	CALIFORNIA	67		67	
ASPEN LUMBER CO	NATIONAL CITY	CALIFORNIA	13		13	
ATKINSON GUY F CO	NATIONAL CITY	CALIFORNIA	20,846		20,846	
ATKINSON MARINE	NATIONAL CITY	CALIFORNIA	479		479	
BAY CITY MARINE INC	NATIONAL CITY	CALIFORNIA	13,969		11,953	2,016
BRAND NAME CONTRACTOR	NATIONAL CITY	CALIFORNIA	859	859		
C P C INTERNATIONAL INC	NATIONAL CITY	CALIFORNIA	930		290	640
CARY K SALES CO	NATIONAL CITY	CALIFORNIA	14		14	
COASTAL RIGGING	NATIONAL CITY	CALIFORNIA	29		29	
COMMERCIAL SERVICE REPAIR	NATIONAL CITY	CALIFORNIA	21		21	
DUNN LEE SMITH & ASSOCIATES	NATIONAL CITY	CALIFORNIA	13		13	
ELECTRO INDUSTRIES	NATIONAL CITY	CALIFORNIA	14		14	

Page 20

Figure 2.4 Department of Defense Prime Contract Awards by City
in Santa Clara County, California -- FY 1982

CITY	AMOUNT	Number of Contractors	Major Contractors (over $5 Million)	Amount
Sunnyvale	$ 1,989,503,000	166	Lockheed	$ 1,470,310,000
			Ford Aerospace	103,403,000
			Westinghouse	95,135,000
			ESL	84,487,000
			ITEK	69,792,000
			United Technologies	35,457,000
			California Microwave	13,755,000
			Stanford Telecommunications	9,631,000
			Argosystems	7,091,000
			Singer	6,770,000
			Control Data	6,132,000
			Eaton	6,101,000
			BR Communications	5,598,000
			Dickman Builders	5,538,000
			General Electric	5,145,000
			Litton	5,002,000
			All Others	60,156,000
San Jose	1,219,499,000	112	FMC	1,115,561,000
			Kaiser	48,754,000
			Watkins-Johnson	16,766,000
			Durham Meat Co.	8,566,000
			Electronic Support	5,537,000
			All Others	24,315,000
Palo Alto	323,027,000	64	Ford Aerospace	132,472,000
			Varian Associates	89,090,000
			Lockheed	36,781,000
			Teledyne MEC	21,039,000
			Hewlett-Packard	12,677,000
			Watkins-Johnson	6,793,000
			Systems Control	6,447,000
			Syntex & Syva	6,181,000
			All Others	11,547,000
Mountain View	254,438,000	87	GTE	214,958,000
			Hewlett-Packard	7,680,000
			Acurex	5,638,000
			All Others	26,162,000
Santa Clara	52,886,000	115	Hewlett-Packard	9,263,000
			Applied Research	6,186,000
			Avantek	6,055,000
			ESD	5,232,000
			All Others	26,150,000
Stanford	24,049,000	6	Stanford University	23,454,000
			All Others	595,000

Figure 2.5 The Cities of California with the Largest Amounts
of DoD Prime Contract Awards in FY 1982

Rank	City	Amount	% of CA
1	Sunnyvale	$ 1,989,503,000	8.8
2	Los Angeles	1,894,153,000	8.3
3	San Diego	1,315,327,000	5.8
4	El Segundo	1,247,694,000	5.5
5	San Jose	1,219,499,000	5.4
6	Pomona	991,614,000	4.4
7	Fullerton	774,510,000	3.4
8	Burbank	693,973,000	3.1
9	Culver City	677,234,000	3.0
10	Anaheim	658,979,000	2.9
11	Hawthorne	552,238,000	2.4
12	Canoga Park	548,251,000	2.4
13	Irvine	507,955,000	2.2
14	Long Beach	499,663,000	2.2
15	Redondo Beach	483,689,000	2.1
16	Torrance	413,310,000	1.8
17	Vandenberg AFB	370,386,000	1.6
18	Goleta	325,211,000	1.4
19	Palo Alto	323,027,000	1.4
20	Oakland	304,650,000	1.3
21	San Francisco	292,966,000	
22	San Pedro	266,565,000	
23	Mountain View	254,438,000	
24	Woodland Hills	253,842,000	
25	Sacramento	251,829,000	
26	Carson	250,465,000	
27	Huntington Beach	235,684,000	
28	Downey	226,021,000	
29	Van Nuys	219,821,000	
30	Newport Beach	216,988,000	
31	Richmond	212,877,000	
32	Azusa	208,816,000	
33	Benicia	208,671,000	
	Rest of California	3,776,698,000	16.6%
	Total California	$ 22,684,547,000	100.0%

Top	Cities have	of California and	of U.S Total
5	33.8%		6.9%
10	50.5%		10.4
15	62.0%		12.7
20	69.6		14.3
25	75.4		15.5
30	80.5		16.5

Figure 2.6 An Example of a Worksheet Used to Determine Total Prime
Contract Awards by City

	11	15	69
32	81	165	34
1,803	30	15	14
308	5,537 *Electronic Support*	30	14
20	155	72	250
47	75	777	381
32	20	69	111
2,242	51	*Page 8* 1,143	20
27	1,?561 *FMC*	15	205
13	18	11	16,766 *Watkins Johnson*
22	38	25	36
204	32	45	17,138
12	126	131	
Page 2 278	10	436	
1,486	333	58	Total = $1,219,336,000
19	64	11	
310	*Page 5* 1,122,147	10	
436	254	742	
23	30	13	
21	61	10	San Jose
11	410	14	FY 1982
18	69	175	
132	42	133	
403	800	17	
14	34	100	
101	1,700	462	
2,979	1,590	10	
270	569	11	
25	14	139	
109	38	146	
46	48,742 *Kaiser*	65	
74	12	10	
583	-191	21	
3,005	302	18	
91	113	12	
8,566 *Durham Meat*	25	905	
86	13	*Page 11* 1,337	
4,410	51,227		
295			
17,560			

Figure 2.7 Examples of Cards Used to Record Prime Contract Data for a Company

Lockheed

Fiscal Year	1975	1976	1977	1978	1979
Santa Clara Valley Rank	1	1	1	1	1
Total Contracts ($000)	885,821	882,979	918,613	1,175,564	1,121,726
L. Aircraft, Palo Alto	338	441	93	98	98
L. Aircraft, Sunnyvale	2,902	4,565	8,806	2,628	1,204
L. Missiles & Space, Palo Alto	4,738	6,992	8,200	8,699	7,968
L. Missiles & Space, Sunnyvale	877,843	870,981	901,514	1,164,139	1,112,017
L. Missiles & Space, Mountain View					439

Fiscal Year	1980	1981	1982	1983	1984
SCV Rank	1	1	1	1	
Total Awards ($000)	1,142,709	1,216,622	1,507,739	1,543,623	
L. Corp., Los Gatos		17	20	100	
L. Corp., Sunnyvale	52,257	45,115	71,101	91,292	
L. Corp., Palo Alto	399	75	628	375	
L. Missiles & Space, Sunnyvale	1,079,020	1,154,117	1,399,209	1,400,387	
L. Missiles & Space, Palo Alto	11,073	17,298	36,781	51,441	
L. Corp., San Jose				28	

FMC Corporation

Fiscal Year	1975	1976	1977	1978	1979
Santa Clara Valley Rank	3	2	2	2	2
Total Contract Awards ($000)	93,878	180,652	143,181	236,870	182,392
San Jose	90,106	176,586	140,348	232,354	180,535
Santa Clara	3,772	4,066	2,833	4,516	1,757

FY	1980	1981	1982	1983	1984
SCV Rank	2	2	2	2	
Total Contract Awards ($000)	486,221	727,832	1,116,965	933,542	
San Jose	480,268	721,568	1,115,561	933,726	
Santa Clara	5,953	6,264	1,404	− 184	

Page 24

Figure 2.8   Santa Clara Valley Top 20 Companies in Prime DoD Contract Awards
-- FY 1982 (October 1, 1981 to September 30, 1982)

Page 1 of 2

COMPANY	LOCATION AMOUNT	TOTAL AMOUNT	Rank in 1981	Growth Over 1981
1. LOCKHEED		$ 1,507,739,000	1.	23.9%
Lockheed Missiles and Space, Sunnyvale	1,399,209,000			
Lockheed Missiles and Space, Palo Alto	36,781,000			
Lockheed Corporation, Sunnyvale	71,101,000			
Lockheed Corporation, Palo Alto	628,000			
Lockheed Corporation, Los Gatos	20,000			
2. FMC Corporation		1,116,965,000	2.	53.5
San Jose	1,115,561,000			
Santa Clara	1,404,000			
3. FORD AEROSPACE AND COMMUNICATIONS		235,875,000	3.	45.0
Palo Alto	132,472,000			
Sunnyvale	103,403,000			
4. GTE		217,759,000	4.	42.9
GTE Products, Mountain View	214,958,000			
GTE Products, Belmont	25,000			
GTE Lenkurt, San Carlos	2,801,000			
5. VARIAN ASSOCIATES		103,164,000	8	75.8
Varian Associates, Palo Alto	89,090,000			
Varian Associates, San Carlos	9,641,000			
Varian Associates, Santa Clara	4,641,000			
Varian Associates, Sunnyvale	33,000			
Varian Associates, Los Altos	21,000			
Varian Associates, Mountain View	13,000			
Varian Data Machines, Palo Alto	74,000			
Varian Graphics, Palo Alto	47,000			
Eimac, San Carlos	39,000			
6. WESTINGHOUSE CORPORATION, Sunnyvale		95,135,000	7	25.5
7. TRW, Inc.		89,135,000	5	5.2
ESL Inc., Sunnyvale	84,487,000			
TRW Inc., Sunnyvale	4,032,000			
TRW Inc., Mountain View	1,132,000			
8. ITEK CORPORATION		75,050,000	6	-11.9
ITEK Corporation, Sunnyvale	69,792,000			
ITEK Corporation, Mountain View	1,360,000			
Applied Technology Associates, Sunnyvale	3,844,000			
Applied Technology Corporation, Sunnyvale	37,000			
ITEK Business Products, Burlingame	12,000			
9. TEXTRON CORPORATION, Dalmo Victor, Belmont		64,895,000	10	39.9

Figure 2.9 An Example of Worksheet Used to Record Prime Contracts in the State
for a Company

Lockheed   FY 1982

County	Contractor	City	Amount
Alameda	Lockheed Corp	Alameda	202
Los Angeles	Lockheed California Co	Burbank	1,940
	Lockheed Corp	Burbank	596,190
	"	Palmdale	231
	"	Sunland	5,127
San Bernardino	Lockheed Aircraft Service Co	Ontario	116
	Lockheed Corp.	Ontario	82,372
San Diego	Lockheed Electronics Co.	San Diego	25
	Lockheed Missiles and Space Co	San Diego	2,291
Santa Clara	Lockheed Corp	Los Gatos	20
	"	Palo Alto	628
	"	Sunnyvale	71,101
	Lockheed Missiles + Space Co	Palo Alto	36,781
	"	Sunnyvale	1,399,204
Solano	Lockheed Corp.	Travis AFB	30
Ventura	Lockheed Electronics Co.	Port Hueneme	26

Total California $2,190,189   62.6%

Calif Rank ②

Total U.S.   3,498,550

Outside of Calif.   1,308,361   37.4%

Figure 2.10 California Top 32 DoD Prime Contractors — FY 1982

Top Twelve = $ 13,614,566,000 or 60.0% of total state prime contracts.
Top Thirty = $ 16,754,836,000 or 73.9% of total state prime contracts.

RANK	COMPANY	AMOUNT	Number of Facilities	Major Facilities (over $50 Million)	City	County	Amount	Rank Last Year	Growth Over Last Year
1.	Hughes Aircraft Co.	$ 2,557,252,000	20	Hughes Aircraft Co.	El Segundo	Los Angeles	$ 759,738,000	1	23.9%
				Hughes Aircraft Co.	Fullerton	Orange	757,457,000		
				Hughes Aircraft Co.	Culver City	Los Angeles	390,326,000		
				Hughes Aircraft Co.	Canoga Park	Los Angeles	330,242,000		
				Hughes Aircraft Co.	Los Angeles	Los Angeles	121,600,000		
				Hughes Communication Serv	Los Angeles	Los Angeles	67,000,000		
2.	Lockheed Corp.	2,190,189,000	16	Lockheed Missiles & Space	Sunnyvale	Santa Clara	1,399,209,000	2	34.0
				Lockheed Corp.	Burbank	Los Angeles	590,100,000		
				Lockheed Corp.	Ontario	San Bernardino	82,372,000		
				Lockheed Corp.	Sunnyvale	Santa Clara	71,101,000		
3.	Rockwell International	2,163,394,000	15	Rockwell International	Los Angeles	Los Angeles	1,289,929,000	4	179.2
				Rockwell International	Anaheim	Orange	491,440,000		
				Rockwell International	Canoga Park	Los Angeles	185,811,000		
				Rockwell International	Seal Beach	Orange	99,585,000		
4.	General Dynamics Corp.	1,424,195,000	21	General Dynamics	Pomona	Los Angeles	956,731,000	3	49.4
				General Dynamics	San Diego	San Diego	421,608,000		
5.	FMC Corp.	1,118,895,000	14	FMC Corp.	San Jose	Santa Clara	1,115,561,000	5	50.4
6.	Ford Motor Co.	841,940,000	7	Ford Aerospace & Communications	Irvine	Orange	416,243,000	8	67.9
				Ford A & C	Newport Beach	Orange	183,655,000		
				Ford A & C	Palo Alto	Santa Clara	132,472,000		
				Ford A & C	Sunnyvale	Santa Clara	103,403,000		
7.	TRW Inc.	690,686,000	16	TRW Inc.	Redondo Beach	Los Angeles	479,699,000	9	75.4
				TRW Inc.	Norton AFB	San Bernardino	107,512,000		
				ESL Inc.	Sunnyvale	Santa Clara	84,487,000		

Figure 2.11 A Sample Page from a Department of Energy (DoE) Contract Listing

RPT-STANDARD1

RUN DATE: SEP 30, 1983

DOE PROCUREMENT AND ASSISTANCE DATA SYSTEM
CONTRACTS IN THE STATE OF CALIFORNIA WHICH
HAD OBLIGATIONS IN FY 1983, NO ASSISTANCE ACTIONS
PROGRAM -- U7594MC.RG83347.DATA

AWARD BIN-----	ORIG AWARD DATE	SUPPORT SERVICE	TOT CONTR VALUE	DESCRIPTIONS OF WORK- - - - -
AWARDEE NAME - - - -	TYPE OF AWARD- - - - - -	CONSULTANT	GOVERNMNT SHARE	
AWARDEE DIVISION - - - - -	EXTENT OF COMPETITION- - - - -		AWARDED SHARE	
ADMINISTRATOR NAME - - -	PRODUCT/SERVICE DESCRIPTION- - - -		CURNT FY CELIGS	
AT03-83ER60171	AUG 03, 1983		$32,802	NO	CANCER STATISTICS AND ENVIRONM
CALIFORNIA UNIVERSITY OF	COST NO FEE		$32,802	NO	ENTAL FACTORS NEAR NUCLEAR F
	UNSOLICITED PROPOSAL		$32,802		ACILITIES
O'BRIEN	R&D/OTHER ENERGY - OTHER				
W-7405-ENG-48	JAN 01, 1940		$7,485,431,406	NO	OPERATION OF LAWRENCE BERKELEY
CALIFORNIA UNIVERSITY OF	COST NO FEE		$7,485,431,406	NO	AND LAWRENCE LIVERMORE LABO
	OTHER NEGOTIATED NON-COMPETITIVE		$449,690,969		RATORIES
MARTINEZ	OPER OF GOVT FAC/R&D GOCO FACILITIES				
AP01-83MA32230	OCT 21, 1982		$2,340	NO	MAINTENANCE AGREEMENT FOR ARCH
CAMBRIDGE SYSTEMS GROUP INC	FIRM FIXED PRICE		$2,340	NO	IVAL SPACE MANAGEMENT SYSTEM
	OTHER NEGOTIATED COMPETITIVE		$2,340		S.
TAZELAAR, DORIS					
AC22-83FC60024	JUN 30, 1983		$38,000	NO	STUDY REPORT ON ZEOLITE CATALY
CATALYTICA ASSOC INC	FIRM FIXED PRICE		$38,000	NO	
	OTHER NEGOTIATED NON-COMPETITIVE		$38,000		
SICILIANO, DALE	R&D/ENERGY - COAL - RESEAR				
AC03-83ER80025	AUG 29, 1983		$19,500	NO	LASAR TREE TRIMMER
CELLULOSE CONVERSION	FIRM FIXED PRICE		$19,500	NO	
	SMALL BUSINESS TOTAL SET-ASIDE		$19,500		
O'BRIAN	R&D/OTHER ENERGY - RESEAR				

Figure 2.12   A Sample Page from Geographic Distribution of Federal Funds -- FY 1980

FEDERAL INFORMATION EXCHANGE SYSTEM
COUNTY SUMMARIES - AGENCY OPERATIONS
[Dollar amounts in thousands]

	PRORATION CODE	CFDA NO.	FY 1980 FUNDS
PHYSICAL DISASTER LOANS		59.008	$935
REGULATORY-OTHER LOANS		59.028	$16
SMALL BUSINESS LOANS		59.012	$200
TOTAL - OTHER FEDERAL FUNDS			$1,269
AGENCY TOTAL - FEDERAL FUNDS			$1,269
INDIRECT FEDERAL SUPPORT *			
SMALL BUSINESS LOANS		59.012	($3,778)
TENNESSEE VALLEY AUTHORITY			
OTHER FEDERAL FUNDS			
TENNESSEE VALLEY AUTHORITY FUND			$14
TOTAL - OTHER FEDERAL FUNDS			$14
AGENCY TOTAL - FEDERAL FUNDS			$14
VETERANS ADMINISTRATION			
OTHER FEDERAL FUNDS			
AUTOS & SPECIAL EQUIPMENT, DISABLED VETS	12	64.100	$16
COMPENSATION TO DEPENDENTS, VETS S/C DEATH	12	64.102	$91
DEPENDENTS INDEMNITY COMPENSATION (DIC)	12	64.110	$1,848
SONS, DAUGHTERS, WIVES & WIDOWS EDUCATION	12	64.117	$256
SPECIALLY ADAPTED HOUSING, DISABLED VETS	12	64.106	$26
VETERANS DEATH PENSION	12	64.105	$1,170
VETERANS DISABILITY COMPENSATION	12	64.109	$6,547
VETERANS DISABILITY PENSION	12	64.104	$1,988
VETERANS INSURANCE AND INDEMNITIES	12	64.103	$1,647
VETERANS READJUSTMENT TRAINING	12	64.111	$3,517
VETS BURIAL AWARDS & OTHER MISC BENEF PMT	12	64.101	$213
VOCATIONAL REHAB. TRNG. FOR DISABLED VETS	12	64.116	$59
TOTAL - OTHER FEDERAL FUNDS			$17,379
AGENCY TOTAL - FEDERAL FUNDS			$17,379
INDIRECT FEDERAL SUPPORT *			
MOBILE HOME LOANS		64.119	($110)
VETERANS GUARANTEED AND INSURED LOANS		64.114	($18,444)
COUNTY TOTAL - GRANT FUNDS			$98,123
COUNTY TOTAL - OTHER FEDERAL FUNDS			$1,092,618
COUNTY TOTAL - FEDERAL FUNDS			$1,190,742

COUNTY-SANTA CLARA
DEPARTMENT OF AGRICULTURE
GRANT FUNDS

	PRORATION CODE	CFDA NO.	FY 1980 FUNDS
AGRICULTURAL CONSERVATION PROGRAM, ASCS		10.063	$22
CHILD CARE FOOD PROGRAM, FNS	10	10.558	$1,628
EQUIP ASST PROG-SCHOOL FOOD SVC PROG, FNS	10	10.554	$60
FARM LABOR HOUSING GRANTS, FMHA		10.405	$73
FOOD STAMP BONUS COUPONS, FNS	1	10.551	$21,510
NATIONAL SCHOOL LUNCH PROGRAM-CASH, FNS	10	10.555	$9,213
NUTRITION PROGRAMS FOR THE ELDERLY, FNS	11	10.550	$255
SCHOOL BREAKFAST PROGRAM, FNS	10	10.553	$1,653
SPECIAL MILK PROGRAM FOR CHILDREN, FNS	10	10.556	$630
SUMMER FOOD SVC. PROGRAM FOR CHILDREN, FNS	10	10.559	$385
SUPP. FOOD-WOMEN, INFANTS & CHILDREN, FNS	10	10.557	$1,958
TOTAL - GRANT FUNDS			$37,386
OTHER FEDERAL FUNDS			
AGRICULTURAL RESEARCH, SEA			$120
COMMODITY INVENTORY OPERATIONS, CCC		10.051	$224
COOPERATIVE RESEARCH, SEA			$259
DAIRY & BEEKEEPER INDEMNITY PAYMENTS, ASCS		10.060	$3
EXP & REFUNDS, INSP & GRADING OF FARM PROD			$988
FEED GRAIN PRODUCTION STABILIZATION, CCC		10.055	$1
FOOD STAMP PROGRAM ADMINISTRATION, FNS	19		$28
FOREST MANAGE, PROTECTION, AND UTILIZATION	18		$128
LAND INVENTORY AND MONITORING, SCS		10.908	$1
NATIONAL WOOL ACT PAYMENTS, CCC		10.059	$4
PURCHASES FOR ELDERLY FEEDING, FNS		10.550	$78
S & E, FARMERS HOME ADMINISTRATION			$92
SOIL AND WATER CONSERVATION, SCS		10.902	$132
SOIL SURVEY, SCS		10.903	**
WATERSHED AND FLOOD PREVENTION OPER., SCS			$58
WATERSHED PLANNING, SCS		10.904	$10
TOTAL - OTHER FEDERAL FUNDS			$2,126
AGENCY TOTAL - FEDERAL FUNDS			$39,512
INDIRECT FEDERAL SUPPORT *			
DONATION OF COMM. TO SCHOOL LUNCH, FNS	10	10.550	($333)
ECONOMIC EMERGENCY LOANS, FMHA		10.428	($1,556)
EMERGENCY DISASTER LOANS, FMHA		10.404	($4,021)
FARM LABOR HOUSING LOANS, FMHA		10.405	($654)
FARM OPERATING LOANS, FMHA		10.406	($281)
FARM OWNERSHIP LOANS, FMHA		10.407	($231)
FOOD DISTRIBUTION TO INSTITUTIONS, FNS	10	10.550	($93)
FOOD DISTRIBUTION TO SCHOOLS, FNS	10	10.550	($3,987)
LOW TO MODERATE INCOME HOUSING LOANS, FMHA		10.410	($43)
TITLE II, PL 480, FOREIGN DONATIONS, CCC			($2)

DEPARTMENT OF COMMERCE
GRANT FUNDS

	PRORATION CODE	CFDA NO.	FY 1980 FUNDS
AID TO STATE MARINE SCHOOLS, MAR		11.506	$2

CALIFORNIA—Con.

	PRORATION CODE	CFDA NO.	FY 1980 FUNDS
ECON DEV-PUBLIC WORKS IMPACT PROJECTS, EDA		11.304	$89
ECON DEV-STATE & LOCAL ECON DEV PLNNG, EDA		11.305	$50
MISCELLANEOUS TRUST FUNDS, ARC			$1
TOTAL - GRANT FUNDS			$142
OTHER FEDERAL FUNDS			
CENSUS SPECIAL TABULATIONS AND SERVICES		11.005	$1
CONSOLIDATED WORKING FUND, CENSUS			$42
CURRENT STATISTICAL PROGRAMS, CENSUS			$10
INFORMATION PRODUCTS AND SERVICES	5		$169
OPER. OF U.S. MERCHANT MARINE ACADEMY, MAR		11.507	$6
OPERATIONS AND TRAINING, MAR			$2
OPERATIONS, RESEARCH, AND FACILITIES, NOAA			$64
PATENT & TRADEMARK TECH INFO DISSEMINATION		11.900	$12
PERIODIC CENSUSES			$2,305
RESEARCH AND DEVELOPMENT, MAR	5		$580
WORKING CAPITAL FUND, NBS	5		$1,029
TOTAL - OTHER FEDERAL FUNDS			$4,221
AGENCY TOTAL - FEDERAL FUNDS			$4,363
INDIRECT FEDERAL SUPPORT *			
FISHERY VESSEL OBLIGATION GUARANTEES, NMFS	5	11.415	($76)

DEPARTMENT OF DEFENSE
GRANT FUNDS

	PRORATION CODE	CFDA NO.	FY 1980 FUNDS
MILITARY CONSTRUCTION, ARMY NATIONAL GUARD	7	12.400	$2
TOTAL - GRANT FUNDS			$2
OTHER FEDERAL FUNDS			
CIVIL FUNCTIONS PRIME CONTRACTS	5		$844
CIVILIAN PAY	15		$45,062
MILITARY ACTIVE DUTY PAY	15		$76,819
MILITARY PRIME CONSTRUCTION CONTRACTS	5		$1,384
MILITARY PRIME RDTE CONTRACTS	5		$373,692
MILITARY PRIME SERVICE CONTRACTS	5		$320,071
MILITARY PRIME SUPPLY CONTRACTS	5		$1,696,799
MILITARY RESERVE AND NATIONAL GUARD PAY	15		$10,978
MILITARY RETIRED PAY	12		$73,037
PRIME CONTRACTS OF LESS THAN $10,000	6		$527
TOTAL - OTHER FEDERAL FUNDS			$2,599,213
AGENCY TOTAL - FEDERAL FUNDS			$2,599,215

DEPARTMENT OF EDUCATION
GRANT FUNDS

	PRORATION CODE	CFDA NO.	FY 1980 FUNDS
ACAD FAC RECON & RENOV-REMOVAL ARCH BARRS		84.001	$25
BASIC EDUCATIONAL OPPORTUNITY GRANT PROG		84.063	$5,968
BASIC SKILLS IMPROVEMENT		84.105	$303
BILINGUAL VOCATIONAL TRAINING		84.077	$247
CAREER EDUCATION STATE ALLOTMENT PROGRAM		84.104	$73
CIVIL RIGHTS TECHNICAL ASST. AND TRAINING		84.004	$561
COLLEGE LIBRARY RESOURCES		84.005	$17
COLLEGE WORK-STUDY PROGRAM		84.033	$1,124
CONSUMERS' EDUCATION		84.082	$84
DOMESTIC MINING & MINERAL FUEL CONSERV PRG		84.085	$101
EDUC DEPRIVED CHILDREN-LEA'S		84.010	$7,781
ESAA-BASIC GRTS TO LOCAL EDUCATIONAL AGIES		84.056	$83
ESAA-MAGNET SCHOOLS UNIVERSITY/BUSINESS		84.102	$381
ESAA-SPECIAL PROGRAMS AND PROJECTS		84.059	$125
FOLLOW THROUGH		84.014	$414
FOREIGN LANGUAGE AND AREA STUDIES-RESEARCH		84.017	$38
FULBRIGHT-HAYS TRNG GTS-FACULTY RES ABROAD		84.019	$379
GRADUATE AND PROFESSIONAL OPPORTUNITIES		84.094	$140
HANDICAPPED PERSONNEL PREPARATION		84.029	$192
HANDICAPPED RESEARCH AND DEMONSTRATION		84.023	$88
INDIAN ED-FELLOWSHIPS FOR INDIAN STUDENTS		84.087	$60
INDIAN ED-GRANTS TO LOCAL EDUCATIONAL AGCY		84.060	$201
INSTITUTE OF MUSEUM SERVICES		84.115	$49
INTERNATIONAL STUDIES PROGRAMS		84.016	$305
INTL STUDIES CTR & FOR LANG ST-FELLOWSHIPS		84.015	$286
LAW ENFORCEMENT EDUCATION PROGRAM			$6
LAW SCHOOL CLINICAL EXPERIENCE PROGRAM		84.097	$42
NAT DIFFUSION PRG (NAT DIFFUSION NETWORK)		84.073	$70
NATIONAL DEFENSE/DIRECT STUDENT LOANS		84.038	$3,628
NATIONAL INSTITUTE OF HANDICAPPED RESEARCH		84.133	$704
NATL DEFENSE/DIR STUDENT LN CANCELLATIONS		84.037	$1,933
REHABILITATION SERVICES-SPECIAL PROJECTS		84.128	$445
REHABILITATION TRAINING		84.129	$60
SAFA-MAINTENANCE AND OPERATION		84.041	$1,757
SPECIAL SVCS FOR DISADVANTAGED STUDENTS		84.042	$141
SUPPLEMENTAL EDUCATIONAL OPPORTUNITY GRTS		84.007	$2,637
TEACHER CENTERS		84.006	$160
TEACHER CORPS-OPERATIONS AND TRAINING		84.045	$114
UPWARD BOUND		84.047	$319
VOCATIONAL ED-PROGRAM IMPROVEMENT PROJECTS		84.051	$16
WOMEN'S EDUCATIONAL EQUITY		84.083	$317
TOTAL - GRANT FUNDS			$31,374
OTHER FEDERAL FUNDS			
HIGHER ED-VETS COST OF INSTRUCTION PROGRAM		84.064	$113

Chapter 3   Major Military Products

Military purchasing agencies issue prime contracts to companies for many different products and services. The companies receive contracts to:

-- Provide food and clothing for military service people;

-- Produce specific pieces of military hardware and equipment (tanks, fighters, bombers, ships, weapons, ammunition, guns, and the electronic devices that control them);

-- Perform research, development, testing, and evaluation (RDTE) of new military hardware;

-- Develop new military strategy;

-- Construct buildings and other facilities;

-- Guard facilities (security);

-- Oversee the work of other contractors and subcontractors (Management and Support);

It is very useful to know specifically what the military contractors in your area are doing for several reasons:

-- To educate the general public on the nature of the military work being performed locally;

-- So you will know the local effect of expansion and cancellation of various weapon systems or programs. For example, if a nuclear Freeze is enacted, you will know what effect this will have in the local area;

-- To inform the people who work for these contractors. Sometimes people who work directly on a product don't know what it is or its use. Those who do clerical work or other support tasks may not have any idea what the company is producing.

People are often outraged when they discover they are working on guided missiles with a first-strike capability, nerve gas, or some other particularly obnoxious product. You may want to highlight these products when describing what the company builds.

Section 3.A. gives an overall idea of how to find out which military products are made (or services rendered, or commodities sold) in your community. Section 3.B. describes in detail the best sources of information for this research. Section 3.C. then gives you information and sources for interpreting contract information and understanding the procurement process. Section 3.D. tells you how to discover the uses of different weapons and Section 3.E. describes some special sources of information for learning about Research and Development (R&D) contracts.

3.A. Procedure for Determining Military Products Made in Your Community

There is no single procedure for determining the military products made in your community. You will want to approach your research in different ways depending on whether you are focusing on a particular company or a particular weapon system, or you are making a complete survey of production in your area. Also, depending on the nature of the products in your area, you may need to proceed in different ways: finding out about production of household commodities used by military personnel is very different than getting information on weapons production or tracking down information on research and development work.

NARMIC is an excellent resource for information on military products. It is wise to call them before searching anywhere else. They may be able to give you just the information you need.

Aviation Week and Space Technology magazine has tables of information about aerospace weapons including the main contractors and their locations (see the Reference section for a more detailed description).

If you are looking at several contractors in your community with numerous contract awards, it is probably best to use the Pentagon report Alphabetic Detail of DoD Prime Contractors over $25,000 (ST18) (or one of the other detailed listings on microfiche). This report lists every contract award and identifies the weapons system by a 3-letter code. For each company, identify the weapons being produced and record the amount for each weapon. Figure 3.1 is a form you can use to record this information.

Alphabetic Detail identifies weapon systems, but doesn't provide much additional information. Commodities and research are identified only in general terms. More detailed descriptions of the contract awards can be found in the listings prepared by Commerce Business Daily (CBD) and by several companies (DMS, Inc., Government Data Publications) that take these listings, rearrange them, and sell them.

If you are researching only a few contracts, CBD has the most detailed descriptions. But you may have to search through dozens of issues, as many as four months after the contract date to find the listing. DMS has good (but expensive) listings by county. However, analyzing many contracts can be quite tedious since the information is not arranged in tabular form.

If there are a few contracts that are especially interesting, you may want to make a Freedom of Information Act (FOIA) request for the contract's work statement and summary. In order to do this, you must write to the appropriate DoD Purchasing Office (PO) and specify the contract number. You can also write directly to the Pentagon and have your request forwarded to the appropriate office, but the request will probably take a little longer.

All the sources mentioned above list contract numbers, but they don't all give you enough information to write to the PO. The Pentagon microfiche reports (ST18, etc.) only reveal the PO if you have the appropriate decoding manual (List of DoD Purchasing Offices, (MN01)). DMS and GDP list the name of the Purchasing Office, but not the address. The free NARMIC publication, How to Read Defense Contract Listings, will give you some of these addresses, but not all. CBD and the Pentagon document Selling to the Military ($6) have all the addresses.

If you are interested in all the contractors for a particular weapon, you can check in The Nuclear Weapons Databook, ask NARMIC for their help, look through magazines such as Aviation Week and Space Technology for the appropriate listings or articles, or subscribe to one of the publications of DMS, Inc.

If your focus is one company, then employees may be the best source of information about what is produced. Also see Chapter 4.

New York Public Interest Research Center (NYPIRC) prepared a listing of all the prime contract awards in FY 1981 for each nuclear weapon made in New York State. They prepared a list of all the codes for weapons in which they were interested, then methodically went through the Pentagon report Alphabetical Detail (ST18) for all of the contractors in New York State, and recorded every company's contracts for those weapons. Their results are contained in their report Production for Destruction: Military Spending in New York State (see Figure 3.2).

The Economic Conversion Task Force of the Connecticut Freeze Campaign performed a similar study for Connecticut contractors working on weapon systems that would be affected by the Freeze. They used DMS data for their work. Their results are shown in their paper Projected Impact of a Freeze on Connecticut.

3.B. Sources of Information on Military Products

There are several primary sources of information that give an indication of the work being performed under prime military contracts. These sources also usually include the amount of the contracts and the DoD Purchasing Office that issued the contract.

DoD Detailed Contract Listings

The Department of Defense (DoD) maintains a computer file that contains every prime contract award over $25,000 issued each year (approximately 400,000 in FY 1982). This database is called the Defense Acquisition Management Data System (DAMDS) (see also Section 2.H.). Most of this information is available on microfiche, listed in various ways. Alphabetical Detail of DoD Prime Contractors over $25,000 (ST18)) ($45) lists every contract according to the alphabetized name of the contractor and then by the city in which the award was made. Detailed listings on microfiche by state and city, in Geographic Detail (ST11), cost $60.

Contracts are also listed on microfiche by Major Weapon System (ST08) ($60) and by Federal Supply Classification (FSC) (ST06) ($65). But these listings have less information than ST18. For example, they list the state but not the city where the award was made. ST08 is useful for determining which companies have prime contracts for a particular weapon nationwide.

The Alphabetical Detail listings (ST18) are probably the cheapest and best of the listings for our purposes. The contract awards on the ST18 microfiche are listed alphabetically by company, then by country, state, and city. The actual contract awards seem to be ordered according to contract number and then chronologically. Following the contracts is a Location Total and a Contractor Total. Conveniently, the microfiche listings correspond exactly to the listings in other DoD reports (Prime Contract Awards over $25,000 by State, County, Contractor, and Place (ST25) for example). Figure 3.3 shows some samples of listings from ST18.

In order to decode this information you need two other DoD documents. The DAMDS Code Translation Manual (MN04) is only 16 pages long and costs $12. Figure 3.4 is a summary of the information in this manual. You can also write to CEC for a photocopy of all 16 pages (please enclose $1.50 to cover the cost of reproduction).

The second document, DoD Procurement Coding Manual, Volume I: Commodities and Services (MN02), explains three of the columns on the microfiche:

    10A = Federal Supply Classification (FSC) code or Service Code (SVC)
    10B = DoD Weapon System Code
    10C = DoD Claimant Program Number

Item 11 spells out most of the FSC information coded in item 10A (see Section 3.C. for a more detailed explanation). Item 10C is sometimes useful, but generally tells you less than the FSC code. However, item 10B indicates exactly what weapon system the contract is for. This is very, very useful. Figure 3.5 is a page from MN02 showing the weapon systems and their corresponding codes.

Note that to determine the exact weapon, you must also know the service branch (Army, etc.) since the same code can refer to several weapons depending on the service. Also note that codes are only listed for weapons already under construction (there are none for weapons still in the R&D phase; see Section 3.E. for some ways to track down information on R&D contracts).

Some reconnaissance aircraft have the same weapons code as the plane on which it is based. For example, the Air Force weapons code ACR means either the C-135 Stratolifter cargo plane or the RC-135 spy plane.

Commerce Business Daily

Every working day the federal government publishes Commerce Business Daily (CBD) listing all the "procurement invitations" from agencies of the federal government for work they wish to have done by outside contractors. CBD provides an interesting up-to-date listing of the military (and civilian) work being contracted. Unfortunately, it lists so many contract requests that it can be overwhelming.

At the end of almost every issue, CBD also has listings of all the unclassified military contracts over $100,000 and all civilian contracts over $25,000 awarded by the government (see Figure 3.6). Each day there are anywhere from 0 to 400 of these contracts listed. The descriptions are often quite detailed, listing the particular device being worked on and its serial number. The contracts are listed in order by Federal Supply Classification (FSC) code (see Section 3.C.) and then by issuing agency. The name, address, and sometimes the phone of the agency issuing the contract (and sometimes the name of the person in this agency responsible for the contract) is listed. This is useful when writing to this purchasing agency for its annual report and for more information on the contract. Generally, though, no information is given about which weapon system the contract is for.

Commerce Business Daily costs $100/year when mailed second-class and $175/year first class. We are able to get it free from a local environmental consulting firm after they are done looking through it for contract opportunities. You might be able to find a similar source. Because there are so many military contracts covering the entire U.S. and they are listed by FSC code rather than by geographical area, the listings are quite overwhelming and usually not that useful in this form. The listings are not easy to read since they aren't in tabular form and you can't scan down the list looking for the largest contract awards.

Several computer database firms have CBD on-line: Lockheed DIALOG Information Services, DMS, Inc. (formerly Defense Marketing Service), and United Communications Group all provide this information in a computer data base file. You can access these data bases and use the computer to search and list the contracts for specific states or cities during a particular time period. For example you could search for Varian Associates in a specific city (Palo Alto) or zip code (943) during FY 1983 (October 1982 - September 1983). In this way you can list all the recent contracts given to companies in your community in a useful order.

Lockheed DIALOG costs $54/hour and a search and listing of several hundred contracts could probably be done in 20-30 minutes (most terminals get information from computers at a rate of about 30 characters/second or about 2 minutes per page -- slower when used heavily by many users). If you have access to a microcomputer and know how to use it well, you can transfer these listings to a disk and then use the computer to sort them by company, city, date, or contract amount (assuming you have the software to do this). Also, many libraries subscribe to DIALOG. A friendly librarian might search for some specific data for you.

Dialogue Information Services, Inc.
3460 Hillview Avenue
Palo Alto, CA   94304
(415) 858-3785
(800) 227-1927

United Communications Group
8701 Georgia Avenue
Silver Spring, MD   20910
(800) 638-7728
(301) 589-8875

DMS, Inc.

DMS,Inc. (formerly Defense Marketing Service) is a private company that takes the military listings from the DoD, Department of Energy (DoE), and National Aeronautics and Space Administration (NASA) over $25,000, sorts them by county, company, and FSC code, and publishes them quarterly. Their subscribers are mostly companies interested in selling products or services to these prime contractors. The listings cost $750/year and are issued about 9 months after the end of the quarter.

The information DMS reports and its format is slightly different than CBD. It may not be completely reliable. The listings are typically not as detailed and many of the words are abbreviated. The purchasing agency name is abbreviated and no address is given. Figure 3.7 shows some examples of contracts listed in the DMS format. The listings are not easy to read since they are not listed in tablular form. As in the CBD listings, DMS listings don't necessarily tell you which weapon system the contract is for.

DMS also has many other publications:

Major Systems Market Forecasts are 2,000 page studies published annually providing comprehensive data on current worldwide military inventories and production with individual program reports and 10-year forecasts (about $2,500). Example: World Armored Vehicle Forecast

Market Studies and Forecasts are similar to the above, but are only 1,000 pages long and cost about $1,200.

Market Intelligence Reports are looseleaf binders covering important military markets and updated with monthly supplements. They have several pages of detailed information for each weapon (about $800). Examples: Military Aircraft, "AN" Equipment

DMS also has various newsletters (about $225/year), budget handbooks ($55), and code name directories (about $200).

DMS information is also accessible on-line on their computer. It costs $6,000 to $7,000 to subscribe originally plus an hourly charge for use of the system.

DMS, Inc.
100 Northfield Street
Greenwich, Connecticut   06830
(800) 243-3852
(203) 661-7800

A Comparison of DMS and DoD Data

The DoD microfiche (ST18) and DMS quarterly data do not, with a few exceptions, contradict each other, but there are substantial differences in their completeness. The DoD data is far more complete, in particular, it includes Defense Logistic Agency (DLA) contracts which DMS rarely carries. Although these contracts are normally not weapons --

and thus of less interest to many activists -- they are economically important, comprising a substantial share of all contract dollars. The DoD data also includes many Army, Navy, and Air Force contracts which DMS excludes with no apparent pattern. On the other hand, DMS includes some NASA, DoE, or Coast Guard contracts that are not included in the DoD data.

The DoD data includes more information for each contract, but much of it is of little interest. Sometimes the DMS listings will tell you more about the contract than the DoD data will, for example, listing the name of the ship being repaired, etc. This can be very useful, especially for Research and Development (R&D) contracts. The DoD listings do not tell you much about R&D work, particularly which weapon it is for.

The DoD data lists the worldwide operations of contractors. This makes the calculation of total contracts and contracts as a percent of sales possible, something which cannot be done easily with the DMS geographic data.

DMS does not always list contracts in the correct quarter and sometimes lists them more than once.

Government Data Publications

GDP is another trade organization. It takes contract information from the CBD, rearranges it, and sells it. Government Prime Contracts Monthly ($96/year) lists prime contracts monthly by 50-60 product categories. Contractors are listed alphabetically under these product categories. This is not a very useful way to get the information since you must look under each product category each month for the company you are interested in.

R&D Contracts Monthly ($96/year) lists all the research and development contracts each month, arranged alphabetically by contractor, geographically by the awarding agency, and also by six categories denoting the nature of the work.

GDP also compiles a Research & Development Directory ($15) organized in the same way as the R&D Contracts Monthly and an annual Government Contracts Directory ($79.50) ordered by product category. The R&D directory might be a useful document if you are trying to track down R&D work.

    Government Data Publications
    1120 Connecticut Avenue, NW
    Washington, DC 20036

Congressional Hearings

Transcripts of the appropriation hearings before Congress are an excellent source of information on the number of weapons planned, costs, and the "mission" of the weapon. See Appendix 3 for more on these hearings.

Wall Street Journal and Electronic News

The Wall Street Journal lists many of the larger contracts awarded each day based on DoD press releases. These listings are indexed in the Journal Index available in most libraries. These announcements sometimes include large subcontracts. Electronic News also carries large awards for electronic equipment.

Company Annual Reports

Company annual reports and 10-K reports often have information on the types of equipment produced by a company. The 10-K report sometimes reports large contracts for a specific system if it represents a major portion of the company's business. See Section 4.D. for more on these reports.

Companies often issue press releases describing new contracts they have received. On request, they may send them directly to you or you may be able to get them from a friendly news reporter.

Freedom of Information Act (FOIA) Requests

Under the provisions of the Freedom of Information Act (FOIA) you can write the Awarding Agency, or Purchasing Office (PO), of the DoD for a copy of any contract that does not compromise national security (most do not) (see Section 3.C. for more on POs). The contract itself may be thousands of pages long, filled with legal contract language that isn't very useful. The title page and work statement are probably sufficient to get an idea of the purpose of the contract work. Fees are usually waived, and if not, usually do not exceed $5 per contract.

Developing an FOIA request requires that you determine as clearly as possible what information you want and which office is responsible for it. The FOI Act includes an appeals process for citizens whose requests have been denied.

For more information on FOIA requests, see the research guide on nuclear free zones published by Mobilization for Survival, Uncovering the Nuclear Industry: A Research Guide. NARMIC, the Council on Economic Priorities (CEP), and the Highlander Center have experience making FOIA requests.

Two organizations offer advice and, if necessary, legal assistance on FOIA requests:

Campaign for Political Rights, 210 Massachusetts Avenue, NE, Washington, DC 20002 (202) 547-4705

Center for National Security Studies, 122 Maryland Avenue, NE, Washington, DC 20002 (202) 544-5380

Employees

Sympathetic employees may be able to give you a lot of information on the products made by their company. Management people, engineers, and scientists usually have the best information, but anyone who works on the product or processes the paperwork for it may be able to tell you about it.

The employee will have to decide how much to tell you about the product since the information may be classified. If it is only classified to provide the company with proprietary protection (so other companies can't steal their work), which is more common than we would like to think, then the employee may feel justified in telling you quite a lot. But if it is information which the Soviet Union is seeking, then it may be hard to get the information and the employee may be jeopardizing her or his security clearance (as well as committing a treasonable act) to tell you about it.

See Chapter 4 for more on interviewing company employees and management and Chapter 5 for more on working with labor unions and technical people.

Data on Commodities

"The Pentagon buys its goods through different purchasing offices that are organized along commodity lines. To identify the leading suppliers of a particular non-weapons commodity, for example, you can obtain a listing: "Contractors Holding Contracts with Largest Aggregate Dollar Value by Purchase Office" from the Defense Logistics Agency (DLA), Cameron station, Alexandria, VA 22314.

"When your research reveals which purchasing office handles which commodity, you can get more data by filing a Freedom of Information request with that office. For example, once you discover that the Defense Fuel Supply Agency buys the military's coal, you get information from DFSA on the shipping point (mine or tipple), destination, tonnage and grade procured from each contractor; the percentage of contracts that were awarded on a set-aside basis for small businesses; or the percentage that were bid non-competitively." [p. 4, How to Research Your Local Military Contractor, Highlander Center]

Other Sources

The business pages of local newspapers sometimes run articles on particular companies describing the things they produce. The New York Times and Newsday (Long Island) are good sources on weapons and the behind-the-scenes political battles which determine who gets the contracts. Job advertisements in the newspaper classifieds sometimes tell about the kind of work the company does. Military trade magazines also describe new weapons work and frequently mention the main contractors (see, for example, the description of Aviation Week and Space Technology in the Reference section). Sympathetic Congressmembers can probably get information quite easily from the contractor or from the DoD Purchasing Office.

3.C. More Information About Contract Listings and Purchasing Offices

Interpreting Contract Listings

The descriptions of the contracts in CBD, DMS, and GDP listings are often difficult to understand. The List of Abbreviations at the end of this workbook should help. As you read more about the various weapon systems and learn more about military contracting, it should be easier to figure out what the contracts are probably for. NARMIC can tell you what other abbreviations and acronyms mean.

Electronic Equipment

Military electronic equipment is denoted by special "AN" codes. These codes indicate the type of equipment, where it is mounted, and its purpose. Figure 3.8 describes the meanings of the AN codes. The September 1983 issue of Defense Electronics has a list of the top 60 military electronics contractors (see the Reference section).

Federal Supply Classification (FSC) Codes

The Federal Supply Classification system has 4-digit codes to describe everything purchased by the government. The first section of the DoD Procurement Coding Manual, Volume I: Commodities and Services (MN02) explains the Federal Supply Classification codes and tells what each one means. Also, NARMIC's short paper "How to Read Defense Contract Listings" and the Pentagon report Selling to the Military have listings of the FSC codes.

The codes are divided into two different types: (1) research, development, test, and evaluation (RDTE), and (2) other services, construction, supplies, and equipment (everything else). The RDTE codes all begin with an "A" (see Section 3.E. for more on RDTE contracts).

DoD Purchasing Offices (Awarding Agencies)

Department of Defense contracts are actually issued by a Purchasing Office (PO) within the Army, Navy, Air Force, or Defense Logistics Agency (in charge of food, blankets, toothpaste, fuel, etc.). These Offices each have a specific area of interest.

A listing of some of the contracting agencies and an abbreviated address is available from NARMIC in their short paper, How to Read Defense Contract Listings. A Pentagon publication directed to small companies looking for contracts called Selling to the Military ($6) lists all the major Purchasing Offices and their addresses and phone numbers and describes the kind of work they do. This list also includes all the military laboratories associated with these Offices. It is very, very useful. See Figure 3.9 for an example of these listings.

The DoD also publishes the decoding manual called List of DoD Purchasing Offices (MN01), (30 pages, $18) which includes the 4-digit Purchasing Office number recorded as Item 5 on the ST18 microfiche.

Our Experience Writing to DoD Purchasing Offices (POs)

As part of their public relations efforts, most DoD Purchasing Offices prepare information about the work they do and the contracts they issue. We chose six of these offices that contracted heavily in our area and wrote to them asking for "information describing your agency, the particular role it plays in our national defense, and the amount and types of contracts you award to private companies."

Five of the six offices responded by sending an annual report or brochures. Generally they provided information on the number of civilian and military employees and total contract amounts. They also explained in greater or lesser detail their particular military role. The sixth, the Army's Communications-Electronics Command in Fort Monmouth, NJ, insisted we make a Freedom of Information Act request and ask for specific information rather than make a "fishing expedition." None gave us information on the companies to which it issues contracts.

One PO, the Maryland Procurement Office, piqued our interest when we were researching contracts, because it issued several contracts to companies in our area, but was not listed in Selling to the Military. The book The Puzzle Palace confirmed our suspicions that this is the purchasing office for the National Security Agency (NSA). The NSA is a very secret agency that breaks foreign codes and engages in electronic eavesdropping of international telephone conversations and other communications.

Defense Contract Administration Services (DCAS)

This DoD agency administers and supervises all prime military contracts except those for shipbuilding, ship repairs, and military construction. DCAS offices are located in each community where there are prime contracts and their addresses can be found in the phone book under the Department of Defense. DCAS offices maintain files on each contract in their jurisdiction including the exact amount of money which has been paid to the contractor to date.

3.D. Descriptions of Weapons Systems

The ST18 microfiche will tell you the code letters of many of the weapons systems. You can then look in the Procurement Coding Manual (MN02) to find the name of the weapon system, but often it is just some code letters like PQM-56, LVTC-7, or AN/UYK-43. The headings in the Coding Manual (see Figure 3.5) give some indication of the purpose of the weapon (the codes above are for a Navy missile, landing vehicle, and electronic communication equipment respectively), but not very much. You must look in other resources for weapon system descriptions:

-- The Department of Defense Appropriation Hearings before the Committee on Appropriations of the House of Representatives have information on all the major weapons systems that are requesting funding for the next fiscal year. The description usually explains how wonderful the weapon is in order to convince Congress to fund it. The description often details how the system will be used in combat, what electronics and armaments it uses, etc. Sometimes it even has a picture. (See Appendix 3 for more on Hearings.)

-- Aviation Week and Space Technology magazine has a lot of information on just about every kind of aerospace product. Articles on particular weapons appear periodically. Sometimes these are written from the perspective of people who work on these weapons all the time and thus contain lots of indecipherable jargon, (but please don't get discouraged). Other military trade magazines may also be helpful.

-- A very good source of information on weapons is the Jane's series of books (Jane's All the World's Aircraft, etc.). These are usually available in a large public or college library. The index quickly directs you to a one or two paragraph description of each weapon. Sometimes it includes very technical information, but you can usually figure out the gist of it.

-- There are also several other informative books available in a good bookstore or library and described in the References section.

You may be interested in the history of cost-overruns and technical problems of a particular weapon made in your area. James Fallow's excellent book National Defense and SANE's Military Budget Manual have this kind of information for many weapons. Also, newspapers, particularly the New York Times and the Wall Street Journal, often bring out criticisms.

3.E. Some Ways of Determining What Work is Being Done under Research and Development Contracts

Most of the listings for research and development contracts don't explain the kind of research being done or which new weapons may employ the results of the R&D. This is unfortunate since some of the most interesting work is done on new weapon systems that are still on the drawing board (like the "stealth" technology which makes airplanes invisible to radar). Also these weapons are the ones that are most easily stopped by Congress (like the midgetman missile). You can, however, determine some things about the research.

The FSC code for R&D work gives some indication of the type of work. The RDTE codes all begin with an "A" and then another letter denoting Agriculture, Education, Medical, etc. The next place is a number detailing the particular sub-area within these broad categories. The last digit tells how far along the research has progressed:

1 Research
2 Exploratory development
3 Advanced development
4 Engineering development

5 Operational systems development
6 Management & support (M&S)

The type of R&D work done for a weapon progresses down the list from research through operational systems development as the weapon gets closer and closer to production.

Management and Support contracts are frequently contracts to oversee several subcontractors. The managing company may decide what subcontracts should be awarded, to whom, and for how much. It then makes sure that the work is done properly and on-time. In this way, the managing company takes on part of the job that would ordinarily be done by the Contract Officer in the Purchasing Office of one of the agencies of the DoD.

Selling to the Military has a 24-page section describing the military Purchasing Offices with major R&D activities. If you know which agency issued the contract, you may be able to guess at the kind of work being performed from this description. You can also write to the agency and ask for its brochure which may have a little more information.

You might also determine the purpose of the research by reading the technical documents that are published describing the work. Non-classified reports are published by the National Technical Information Service (NTIS). They are abstracted and indexed in Government Reports Announcements and Index according to keyword, personal authors, corporate author, contract number, and NTIS report number. This abstract should be available in any Federal Government Depository (library).

Every two weeks the Defense Technical Information Center (DTIC) publishes Technical Abstract Bulletin (TAB) describing all of the classified and unclassified-limited-distribution technical publications issued by the DoD and its contractors. These abstracts can give you some sense of the kind of R&D a company is doing. TAB is indexed in the same way as Government Reports Announcements.

For example, when NARMIC was researching the military work done by MIT's Lincoln Labs, they discovered a listing in TAB for a report called "Modeling of Cruise Missile-Like Signatures" describing the ways to model the identifying characteristics of these missiles. They were then able to order this report and determine specifically what work the Labs were doing.

NARMIC received the TAB index and abstracts for calendar years 1978 through 1982, but these abstracts were classified by the government in 1983. NARMIC is suing the government to release TAB, but this probably will take many months.

Figure 3.1 Weapon and Prime Contract Award Form

Today's Date: _____   Fiscal Year: _____

Company: _____   Location: _____

Number	Military Service	Weapon System Code	Weapon Name and Description
1.	____	____	_____
2.	____	____	_____
3.	____	____	_____
4.	____	____	_____

Military Service = Army (A), Navy (N), Air Force (AF), Marines (M), Defense Logistics
   Agency (DLA), or Other (DMA, DCA, DNA, MDA, etc.)

Contract Awards ($000) _____

Weapon 1.		Weapon 2.		Weapon 3.		Weapon 4.	
Mon/Yr	$ Amount	Mon/Yr	$ Amount	Mon/Yr	$ Amount	Mon/Yr	$ Amount

Total _____   Total _____   Total _____   Total _____

Figure 3.2   A Page from NYPIRC's <u>Production</u> <u>for</u> <u>Destruction</u>: <u>Military</u> <u>Spending</u>
<u>in</u> <u>New</u> <u>York</u> <u>State</u>

NEW YORK NUCLEAR WEAPONS SYSTEMS PRODUCTION 1981
(Thousand dollars)

SYSTEM / CONTRACTOR	AMOUNT
MX Missile*	
Grumman Corp.	10,000 **
Parsons Brinckerhof/Quade Douglas	360
Trident Missile*	
Gould Inc.	30
Sperry Corp.	20,085
Pershing Missile*	
Deutsch Relays Inc.	83
Eastman Kodak	1,179
Espey Mfg. & Electronics	95
Eur Pac Corp.	45
General Electric	100
Litton Industries	20
Moog Inc.	46
Roanwell Corp.	116
Stewart & Thomas Ind.	66
	1,750
Tomahawk SLCM*	
Line Fast Corp.	21
Minuteman Missile	
Amperex Electronic Corp.	47
BG Electronics	30
Buffalo Forge Co.	20
Bulova Systems & Instruments	34
Bulova Watch Co.	14
Carrier Transicold	1,387
Kinemotive Corp.	43
Lorben Corp.	43
Mohawk Data Sciences	46
Moog Inc.	131
Teledyne Gurley	127
	1,922
Nike Hercules	
Aeroflex Labs Inc.	22
Alton Ironworks Inc.	45
Applied Research Inc.	21
Arko Precision Machinists	12
General Electric	2,620
H & R Parts Co. Inc.	13
Hewlett-Packard Co.	16
Inscom Electronics	56
MW Microwave Corp.	19
Moda Magnetics Corp.	29
Modular Devices Inc.	56
Precision Electronics	61
Sierra Research Corp.	945
Struthers Electronics Corp.	27
Union Carbide Corp.	33
	3,975
Titan Missile	
Amperex Electronics Corp.	42
Becton-Dickinson Co.	569
Wright Components Inc.	79
	690

SYSTEM / CONTRACTOR	AMOUNT
Polaris Missile	
A&M Instruments Inc.	15
Bendix Corp.	20
Eastman Kodak	124
Frequency Electronics	117
North Atlantic Industries	29
Sperry Corp.	2,049
	2,354
Safeguard ABM	
Calspan Corp.	49
Missile/Space Program	
Fairchildd Industries	157
Grumman Corp.	616
Riverside Research Inst.	712
Textron Inc.	270
Ehrenphreis David	230
	1,985
Trident Submarine	
General Electric	60,285
Sperry Corp.	56,369
	116,654
B-1B Bomber*	
Eaton Corp.	8,214
B-52 Bomber	
Arista Devices	29
Bendix Corp.	718
Boeing Co.	145
CF Electronics Inc.	81
Chloride Electro Networks	12
Computer Instruments Corp.	43
Cox and Co. Inc.	11
Frequency Control Products	53
GSE Dynamics Inc.	460
General Electric	102
General Signal Corp.	627
Gull Airborne Instruments Co.	76
Harris Corp.	11
IBM Co.	34,381
Lourdes Industries	100
Mar Mac Precision Co.	73
Metermod Instrument Corp.	12
Moda Magnetics Co.	73
Numax Electronics Inc.	119
Orowac Industries	14
Pickard & Burns	102
Premier Microwave Corp.	110
SMS Instruments & Acessories	236
SECS Inc.	32
Singer Co.	110,006
Transworld Optics	75
US Dynamics Corp.	323
Venus Scientific Inc.	241
Westinghouse Electric Corp.	3,128
	151,393

SYSTEM / CONTRACTOR	AMOUNT
Submarine FBM-SSBN	
American Standard	23
Arista Devices Inc.	13
Figgie International	11
Ingersoll Rand Co.	23
Rollson Inc.	15
Sperry Corp.	8,062
	8,147
Submarine Nuclear SSN	
Aluf Industries Inc.	429
Arista Devices Inc.	42
Buffalo Forge Co.	13
Carrier Transicold Co.	18
General Electric Co.	184,773
Oceanetics	12
	185,287
Lance SRBM	
Alton Iron Works	48
GSE Dynamics Inc.	68
SRAM AGM-69	
General Signal Corp.	83
Moog Inc.	73
M-109 Howitzer	
BAM Machine Co.	63
Eur Pac Corp.	38
Forest Scientific Inc.	53
H&R Parts Co. Inc.	84
Hydrodyne Industries	131
Kasco Metal Products Corp.	24
M&M Ordnance Corp.	15
Ronal Industries Inc.	23
ZB Precision Products	45
	476
M-109 Medium Speed Howitzer	
Aluf Industries	414
H&R Parts Co. Inc.	32
Lunn Industries	101
Maximum Precision Metal Products	94
Ronal Industries	1,920
	2,561
M-110 Howitzer	
Breton Industries	89
Dunlin Corp.	49
General Signal Corp	155
Humbert Machine Corp.	29
PTE Inc.	12
RAN Associates	33
Ronal Industries	574
	941
Walleye Missile	
Applied Design Co.	230
NY TOTAL	517,396

*Systems affected by a freeze (as specified elsewhere)
**This is a subcontract (see Appendix A)

SOURCE: *Prime Contract Awards over $10,000 by State County, Contractor and Place New York*: FY 1981 (DOD Publication #P12

DOD Procurement Coding Manual, Volume 1, Commodities and Services (Applicable to FY 1981—DOD Publications # MN02

Alphabetic Detail Listing of DOD Prime Contractors: FY 1981 (DOD Publication # ST 613)

Geographic Detail Listing of DOD Prime Contractors: FY 1981 (DOD Publication # ST 615)

Prime Contract Awards over $10,000 by Major Systems, Work Performed and Awarding Department (DOD Publication # ST04)

Figure 3.3 A Few Samples from Alphabetic Detail of DoD Prime Contractors over $10,000 (ST18), FY 1982

```
S M
C O            1111 222222 22 22222  5 7  9 9 9 9                        1 1 1 1 1        1 1 9 2 2 2
V N           5555 AAAAAA BB CCCCC   3 A C 8 999 A B C D 10A 10B 10C 11  2 3 4 5 6 1717   8 9 A 0 1 3  24  $$$$$(000)

LOCKHEED CORP                        SUNNYVALE      CALIFORNIA          555240  6920  05
1 A AK50 0071 DAAK50-79-C0025  D C A 5 1 1 2 2 AC14 DBS A1A RDTE/AIRCRAFT  8 A 7 5 B 11    2 B 1 W 2 A L3  13,500
1 C AK50 0109 DAAK50-79-C0025  D C A 5 1 1 2 2 AC14 DBS A1A RDTE/AIRCRAFT  8 A 8 5 B 11    2 B 1 W 2 C L3   4,000
1 C AK50 0110 DAAK50-79-C0025  D C A 5 1 1 2 2 AC14 DBS A1A RDTE/AIRCRAFT  8 A 7 5 B 11    2 B 1 W 2 C L3   7,442
1 E AK50 0170 DAAK50-79-C0025  D C A 5 1 1 2 2 AC14 DBS A1A RDTE/AIRCRAFT  8 A 8 5 B 11    2 B 1 W 2 E L3      54
1 F AK50 0211 DAAK50-79-C0025  D C A 5 1 1 2 2 AC14 DBS A1A RDTE/AIRCRAFT  8 A 8 5 B 11    2 B 1 W 2 F L3  20,958
1 F AK50 0212 DAAK50-79-C0025  D C A 5 1 1 2 2 AC14 DBS A1A RDTE/AIRCRAFT  8 A 3 5 B 11    2 A 1 W 2 F L3     500
1 J AK50 0002 DAAK50-79-C0025  D C A 5 1 1 2 2 AC14 DBS A1A RDTE/AIRCRAFT  8 A 7 5 B 11    2 B 1 W 2 J L3   3,100
1 K AK50 0017 DAAK50-79-C0025  D C A 5 1 1 2 2 AC14 DBS A1A RDTE/AIRCRAFT  8 A 7 5 B 11    2 B 1 W 2 K L3  11,000
1 K AK50 0028 DAAK50-79-C0025  D C A 5 1 1 2 2 AC14 DBS A1A RDTE/AIRCRAFT  8 A 8 5 B 11    2 B 1 W 2 K L3      54
1 L AK50 0054 DAAK50-79-C0025  D C A 5 1 1 2 2 AC14 DBS A1A RDTE/AIRCRAFT  8 A 8 5 B 11    2 B 1 W 2 L L3     295
1 H AK50 0258 DAAK50-79-C0025  D C A 5 1 1 2 2 AC14 000 S1  RDTE/AIRCRAFT  8 A 7 5 B 11    2 B 1 W 2 H F5     249
1 I AK50 0328 DAAK50-79-C0025  D C A 5 1 1 2 2 AC14 DBS A1A RDTE/AIRCRAFT  8 A 7 5 B 11    2 B 1 W 2 I F5   2,087
1 I AK50 0314 DAAK50-79-C0025  D C A 5 1 1 2 2 AC14 DBS A1A RDTE/AIRCRAFT  8 A 8 5 B 11    2 B 1 W 2 I F5   3,500
1 K AK50 0007 DAAK50-79-C0025  D C A 5 1 1 2 2 AC14 DBS A1A RDTE/AIRCRAFT  8 A 7 5 B 11    2 B 1 W 2 J L3   1,100
3 I HC48 0065 F04701-82-C0121  B C A 5 1 1 2 2 AR33 000 A2  RDTE/SPACE TRANSPORTATION S 8 A 3 5 A 11  4 A 1 W 2 I D6   3,000
3 H FJ04 6557 F09603-82-C4350  B C A 5 1 1 2 2 1270 ACD A7  AIRCRAFT GUNNERY FIRE CONTRO 8 A 3 5 A 1015 1 B 1 J 1 H A3    138
3 B HR01 0162 F33615-81-C3220  B C Z 5 1 1 2 2 AC12 000 A1C RDTE/AIRCRAFT  8 A 7 5 B 11    2 B 1 U 1 B F3      33
3 K HR01 0071 F33615-81-C3220  B C Z 5 1 1 2 2 AC12 000 A1C RDTE/AIRCRAFT  8 A 7 5 B 11    2 B 1 U 1 K F3      39
3 G HR01 0183 F33615-81-C3220  B C Z 5 1 1 2 2 AC12 000 A1C RDTE/AIRCRAFT  8 A 7 5 B 11    2 B 1 U 1 G F3      52

                      LOCATION  TOTAL                                                                           19     71,101
```

Explanation:

These are all the contract awards issued to Lockheed Corporation in Sunnyvale (this is the parent corporation of Lockheed Missiles and Space that is located in the same place). It is establishment 555240 at location 6920 (Sunnyvale) in state 05 (California). At this location the company had 19 contracts totalling $71,101,000 in FY 1982.

The first 14 listings are all for contract number DAAK50-79-C0025. This is an Army contract first issued in 1979. It is administered by purchasing office number AK50 (unknown). This is a Mulit-Year Procurement (Column 7C). The AC14 in Column 10A is the code for Engineering Development of Aircraft. The DBS in Column 10B indicates that this is work on a Remotely Piloted Vehicle. The A1A in Column 10C indicates this is work on Airframes and Related Assemblies and Spares. The one contract with a S1 in this column is for Services, probably field service work on this remotely piloted vehicle. Column 14 reveals that these are all Modifications, either a Funding Action (7) or a Change Order (8). Column 15 indicates these contracts were negotiated without advertising. Column 1717 says this is because this is Experimental, Development, Test or Research work. But Column 18 says they were competitively negotiated on the basis of Design, Technical, or Other. Column 20 says they were all Cost-Plus-Incentive Fee -- Without Performance Incentive awards. Most of these awards are estimated to be completed in December 1983 (Column 24) except for three which will be completed in June 1985 (coded as F5). The total amount awarded for this contract this year is $67,839,000 (found by adding the 14 entries in Column $$$$).

Figure 3.3 (continued)

There is one $138,000 contract award from the Air Force for aircraft gunnery fire control components (1270 in Column 10A) for a C-130 Hercules Cargo Transport airplane (Column 10B) and this is Electronics and Communication Equipment (Column 10C). The 1015 code in Column 1717 indicates this is Replacement Parts for Specially Designed Equipment. The other Air Force contracts are for Exploratory Development of Aircraft (AC12 in Column 10A) and Advanced Development of Space Transportation Systems (AR33). These weapons don't yet have weapons codes (000 in Column 10B).

```
S M
C O         1111 222222 22 22222  57    9 9 9 9                                  1111 1   1 1 9 2 2 2
V N  5555 AAAA AAAAAA BB CCCCC 3 A C 8 999 A B C D 10A  10B 10C 11 DESCRIPTION OF CMDTY/SRVC  2 3 4 5 6 1717 8 9 A 0 1 3 24 $$$$$(000)

LOCKHEED CORP                  PALMDALE        CALIFORNIA    555240 5080 05
3 I HU18 0070 F33657-79-E0005  B C A 5  1 1 2 2 ZI53 ARA C2 MAINT-REPAIR-ALTER/PRODUCTIO 8 A 6 5 A 1016 4 B 1 S 1 1 D3   96
3 E HU03 0058 F33657-82-M2092  B C B 5  3 3 2 2 9130 AFA A8A LIQUID PROPELLANTS & FUEL PE 8 E 3 J          E E2        12
```

Explanation:

This is an excerpt from the listing for Lockheed Corp. in Palmdale. The first contract is from the Air Force for Additional Work (6 in Column 14) of Maintenance, Repair, or Alteration of Real Property — Production Buildings (ZI53 in Column 10A). This work is connected with the SR-71 Blackbird Reconnaissance aircraft (ARA in Column 10B) and is for facilities which will be owned by the government (C2 in Column 10C). The second contract is another Air Force contract for Liquid Propellants & Fuel, Petroleum Base (9130 in Column 10A) for a F-5 Freedom Fighter. This is a Foreign Military Sale (J in Column 15) which means that it was purchased through the DoD, but was actually bought by a foreign country.

```
OPTICAL COATING LABORATORY INC   SANTA ROSA     CALIFORNIA    657510 6380 05
2 I 1674 1011 N60530-81-C0151  B C A 1  1 1 2 2 AC64 000 A7 RDTE/ELECTRONICS AND COMMUNI 8 A 7 5 A 11  5 A 1 U 2 F K2   178
2 I 1674 1012 N60530-81-C0151  B C A 1  1 1 2 2 AC64 000 A7 RDTE/ELECTRONICS AND COMMUNI 8 A 7 5 A 11  5 A 1 U 2 F K2   32
3 I HM02 0383 F08651-82-M4792  B C A 5  1 1 2 2 5915 000 C9E FILTERS AND NETWORKS       8 E 3 3 J 0000 0   J 1 1 K2    14
3 G HK02 0354 F29650-82-CE004  D C A 5  1 1 2 2 6650 000 C9E OPTICAL INSTRUMENTS        8 A 3 5 B 1001 5 B 2 J 1 G C3  64
3 F HR06 0240 F33615-82-C2232  B C Z 5  1 1 2 2 AC12 000 A1C RDTE/AIRCRAFT             8 A 3 5 A 11  2 B 1 U 1 F E4    81
                  LOCATION TOTAL  5                                                                                   369
```

Explanation:

This is the listing for Optical Coating Laboratory Inc. in Santa Rosa, California. The first two contracts are from the Navy. They are for Engineering Development of Electronics and Communication Equipment (AC64 in Column 10A and A7 in Column 10C). They are Cost-Plus-Fixed Fee contracts (U in Column 20) and were negotiated just with Optical Coating Labs because it is Experimental, Development, Test or Research work (11 in Column 1717). The other contract listings are equally unenlightening. It is very difficult to learn the purpose of the RDT&E work from this report.

Page 44

Figure 3.4 Summary of the <u>Defense Acquisition Management Data System</u> (DAMDS)
<u>Code Translation Manual</u> -- <u>Fiscal Years 1981/1982</u> (MN04)

Column Heading	Data Item	Explanation Summary (see the MN04 manual for full details)
SVC	Service Reporting Function	1=Army 2=Navy 3=Air Force 4=Defense Logistics Agency (DLA) 5=Army Corps of Engineers (Civil Functions)
MON	Report Month	A=January ... L=December
5555	Purchasing Office	Find in <u>List of DoD Purchasing Offices</u> (MN01)
1111 AAAA	Report Number	Number assigned by the purchasing office

--- CONTRACT NUMBER ---

222222 AAAAAA	Department or Activity	DA=Army N=Navy F=Air Force M=Marines DLA=Defense Logistics Agency DMA=Defense Mapping Agency DCA=Defense Communications Agency DNA=Defense Nuclear Agency MDA=Miscellaneous Defense Activities
22 BB	Fiscal Year	Fiscal year in which basic contract number was initially assigned.
22222 CCCCC	Serial Number	Assigned by Purchasing Office. See Section XX of <u>Defense Acquisition Regulations</u> (DAR) for further info.

3	Correction of Prior Report	Blank=Initial Entry 1=Corrected Entry 2=Reversal of Initial Entry
5 A	Small Disadvantaged Business	A=Yes B-F=No for various reasons
7 C	Multi-Year Procurement	A=Yes C=No
8	Subject to Statutory Regs	A-B=Walsh-Healy Act C=Service Contract Act E=Davis-Bacon Act Z=No
999	Labor Surplus Area	1-3=Yes, various kinds 5-8=Other
9 A	Affirmative Action Plan on File	1=Yes 2=No 3=Exempt
9 B	Affirmative Action Plan Previously	1=Yes 2=No 3=Exempt
9 C	Woman-Owned Business	1=Yes 2=No 3=Not Certified

9 D	Consultant Type Service	1=Yes 2=No
10A	Federal Supply Classification (FSC) Code	See <u>DoD Procurement Coding Manual, Volume I</u> (MN02)
10B	Weapons System	See manual above
10C	DoD Claimant Program Number	See manual above
11	Description of Commodity or Srvc	Text of code listed in column 10A
1 2	Coordinated Procurement	1-6=Various types 7=Outside the U.S. 8=Other
1 3	Synopsis of Procurement	A=Synopsized E=Not: Original Est. under $10,000 1-9=Not: Other reasons
1 4	Kind of Procurement Action	1=Initial Letter Contract 2-4=Definitive Contract 6-9=Modification of various kinds
1 5	Contract Placement	J=Foreign Military Sale (FMS) 1=Intragovernmental 2-3=Formal Advertising 4-6= Other various
1 6	Type of Business Concern	A-D=Large business for various reasons J=Small business L=Work outside U.S. R=Overseas firm for work in U.S. M-P=Non-profit institutions, various types
1717	Negotiation Exception	For awards not formally advertised, various reasons. A few examples: 1001=Sole source 1005=Utilities 11=RDT&E 12=Classified purchases
1 8	Extent of Competi- tion in Negot.	1-2=Competitive, various reasons 3-6=Non-competitive 7=Not applicable
1 9	Certified Cost or Pricing Data	A=Required B=Not required
1 9 A	Cost Accounting Clause	1=Includes or is subject to clause 2=Not included or not subject
2 0	Type of Contract	A-M=Fixed price, various types R-W=Cost plus, various types Y-Z=Other types
2 1	Subcontracting Program Plan Clause	1=No clause 2-4=Clauses of various types
2 3	Award Month	A=January ... L=December
2 4	Estimated Completion Date	A=January ... L=December + Last digit of calendar year
$$$$$	Contract Amount	Dollar amount, rounded to nearest thousand

Figure 3.5 A Sample Page from <u>DoD Procurement Coding Manual, Volume I: Commodities and Services</u> (MN02)

NAVY SYSTEM OR EQUIPMENT CODES

DESCRIPTION	CODE	DESCRIPTION	CODE
		AGM-83 BULLDOG	CNT
ROCKET LAUNCHER LAU-51	CLG	AGM-84 HARPOON	CNU
ROCKET LAUNCHER LAU-68	CLH	RIM-85	CNM
		AGM-87	CNO
		AGM-88 HARM	CNP
MISSILES	(CM)(CN)	BQM-90	CNR
	(CP)	AIM-95 AGILE	CNV
RIM-2 TERRIER	CMA	UGM-96 TRIDENT	CNJ
RGM-6 REGULUS I	CMR	RIM-101	CNW
AIM-7 SPARROW	CMB	BGM-109 TOMAHAWK	CNY
RIM 7-H-2 NATO SEA SPARROW	CNA	AEGIS	CNZ
RIM-8 TALOS	CMC	CHAFF DECOY WARHEADS	CMZ
AIM-9 SIDEWINDER	CMD	FIREBRAND TARGET	CPA
CMQ-10 BOMARC	CNB	STINGER	CNX
ATM/AGM-12 BULLPUP	CME		
RGM/MQM-15 REGULUS II	CMW		
MIM-23 HAWK	CNC	ROCKETS	(CR)
RIM-24 TARTER	CMU	MGR-1 HONEST JOHN	CRA
UGM-27 POLARIS	CMF	RUR-4 WEAPON ALPHA	CRE
BQM-34 FIREBEE	CMG	RUR-5 ASROC	CRF
MQM-36 TARGET DRONE	CMH	ADR-8 CHAFF ROCKET	CRH
AQM-37 TARGET DRONE	CMI	AGR-14 ZAP	CRJ
AQM-38	CND	MQR-16	CRK
MQM-39	CNE	5" SPIN STABILIZED ROCKET	CRI
AQM-41 PETREL	CNF	5" ZUNI	CRC
FIM-43 REDEYE	CMS	2.75" ALL TYPES	CRG
UUM-44 SUBROC	CMJ	3.5 HEAT M29	CRD
AGM-45 SHRIKE	CMK	MK-56 MOD 2 ROCKET MTR	CRL
RIM-46 SEA MAULER	CNH	66 MM INCEND RKT	CRB
QH-50 DASH	CMY		
RIM-50 TYPHON	CMT		
AGM-53 CONDOR	CMX	VEHICLES	(D)
AIM-54 PHOENIX	CML		
RIM-55 TYPHON	CNK		
PQM-56	CNL	VARIOUS	(DB)
ZRGM-59	CNN	LVTC-7	DBL
AGM-62 WALLEYE	CMM	LVTE-7	DBN
ZAGM-63	CNQ	LVTP-7	DBK
RIM-66 STANDARD MISSILE(MED)	CMN	LVTR-7	DBM
RIM-67 STANDARD MISSILE(EXT)	CMP	MK-30 MOD-0 MOBIL ASW TGT V	DBE
MGM-71 TOW	CNG	M88 RECOVERY VEHICLE	DBT
MIM-72 CHAPARRAL	CMV		
ZUGM-73 POSEIDON	CMQ		
MQM-74	CNS	CARRIER	(DC)
XM-77 DRAGON	CNI	MK-11 ARMRD TROOP CARRIER	DCA
AGM-78 STANDARD ARM	CMO		

Figure 3.6   A Sample Page from Commerce Business Daily Showing Contract Awards

---

COMMERCE BUSINESS DAILY   **Issue No. PSA-8529; Thursday, February 23, 1984**

---

locator designator (G/VLLD) System—FY84 production for 200 ea—DAAH01-84-C-A062 (DAAH01-84-R-A870)—Hughes Aircraft Company, 2101 El Segundo, CA 90245—$29,451,900.

U.S. Army Armament Munitions and Chemical Command, Attn: DRSAR-PCP-SP 309-794-4664 or 4166, Rock Island, IL 61299.

12—**TELESCOPE, PANORAMIC**—NSN 1240-00-895-9106—DAAA09-84-C-0025/P00001—Date of award 26 Jan 84—Qty 100 ea—$479,800—Small business—Opto Mechanik, Inc, PO Box 640, Melbourne, FL 32901.

12—**M1A1 COLLIMATOR MOD KIT**—NSN 1240-00-332-1779—Contract DAAA09-84-C-0189—Date of award 10 Feb 84—Bid DAAA09-83-R-4670—Qty 1,405 ea—$285,172—Small business—ADE Technology Corp, 7301 W Wilson Ave, Harwood Heights, IL 60656.

---

13 Ammunition and Explosives

Directorate of Contracting & Manufacturing, Ogden Air Logistics Center, Hill AFB, UT 84056, Attn: PMXOD.

13—**INITIATOR** (1377-01-054-2912) & data, appl F-16 acft, Contract F42600-84-C-0154 dated 31 Jan 84—2 line items—$117,306—OEA Inc (S), 34501 E Quincy Ave, Denver CO 80210.

13—**REMOVER** (1377-01-058-0122) & data, appl F-16 acft, Contract F42600-84-C-0153 dated 2 Feb 84—2 line items—$355,716—OEA Inc, 34501 E Quincy Ave, Denver, CO 80210.

13—**REMOVER** (1377-01-057-5431) & data, appl F-16 acft, Contract F42600-84-C-0309 dated 2 Feb 84—2 line items—$367,524—OEA Inc, 34501 E Quincy Ave, Denver CO 80210.

13—**EXPLOSIVE CHARGE** (1336-00-931-3590), explosive charge (1336-00-076-4715), explosive charge (1336-00-932-2434), explosive charge (1336-00-051-3571) & data, appl LGM-30F/G, LGM-30B/F, Contract F42600-84-C-0302 dated 2 Feb 84—6 line items—$96,940—Unidynamics/Phoenix Inc, PO Box 2990, Phoenix AZ 85062-2990.

Navy Ships Parts Control Center, Code 02623 PO Box 2020, Mechanicsburg, PA 17055.

13—**LOAD MC50**, P/N 126AS125, NSN 1377-00-263-4126, Contract N00104-84-G-0200 (Negn N00104-83-N-A575) Ord 0002—Dated 27 Dec 83—1366 ea—$192,108—OEA Inc, PO Box 10488, Denver, CO 80210.

13—**CIRCUIT CARD ASSEMBLY**, NSN 7H 1355-01-059-6235, Contract N00104-78-A-0242 (Negn N00104-83-Y-VK29) Ord 0146 dated 28 Oct 83—66 ea—$75,438—Gould Inc, 18901 Euclid Ave, Cleveland, OH 44117.

13—**SHELL, EXERCISE**, NSN 7H 1355-01-140-6827, Contract N00104-78-A-0242 (Negn N00104-83-X-C661) Ord 0148 dated 1 Oct 83—34 ea—$187,782—Gould Inc, 8901 Euclid Ave, Cleveland, OH 44117.

13—**FIN ASSEMBLY, TORPED**, NSN 1H 1355-00-977-2831, Contract N00104-80-G-0015 (Negn N00104-83-X-D408) Ord 0019 dated 30 Sep 83—590 ea—$206,500—TRW Inc, 2355 Euclid Ave, Cleveland, OH 44117.

13—**CABLE ASSEMBLY**, P/N 2509523, NSN 1H 1355-01-029-9583, Contract N00104-83-C-2848 (Negn N00104-83-Y-TB17) dated 27 Oct 83—119 ea—$35,331—Cable Systems & Assembly Co, 210 Broadway, Everett, MA 02149.

13—**PLUG ASSEMBLY**, P/N 2507616, NSN 1H 1355-01-029-2993, Contract N00104-83-C-2858 (Negn N00104-83-T-E187) dated 11 Oct 83—566 ea—$26,319—Orlotronics Corp, 3201 Arch St, Philadelphia, PA 19104.

13—**PRESSURE CYLINDER**, Dwg PL5268574, NSN 4T 1356-01-123-4744, Contract N00104-83-C-A024), (Negn N00104-83-C-A024 (IFB N00104-83-B-0718) dated 23 Nov 83—146 ea—$278,468—Cartridge Actuated Devices Inc, 123 Clinton Rd, Fairfield NJ 07006.

13—**CTG, CAL .45, CENTERFIRE MATCH BALL 185 GR WADCUTTER**, Dwg 10521458-E, NSN 2T 1305-00-892-4230-A482, Contract N00104-84-C-A020 (IFB N00104-83-B-0784) dated 22 Nov 83—300,000 ea—$42,675—Federal Cartridge Corp, 2700 Foshay Tower, Minneapolis, MN 55402.

U.S. Army Armament Munitions and Chemical Command, Attn: DRSAR-PCP-SP 309-794-4664 or 4166, Rock Island, IL 61299.

13—**SIMULATOR M22 (ATWESS)**—NSN 1370-01-085-2601—DAAA09-84-C-0144—3 Feb 84—IFB DAAA09-83-B-4940—633,430—$1,488,560—Dela-Tek Inc, Sub of Technical Ordnance, Inc, 2000 N Vavages Ave, PO Box 1407, Coolidge, AZ 85228.

13—**EXPULSION CHARGE CUP**—NSN 1320-01-M30-1802—P/N C15-12-289—DAAA09-84-C-0230—31 Jan 84—DAAA09-83-B-5033—43,418 ea—$58,310—Gayston Corp, 55 Janney Rd, PO Box 239, Dayton, OH 45404.

13—**76MM PROJECTILE BODY**—NSN 1315-01-064-8424—DAAA09-84-C-0276—31 Jan 84—DAAA09-84-R-0047—69,946 ea—$4,580,763—Lansdowne Steel and Iron Co, Highland Ave, Morton, PA 19070.

13—**PRIMER, ELECTRIC MK 153 MOD 1**—NSN 1390-01-035-1842—DAAA09-84-C-0232—10 Feb 84—DAAA09-83-R-3069—3,897 ea—$99,178—Propellex Corporation, PO Box 387, Edwardsville, IL 62025.

Whittaker Corp, Bermite Div, Saugus, CA.

---

14 Guided Missiles

U.S. Army Missile Command, Directorate of Procurement and Production, Redstone Arsenal, AL 35898.

14—**PARTS KIT, FLUID, PRE**—NSN 1430-00-076-1888—APN 5959133—Qty 627 ea—Awarded to Fluid Conditioning Products, Inc, Lititz, PA—DAAH01-84-C-0262 (DAAH01-84-B-A005)—Contract amount $37,475.

14—**CONTROL SIGNAL, COMPARATOR**—NSN 1430-01-040-3750—APN 10276490—Qty 712 ea—Contract DAAH01-84-C-0220—Date 27 Jan 84—Amount of contract $1,643,139—Contract issued to McDonnell Douglas Corp, PO Box 600, Titusville, FL 32780.

14—**TARGET GROUP SETS**, Mdl 685-1, thirty-six ea, for use with the Target Tracking Control System (TTCS) in the Missile System test and evaluation programs—Delivery to Fort Bliss, TX by 31 Oct 84 Priced Order 0035 under Basic Ordering Agreement DAAH01-81-G-A037 in the amount of $730,152 awarded 24 Jan 84 to General Indicator Corporation, Vega Precision Laboratories Division (A), 800 Follin Lane, Vienna, VA 22180.

14—**M70 A-2 TRAINER ADAPTER CABLE** Kit, 391 ea plus 1 first article—P/N 5425634, with an option of 432 ea—Contract DAAH01-84-C-0141—Awarded 24 Jan 84 to PBR Electronics, Inc, 1601 W Hoobs St, Athens, AL 35611—Total amount $272,020.

14—**GEAR**—NSN 1430-01-071-1442—APN 10668615-3—Qty 805 ea—Delivery Dec 84—Contract DAAH01-84-C-0234—Sol DAAH01-83-R-A779—$106,509—Awarded to Lear Siegler, Inc, Romac Division (S), 241 South Abbie Road, Elyria, OH 44035

14—**POWER SUPPLY**—APN 11510968—NSN 1430-01-064-8126—Qty 30 ea—One ea required for testing and approval—Contract DAAH01-84-C-0244—(DAAH01-84-B-A001)—$50,520—Ship to: Sharpe Army Depot, Lathrop, CA—Sentinel Electronics, Inc, PO Box 122, Bristol, PA 19007.

14—**XM HOISTING BEAMS AND VARIOUS HAWK MODIFICATION KITS**—DAAH01-84-C-0251—$1,717,753—Dated 3 Feb 84—Raytheon Company, Missile Systems Div, 350 Lowell Street, Andover, MA 01810.

14—**HAWK TAILCONE ASSEMBLY**—NSN 1420-01-034-8725—DAAH01-84-C-0269—31 Jan 84—(DAAH01-83-B-0292)—400 ea plus 1 first article—$75,777—Ainslie Corporation, 531 Pond Street, Braintree, MA 02184.

14—**ELECTRICAL CONTRACT ASSEMBLY**—NSN 5999-00-350-4073—APN 10672017—Qty 434 ea—Delivery Nov 84—Contract DAAH01-84-C-0239—(DAAH01-84-B-A032)—$109,368—Awarded to Agustin Industries, Inc, Rd 5 Thomas Avenue, Williamstown, NJ 08094.

14—**GENERATOR**—NSN 1430-00-968-7617—APN 10049206—Qty 4 ea—Awarded to ICSD Corporation, Kissimmee, FL—DAAH01-84-C-0238 (DAAH01-84-R-A027) Contract amount $69,996.

14—**TOWED CHAPARRAL MISSILE SYSTEMS**—13 ea—And towed Chaparral peculiar spare—Contract DAAH01-84-C 0224—Awarded 30 Jan 84—Contract amount $10,632,500—Ford Aerospace and Communications Corporation, Aeronutronic Division, Ford Road, Newport Beach, CA 92660.

---

15 Aircraft and Airframe Structural Components

Directorate of Contracting & Manufacturing, Ogden Air Logistics Center, Hill AFB UT 84056, Attn: PMXOD

15—**DUCT ASSBLY**—1560-00-918-6394BF—Appl F-4 acft—Contract F42600-84-C-4303 dated 19 Jan 84—116 ea—$364,550—Metal Bellows Corp, 20960 Knapp St, Chatsworth CA 91311.

15—**CORE TE STABILOR**—1560-01-149-7453BF—Appl F-4 acft—Contract F42600-84-C-4434 dated 19 Jan 84—231 ea—$69,242—Brunswick Corp, 4300 Industrial Ave, Lincoln NB 68504.

15—**COVER, ACCESS**—1560-00-953-3666BF—Appl F4B/F4C/D/E/RF4C—Contract F42600-84-C-4379 dated 16 Jan 84—224 ea—$35,784—Flameco Engineering Inc, 2951 Pennsylvania Ave, PO Box 1534, Ogden UT 84402.

15—**TIP ASSY, WELDED, ACFT**—1560-00-404-1951BF—Appl F4—Contract F42600-83-G-7508-0014 dated 16 Jan 84—85 ea—$36,133—Flameco Eng Inc, 2951 Pennsylvania Ave, Ogden UT 84401.

15—**SUPPORT ASSY**—(1560-00-785-8435BF)—Support assy—(1560-00-785-8434BF)—Appl F-4 acft—Contract F42600-84-C-4249 dated 11 Jan 84—$67,216—KT Aerofab, Inc, 203 N Johnson Ave, El Cajon CA 92020.

15—**DRAIN ASBLY**—(1560-00-759-9011BF)—Appl F-4 acft—Contract F42600-84-C-4354 dated 10 Jan 84—881 ea—$36,658—Western Pacific Enterprises, 8110 Remmet St, Canoga Park CA 91304.

15—**DISCHARGER**—(1560-01-116-5688WF)—Appl F16A/B—Contract F42600-84-C-4088 dated 6 Jan 84—2695 ea—$62,389—Chelton Inc Chelton (Electrostatics) Ltd, PO Box 711, Lewisville TX 75067.

15—**SKIN**—(1560-00-825-5032BF)—Appl F-4 acft—Contract F42600-84-C-4334 dated 5 Jan 84—90 ea—$33,660—Algonquin Parts, 667 Conn Ave, S Norwalk CT 06854.

Figure 3.7 Contract Award Listings in the DMS Format

```
SANTA CLARA
 ESL INC
  (AC64)-C-E SYSTEMS ENGINEERING R&D  01/02/82
  $3,299,000 DAAK20-80-C-0528 CSG ESL INC SUNNYVALE,
  CALIFORNIA 94086 USA ELECTRONICS R&D COMMAND
```

Listing Information	Explanation
SANTA CLARA	The name of the County where the company or division of the company which received the contract is located.
ESL INC	The name of the company or division.
(AC64)	The Federal Supply Classification (FSC) code describing the type of work to be performed. In this case, AC64 means "Electrical and Communication Equipment, Engineering Development".
C-E SYSTEMS ENGINEERING R&D	A short description of the type of work to be done. Often this description is more detailed than the code number description, sometimes listing the name of the weapon system it is part of. Other times it is very terse, such as "SPARE PARTS" or "OTHER RESEARCH." The abbreviation EA means Each. 500 EA means that 500 devices will be delivered.
01/02/82	The date of the contract. Note that this is listed in the form DD/MM/YY so this is for February 1, 1982 not January 2, 1982.
$3,299,000	The amount of the contract award. The abbreviation TTD means Total To Date (this is total amount awarded on this contract to date including funds paid out in previous years.
DAAK20-80-C-0528	The contract number. A lot of information can be extracted just from this alone.
DAAK20	This is a unique code for the awarding agency. The letter prefix specifies which branch of the armed forces: F=Air Force, N=Navy, DAA=Army, DLA=Defense Logistics Agency
80	The fiscal year in which the contract was originally awarded. In this case, this is an extension to a contract originally awarded in FY 1980.
0528	The 528th contract awarded by this agency this fiscal year.
CSG	(unknown)
ESL INC SUNNYVALE, CALIFORNIA 94086	The name of the company/division and its address receiving the contract. ESL is owned by TRW, but this is not reported here.
USA ELECTRONICS R&D COMMAND	The name of the contracting agency. In this case, it was awarded by the U.S. Army Electronics R&D Command.

Figure 3.8 The Code Letters for "AN" (Electronic) Equipment

Electronic equipment is designated by an "AN" code. A typical AN code looks like this:

AN/TLG-5A

AN	Indicates an "AN" system	G	Purpose
T	Installation location	5	Model number
L	Type of equipment	A	Modification

Installation Location Codes

A   Aircraft
B   Submarine
D   Pilotless carrier
F   Fixed
G   Ground, general use
K   Amphibious vehicles
M   Ground, mobile (in vehicle designed
        especially for this equipment)
P   Pack or portable (animal or person)
S   Water surface craft (ship or boat)
T   Ground, transportable
U   General utility (can be used multiple
        places)
V   Ground, vehicular (mounted in a
        vehicle used for other purposes such
        as a tank)
W   Water surface and underwater

Type of Equipment

A   Invisible light, heat radiation
B   Pigeon
C   Carrier
D   Radiac
E   Nupac
F   Photographic
G   Telegraph or teletype
I   Interphone and public address
J   Electro-mechanical (other)
K   Telemetering
L   Countermeasures (jamming)
M   Meteorological
N   Sound in air

P   Radar
Q   Sonar and underwater sound
R   Radio
S   Special types, magnetic, etc. or
        combinations of types
T   Telephone (wire)
V   Visual and visible light
W   Armament (peculiar to armament)
X   Facsimile or television
Y   Data processing

Purpose

A   Auxiliary assemblies (parts and
        components)
B   Bombing
C   Communications (receiving and
        transmitting)
D   Direction finder and/or
        reconnaissance
E   Ejection and/or release
G   Fire control or searchlight
        detecting
H   Recording and/or reproducing
K   Computing
M   Maintenance and test assemblies
        (including tools)
N   Navigation aids
Q   Special or combination of purposes
R   Receiving, passive detecting
S   Detecting and/or range and bearing
T   Transmitting
W   Control
X   Identification and recognition

Components of larger systems are identified as follows:

AS-289/APS-33

AS	Component indicator (this one means "complex antennae")
289	Model number
APS-33	Basic AN system to which component is part

There are 108 component codes. They usually aren't very useful, but call NARMIC or CEC for more information if you need it.

Figure 3.9 A Sample Page from <u>Selling</u> <u>to</u> <u>the</u> <u>Military</u> Describing Purchases Offices (POs)

DEPARTMENT OF THE ARMY MAJOR BUYING OFFICES (Continued)

NASA Langley Research Center
Hampton, Virginia 23605
804/827-1110

Propulsion Laboratory
NASA Lewis Research Center
Cleveland, Ohio 44135
Tel: 216/433-4000

U.S. Army Troop Support and
Aviation
Materiel Readiness Command
(TSARCOM) ATTN: DRSTS—V
4300 Goodfellow Blvd.
St. Louis, MO 63120
Tel: 314/263-2222

Integrated commodity management and procurement responsibility for the following types of equipment: surface transportation (other than tactical wheeled and general purpose vehicles): aircraft both fixed and rotary wing; electric power generation, and services; barrier equipment (including mine and dispensing; general support and supplies (fire fighting, industrial engines, heating and air conditioning, water purification, etc.); test equipment that is apart of, or used with assigned materiel, and aerial delivery equipment.

U.S. Army Missile Command
(MICOM)
ATTN: DRSMI—B
Redstone Arsenal, AL 35809
Tel: 205/876-5441

Areas of responsibility include (1) design and development, (2) product, production, and maintenance engineering; and (3) new equipment training design of pertinent training devices. The U.S Army Missile Command is responsible for integrated commodity management of free rockets, guided missiles, ballistic missiles, targets, air defense, fire control coordination equipment, related special purposes and multisystem test equipment, missile launching and ground support equipment metrology and calibration equipment, and other associated equipment.

U.S. Army Tank-Automotive
Command (TACOM)
ATTN: DRSTA—CB
Warren, Michigan 48090
Tel: 313/573-5388/5406

Associated Installations

Keeweenaw Field Research
Center
Houghton, Michigan 49331

The U.S. Army Tank-Automotive Command (TACOM) is responsible for research, design, development, engineering, test management, modification, product assurance, integrated logistics support, acquisition, and deployment of the following items: Combat, tactical, special purpose vehicles, (e.g. automotive systems, subsystems, and engines, transmissions, suspensions, electrical, peculiar diagnostic test equipment, armor materials application and vehicle survivasbility, and miscellaneous vehicular components), carriers (e.g. personnel, cargo, missile, and rearm), trailers, tractors, special tools, and special purpose kits.

Detroit Arsenal
Warren, Michigan 48090

Pontiac Storage Facility,
Pontiac, Michigan 48657

Army Tank Center
Lima, Ohio 45804

TACOM Support Activity-Selfridge
Selfridge ANG BASE
Selfridge, Michigan 48046

TACOM has the responsibility for the procurement production, maintenance, supply, and repair parts support of the US Armed Forces vehicle fleet, general purpose, construction equipment, material handing equipment, and tactical vehicles for the DoD and our foreign allies.

U.S. Army Test and Evaluation
Command (TECOM)
Aberdeen Proving Ground, MD
21005
Tel: 301/278-4790

The mission of the U.S. Army Test and Evaluation Command is to direct those assigned research activities, proving grounds, installations, boards, and facilities required to test equipment, weapons, and materiel systems to plan and conduct tests of materiel intended for use by the U.S. Army, or developed by the Army for use by other departments of the Government, and to assure efficient and economic use of test facilities.

Chapter 4

Researching Specific Companies and Military Bases

There may be one or a few local companies you particularly want to learn more about. It may be the largest military contractor, one growing rapidly, or one where some of the employees or management are concerned about its military contracts. Or it may be a company you believe is a good candidate for conversion away from military production to civilian production.

Section 4.A. gives examples of questions you might want to ask about a company and presents a form for recording this information. It also gives a procedure for determining what percentage of the company's work comes from prime military contracts. Section 4.B. discusses how to find out what parent corporation owns which subsidiaries. Section 4.C. talks about the issue of profitability, a major driving force for all business decisions including whether or not to produce military equipment. Section 4.D. tells how to request annual reports and 10-K reports. Section 4.E. lists numerous sources for tracking down information on companies. And Section 4.F. discusses how to get information on military facilities.

4.A. Collecting Information on Companies

Several things you might want to know about a company:

-- What is the company's total sales? What percentage of its sales is for military work? Is this percentage growing or shrinking over the years? (see Chapter 2 for information on how to obtain the amount of military sales.)

-- How much taxes does the company pay to the local community?

-- Who works for the company? How many production workers, clerical staff, technical support, and management people are there? Are they concerned about working on military products? What skills do they have? What other products could they make? Is there a labor union representing all or some of the workers?

-- What is the plant's total production capacity? How much of it is idle?

-- What is the company's profit margin on military sales versus civilian sales?

-- Who makes decisions for the company? Are they connected with other military contractors or the Pentagon? Do they want to increase the percentage of military sales to civilian sales or decrease it? Why?

Recording the Most Interesting Information on Companies

Publicly-held corporations are those whose stock can be bought by anyone. Stock in these corporations is traded in one or more of the stock exchanges around the country or it is traded "over the counter." There is a lot of information about publicly-held corporations available to potential investors so they can determine whether the corporation is a good investment prospect. This includes information on the corporation's finances, plant, equipment, and employee relations. It is more difficult to get information on privately-held companies, but not impossible. Much of this information is available from public sources as described below. (Also see the discussions in Chapters 2 and 3.)

There is no single procedure for obtaining information on companies. Some resources are better than others for particular kinds of information. You must simply try different sources until you get what you need.

Figure 4.1 is a form you can use to record some of the more important information about a company from its annual report, 10-K report, and elsewhere. Only some of this information may be relevant for your purposes and worth collecting, depending on how you intend to use it. The Bay State Center for Economic Conversion (BSCforEC) has prepared a much longer and very excellent questionnaire/form for recording important information about a company (see the Resource Center section).

The New York Public Interest Center (NYPIRC) recently published a description of the top 25 military contractors in New York state. Examples of company descriptions from their report, <u>Production</u> <u>for</u> <u>Destruction</u>: <u>Military</u> <u>Spending</u> <u>in</u> <u>New</u> <u>York</u> <u>State</u>, are shown in Figure 4.2. You might want to prepare similar descriptions of the companies in your area.

Determining What Percent of A Company's Business is Military-Related (Prime Contracts)

You can determine the importance of military contracts to the company's business using the following procedure:

1. From the annual report, determine the company's total sales for the year that you have military contract data. This figure is usually listed prominently in the report.

2. Find the amount of money the company has received worldwide in prime military contracts. For the 100 largest military contractors, the easiest source of this information is the Pentagon report <u>100</u> <u>Companies</u> <u>Receiving</u> <u>the</u> <u>Largest</u> <u>Dollar</u> <u>Volume</u> <u>of</u> <u>Prime</u> <u>Contract</u> <u>Awards</u> (P01) or its reprint in <u>Aviation</u> <u>Week</u> <u>and</u> <u>Space</u> <u>Technology</u>, or the annual compilation done by CEP. For smaller companies, the best source for this is probably the Pentagon's <u>Alphabetical</u> <u>Detail</u> <u>of</u> <u>DoD</u> <u>Prime</u> <u>Contractors</u> <u>over</u> <u>$25,000</u> (ST18). This lists all the prime contracts for all the company's facilities around the world and the total for the company. Don't forget to include all of the company's subsidiaries (see Section 4.B. below).

3. Divide the company's total military prime contract awards (at all locations) by total sales. This is a rough estimate of the amount of the company's business which is due to military (prime) contracts. Note that the company's annual year may not correspond to the government's Fiscal Year.

Unless the company has only one location, you will probably only be able to derive this statistic for the whole company, not a figure for your community alone. It is usually difficult to learn the amount of sales generated by a single location. Try asking people at the local company office. Business reporters for the local newspaper may be able to find out for you. Also, check the information available from <u>Sales</u> <u>Marketing</u> <u>and</u> <u>Management</u> magazine (see the Reference section).

4. Divide the amount of prime contracts the company receives in your community by the total amount it receives worldwide to determine what percentage of the company's military contracts are spent locally.

4.B. Who Owns Whom?

Companies are continually buying and selling other companies. Very often the name on the company stays the same even though the corporate owner changes. It can be very difficult to find out just who currently owns a particular division. Here are some sources of information for determining who the corporate parent is for a company in your area.

Each year the DoD publishes 100 Companies Receiving the Largest Dollar Volume of Prime Contract Awards, (P01) ($12). This lists each of the Top 100 Prime Military contractors with all of its subsidiaries which received contracts over $25,000. In April or May of each year Aviation Week and Space Technology reprints this list (see Figure 4.3). You can skim over this list to find subsidiary names that might be part of a larger conglomerate. For some companies, like The Signal Companies, the subsidiaries all have names quite unlike the parent, but others, like Teledyne, all have names starting with the parent name.

For companies not among the Top 100 contractors, you can look up their parents and subsidiaries in two standard references and two references which specifically focus on subsidiaries and parent corporations. These four references (listed in order of our preference) are:

> The Million Dollar Directory
> America's Corporate Families/The Billion Dollar Directory
> Standard and Poor's Register of Corporations
> Directory of Corporate Affiliations -- "Who Owns Whom"

See Appendix 1 for more information on these standard references.

Also, annual reports and other company documents usually have a complete listing of the company's subsidiaries (see Section 4.D.).

4.C. Company Profitability

Most companies do military work not for ideological reasons, but simply because it is a good business in which to make money and turn a profit without much risk. When studying a company, you may want to take particular note of its profit margin so you can point out how the government has allowed the company to make large, easy profits from its military contracts. The contrast between the profits from military and civilian work may be particularly striking if you can get this information. For example, an employee at Rolm Corporation in Santa Clara, California told us that its MIL-SPEC (military specification) division only provides 14% of the sales revenues, but 50% of the company's profits.

Jacques Gansler's book The Defense Industry discusses the profitability and economics of military industry and strategies to strengthen the industry. Appendix 2 describes why companies like military contracts from an economic perspective and shows how to determine the profitability of a company.

4.D. Annual Reports, 10-K Reports, and Other Company Documents

Company Annual Report and 10-K Report

Some of the best sources of information about a company are its annual report and 10-K report. All publicly-held corporations with stock held by over 500 people and assets of over a million dollars must file a 10-K report with the Securities and Exchange Commission (SEC) each year. Both of these reports are sent to shareholders. Some private companies also prepare annual reports and will send them to you. This is particularly true if the company is considering selling stock ("going public").

The annual report and 10-K report frequently have information on the number of employees, sales, earnings, management personnel, land holdings, company organization, major products, outstanding litigation that could affect the stockholder's interests, union relations, and sometimes even the amount of work going to the military.

You can get these reports from the Securities and Exchange Commission (SEC), but they charge 10 cents per page plus postage. It is much easier to write or call the company directly. The local company office may be able to send you these reports, but you may have to call or write the U.S. headquarters.

Extremely informative data about a company's military work is often found in its annual report, especially if the company is primarily involved in the military business. They often brag about their military business -- particularly now that military contracts seem to be a "growth industry" -- and include lots of glossy photos which are great for leaflets and reports. Names of directors and officers are useful for personalizing the company in a protest demonstration, etc., as well as for examining former military connections and interlocking directorates between companies.

Other Company Documents

A company prospectus (an offer to sell shares) is another good source of information from a company, particularly one that is just going public. The company must prepare a prospectus whenever it offers a block of stock for sale. It outlines the company's long-range plans, lists all shareholders owning more than 5% of the corporation's stock, and lists the stockholdings and salaries of the company's directors and senior executives. You can get a prospectus by writing or calling the company, writing to the Securities and Exchange Commission, or talking to a broker. Two other documents available from the company, the notice of its annual meeting and the proxy statement for stockholder proposals, provide similar information and some biographical information on the proposed new directors.

You should also ask for a company history (some companies have whole books on their history) and, for any company you want to follow, ask to be put on the mailing list for press releases and the company newspaper, which can sometimes be very useful -- see Rockwell News for a good example of this.

Detailed information on the ownership of the company's stock can be very useful for proxy battles and looking for interlocking ownership between companies (and between companies and banks), and the influence of rich families. Contact Steve Johnson at the Pacific Northwest Research Center for a bibliography of good sources and tips on how to find this information.

Our Experience Writing for Annual and 10-K Reports

Since we wished to create a continuing file of information on all the military contractors in our area and the largest ones in California, we chose to write a form letter to 100 companies of interest. In order to write for these reports, one must know who the parent company is, its address, and whether it is incorporated and publicly-held. Several of the references we consulted have a symbol code indicating that the company is incorporated, but it doesn't indicate whether it is publicly-held. You can check if a company is publicly held by looking in Directory of Companies Required to File Annual Reports with the Securities and Exchange Commission. This takes some time, but may be worth the effort. (See Appendix 1 for a full description of the Standard References on Companies mentioned below.)

We consulted the following references in the order shown:

-- Ward's 55,000 Corporations 1981 has a table of 55,000 companies with addresses.

It is the easiest to consult, but the 1981 version was the only one available and it seems to be outdated.

-- Dun & Bradstreet's Million Dollar Directory seems to have the most complete listings. It is easy to find the company in the index and then turn to the appropriate volume (usually Volume 1) for the description.

-- Standard & Poor's Register has some listings that the Million Dollar Directory lacks, but it doesn't have some that are found in the Million Dollar Directory. No one source seems to have a monopoly on information!

-- The California Manufacturer's Register seems to be fairly casual about whether a company is based in California or not and it has no information on whether a company is publicly-held or incorporated.

-- Rich's Complete Guide to Santa Clara County's Silicon Valley lists most facilities in the Valley, but it doesn't list the head office of a company unless it is located in Santa Clara County.

-- The Santa Clara County Industrial Directory seems to be very casual about all of its information and we don't trust it to be very accurate.

-- The local telephone book doesn't indicate anything about ownership, etc., but does give the address and phone.

Occasionally a listing was difficult to find. Companies like FMC Corp. are sometimes listed in strict alphabetical order and sometimes listed at the beginning of the F's. Companies with hyphens might be in several places. Argosystems Corporation fooled us by being one word when it seemed like it should be two. We discovered in these guides that a few local companies have recently been bought by large companies.

Some of the information from our references was outdated or wrong, resulting in returned letters, but eventually we were able to find the addresses of all the companies in which we were interested except two.

We wrote to the Top 32 Prime Military Contractors in California and the Top 100 Contractors of Santa Clara Valley (excluding the food suppliers, construction firms, and janitorial, garbage, and security guard services). We sent our request on Pacific Studies Center letterhead (our sister organization), assuming it was more likely to be answered.

For publicly-held California corporations we asked for the annual report and 10-K. For out-of-state, publicly-held corporations we asked for the two reports and also for any literature they had describing their operations in California. For large conglomerates we further asked for specific information on the divisions or subsidiaries which do most of the military work. For example, we wrote Ford Motor Company and asked for information about Ford Aerospace and Communications Corporation. We received 5 brochures including two on the Aeronutronic Division which seems to do most of the military electronics work. For privately-held corporations and unincorporated companies, we asked for general information about the company including a brief description of their product line and operations.

Locating the addresses and status (whether publicly- or privately-held) of these 100 companies took a total of about 12 hours and typing the information into a word-processor and printing the form letters took another 12 hours. The annual reports then arrived over the next 5 weeks. We received 71 responses. Unfortunately, some of the companies of most interest didn't send us anything.

The responses took many forms: some companies sent a lot of information, loudly proclaiming their military products. Several companies we had guessed were publicly-held told us they were privately-held and, therefore, didn't have annual reports or 10-Ks available to the public. They sent us nothing. For some of these companies, it probably would have been better to ask only for a description of their product line and operations since we are more interested in this information than in the financial information which they are more reluctant to give out. Other companies seem to want no one to know what they are doing and since they contract mostly with the DoD, aren't very concerned about maintaining a good image in the community or losing potential sales. Most of the large out-of-state conglomerates only sent us their annual reports, 10-Ks, and a very general brochure. For these companies, it would probably be useful to write to the local facility and ask for a description of its operations. We learned that several of the smaller companies had been bought by larger companies, making it clear that Dun & Bradstreet and Standard & Poor's make mistakes.

Since we have access to Pacific Studies Center's files, we learned about some of the more unresponsive companies there. We also obtained good information about some of the smaller companies from employees we knew.

4.E. Sources of Information

There are numerous sources of information on military companies. Because they are companies like any other, they are discussed in many newspapers and business magazines, listed on stock exchanges, and tracked by government agencies, employment placement centers, etc. And since they do military work for the government, there are a few additional sources of good information. After you have some sense of the company, you can profitably interview people who work there for additional information.

This section is divided into three sub-sections detailing these three sources of information.

General Business Information

Business School Libraries

Business School libraries at local colleges are often a good source of information on local companies. For example, Stanford University's Business School uses local companies as case studies for students to learn how to manage companies. These case studies are filed at the library. Most schools have a very complete set of business magazines and references. Some though, like Stanford, charge a fee for access to anyone except students and alumni.

Public Libraries

Public libraries usually have several standard references describing companies. Each library usually has either Standard and Poor's Register of Corporations or Dun and Bradstreet's Million Dollar Directory. They also have a few other references, some useful, some not so useful (see Appendix 1 for a full description of the Standard References on Companies). Because money is tight, many libraries share their resources with other nearby libraries. One may specialize in business and have a much more extensive collection on this topic.

Libraries may have some company annual reports -- often companies will send their annual report to the local city library. One library in our area has annual reports for the first 100 of the Fortune 500 Corporations. Very few have any 10-K reports and those that do only have a few.

By calling around, we found that the Oakland Business Library (45 miles from us) has annual reports for most California-based corporations, but very few 10-K reports. The

Social Science library at the University of California Berkeley campus (also 45 miles away) has a set of microfiche with annual reports for thousands of corporations.

Two good indexes for business magazines are <u>Business Periodicals Index</u> and <u>F + S Index</u>. <u>F + S</u> covers more journals, but the format of <u>Business Periodicals Index</u> is more familiar. The <u>Wall Street Journal Index</u> covers articles in this business newspaper.

Fortune 500

Each year, <u>Fortune</u> magazine publishes a listing of the 500 largest U.S. industrial corporations, known as the Fortune 500. This year this list was in the April 30, 1984 issue. They also publish the 500 largest U.S. non-industrial corporations (June 13, 1983) which includes the Top 100 diversified financial, diversified service, and commercial banking companies, and the Top 50 life insurance, retailing, transportation, and utility corporations. They also publish a list of the 500 largest foreign industrial corporations (August 23, 1982). Each company is ranked by its annual sales and for each company is listed the sales, assets, net income (profit), stockholder's equity, number of employees, 2-digit SIC code, and net income as a percent of sales and as a percent of stockholder's equity. There is also an alphabetical index.

<u>Business Week</u> Scoreboard

The March 21, 1984 issue of <u>Business Week</u> contains the annual survey of 1,200 of the largest U.S. corporations. This issue has data on sales, earnings, profits, stock price and book value, earnings per share, return on equity, price-earnings ratio, assets, total debt, top executive compensation (pay), R&D spending, and pension assets. It also has data on 930 foreign companies and 200 banks. [<u>Forbes</u> magazine also has similar listings.]

<u>Inc.</u> 500

<u>Inc.</u> magazine publishes a listing each year of the 500 fastest-growing U.S. private companies, known as the <u>Inc.</u> 500. Last year this list was in the December 1983 issue. The list is composed of privately-held companies with a sales history of at least 5 years, with 1978 sales of $100,000 to $25 million, and with a net growth in 1981 to 1982. They are ordered according to sales growth over the last 5 years and for each company is listed the 1978 and 1982 sales, a profit range for these two years, the number of employees for these two years, date founded, <u>Inc.</u> rank in 1982, number of acquisitions of other companies, and a 2-word description of their business.

The <u>Wall Street Journal</u>

The <u>Wall Street Journal</u> often has very good articles on businesses and industries. Articles are indexed in the <u>WSJ Index</u>. Most good libraries carry the <u>Journal</u> and <u>Index</u>.

Local Sources

If you have connections with a brokerage firm, they may be able to supply you with annual reports, 10-K reports, and other information. They may also have inside "scuttlebutt" which could be useful.

"The County offices that maintain property records keep information on the contractor's real and personal holdings. The property tax rolls reveal how much tax the contractor is paying for land and equipment -- and how much comparable landholders and businesses in the area are paying. The county deed books will tell you if the contractor is buying or leasing land.

"The local courthouse also contains a wealth of information about company practices. Records in the deeds and property offices may reveal such data as the company's home office address, its local agent, or sources of credit -- in addition to describing land transactions. And always check the court records: federal, state, or local. If a company has sued someone or has been sued, the case file may reveal a lot about them. These files are open to the public.

"Despite all the documents you can glean from the above sources, remember: people are usually your best source of insights into corporate practices. Plant workers, truckers, residents, insurance agents, doctors, and others know a lot about what's going on, or have heard rumors that you can help investigate. Journalists and public officials also have a lot of knowledge about the community." [How to Research Your Local Military Contractor, Highlander Center]

Other Information Sources

Local newspapers may have very detailed and up-to-date articles on the industry in the area. The business reporters and editors may also be able to give you good information from their own knowledge and their files. Job advertisements will frequently have lots of information about the company.

Your local telephone book, especially the Yellow Pages, is a valuable resource. Your local Chamber of Commerce may have brochures which will give a good overview of the local economy. They might have a history of the commercial development in your area. State government offices maintain files of information on corporations in your state.

Another source of information is employment placement centers. For example, the Career Planning and Placement Center at Stanford University has employment brochures for many of the large companies in the area which try to recruit engineers and other employees. These brochures seem to come in two types: some companies seem to be embarassed by their military work and so downplay it -- instead emphasizing every other product they manufacture. Other companies seem to be very proud of their military connections and usually make some fairly strong statements about the danger of the Soviet threat and how they are helping to protect America.

Other places that may have similar information are job agencies, women's employment centers, and temporary job agencies.

For more sources of information, see Business Information Sources by Lorna Daniels who is the head reference librarian at the Harvard Business School Library.

Information Specific to Military Contractors

The Contract Document

Copies of the actual contract with the Department of Defense can be very useful, particularly to investigate the company's failure to meet contract specifications or its unfair labor practices, etc. The contract itself lays down rules that contractors often violate. Those violations offer educational and organizing opportunities. You must file a request under the Freedom of Information Act in order to get this contract document (see Section 3.B on how to do this).

The Pre-Award Survey and Other Contract-Related Documents

"Once you know the name and location of the office that administers the contract, you can file a Freedom of Information request for documents about the awarding and performance of the contracts. One extremely useful source is the Pre-Award Survey, which contains information on the contractor's physical plant, workforce, financial capacity, production capacity, and performance record. The performance record may be especially useful, as it contains the contract administrator's analysis of the company's record of timeliness, quality, and integrity in dealing with the government.

"Once the contract has been awarded, the Pentagon and the company correspond over such issues as cost-overruns, delivery schedules, and the quality of the products. Some of these exchanges result in contract modifications, e.g. a new delivery schedule or a place of performance change. Occasionally the correspondence includes other important items like the way management is trying to deal with a union, with potential plant closing, or with a thorny workplace hazard. These documents reveal much of the flavor of the relationship between the contracting office, contract administrator, and the company. Unless you are seeking information on just one particular item, it is generally useful to make a broad FOI request for all correspondence and contract modification records regarding the contract.

"Military officials may refuse to provide some parts of the pre-award survey or other documents because they or the contractor consider them proprietary business information. You can challenge those decisions, as outlined in the FOI section. And remember that the search for information does not end with final denials or excised words. In some cases, courts or government agencies have subpoenaed (or could subpoena) such documents in their unsanitized form. Once introduced into a court or a public hearing, they become public record." [p.6, How to Research Your Local Military Contractor, Highlander Center]

Interviewing Company Personnel

Talking with a company's public relations director, employees, union leaders, and management will often turn up a wealth of information not available from other sources. Workers generally know a lot about a company's pattern of business: where the company gets its equipment, what political connections it has in the community, etc. The officers of the union local will have information on the work force, strike history, and current issues. Management, of course, knows more than anyone else.

In general, it is a good idea to do interviewing last. You need to know what questions to ask and how to interpret the answers. Also, people will generally tell you more if they believe you already know a lot. This is particularly true with management; the more informed you appear, the more they feel compelled to talk to your level of understanding.

It is always helpful to begin your conversation with management by asking general questions. This will allow time for both of you to become relaxed. Save the more involved questions and the "cross-examination" for last. If the person you are interviewing seems to be giving you "misleading" information, avoid reactions that might be antagonistic. Instead respond in a manner which keeps the conversation open, for example: "Gosh, I thought ..." Write down your questions beforehand in case you get a little nervous. Ask your interviewees if they mind if you tape the conversation with a cassette recorder.

Another strategy for getting information from a company is to pretend you are looking for a job. A phone discussion with people in the employment office may reveal some good information. If not, set up a job interview and ask all your questions that don't seem too outrageous in that context. Be careful though -- you might get hired.

Be aware of the dangers in interviewing regular employees of a company. They may get in trouble if their employer or the government finds out they are helping researchers. Opponents of a researcher's work can transform the political climate in a community by discovering a whistleblower's identity and making an "example" of her or him. When other workers see that whistleblowing leads to serious reprisals, they may be reluctant to talk with you. Finding and then protecting sources can be difficult.

There are several very good guides to doing corporate research and interviews. See the Reference section for a list of some of the best.

4.F.   Researching Local Military Bases, GOGOs, and GOCOs

The simplist way to get information about a local military bases is to just write or call and ask for information on the history, current operation and mission, number of armed service personnel and employees, etc. Most bases have a Public Relations office to stay on good terms with the local community. You may be able to get information on job categories, etc. if you are persistent.

Other sources of information:

-- Building permits and environmental impact reports (EIRs) filed with the local government for new facilities may have a lot of information.

-- The House Armed Services Committee hearings on military construction is indexed and has maps of military bases, Government-Owned Government-Operated (GOGO) facilities, and Government-Owned Contractor-Operated (GOCO) facilities. (See Appendix 3 for more on hearings.)

-- A Census Bureau report, <u>Manufacturing</u> <u>Activity</u> <u>in</u> <u>Government</u> <u>Establishments</u>, shows the number of employees and value of shipments of GOGOs in the U.S.

-- <u>Air</u> <u>Force</u> magazine has a listing of Air Force bases.

-- CEP has a copy of a useful report on Army GOCOs: <u>U.S.</u> <u>Army</u> <u>Industrial</u> <u>Reserve</u> <u>Plant/Maintenance</u> <u>Facilities</u> <u>Report</u> (Department of the Army, January 1980). It lists good information on the operator of the plant, area of land, and weapons manufactured (usually). There are similar books for the Navy and probably the Air Force too.

The Experience of Coastsiders for A Nuclear Free Future (CNFF)

In early 1983, Coastsiders for a Nuclear Free Future (CNFF) in Half Moon Bay, California decided to find out exactly what the Pillar Point Air Force Station (PPAFS) does, especially its role in tracking test launches of ballistic missiles (specifically MX Missiles) from the Vandenberg Air Force Base. Members of CNFF contacted PPAFS and were directed to Vandenberg. The Public Affairs Office there sent an Air Force fact sheet and photo of the Pillar Point AFS, but asked that all further questions be sent by letter to determine if the information was "releasable." CNFF then asked their local Congressmember, Tom Lantos, to arrange to get answers to their questions. Lantos did get answers and sent them along to CNFF. He also arranged with Vandenberg officials for a tour of PPAFS for 12 CNFF members.

CNFF learned about the work performed at PPAFS, the equipment and facilities, operating procedures and safety concerns, the effects of living near the station such as the consequences of electromagnetic radiation emitted by the facility, and the effect on the local economy of the 33 people who work there. They also learned about PPAFS's role in the testing of ballistic missiles.

This process seems to be a good one if your local Congressmember is at all sympathetic. For copies of the letter to Lantos and the report CNFF prepared on PPAFS, write to CNFF at Box 951, El Granada, CA 94018.

Figure 4.1 Company Information Form

Fiscal Year: _____   Today's Date: _____

Local Company Name   Founded   Parent Company Name   Founded

Local Address & Phone   Parent Address & Phone

Local Sales   Local Employment   Overall Sales   Overall Employment

Local Prime Contracts Amount   Total Prime Contracts Amount Nationwide

Military Rank   Percent Prime Contracts / Total Sales

Locally: _____   Locally: _____

Nationwide: _____   Nationwide: _____

Division	Location/Facility	Total Sales	Major Military Products	Prime Contract Amount

Other Useful Information (SIC Codes for Major Products, Board of Directors, Executives, Bank, Accountants, Military Profits, Overall Profits, Unions, Ownership of Company, Facilities, Stock Exchange Symbol, etc.): _____

Figure 4.2   A Sample of Company Descriptions from NYPIRC's <u>Production for Destruction:</u>
<u>Military Spending in New York State</u>

2. General Electric Co.

General Electric (GE) is a prime example of the involvement of big business in the weapons industry. The appliance giant dwarfs even Grumman in military business — it ranks fourth in contracts in the U.S. — but because of its huge size, military money made up only 11% of sales in 1981. GE is spread out across the country, but it has four large plants in New York. The company builds a variety of products for the military. Its most well—known contracts are jet engines for the F-18 fighter and the B-1B bomber. However these are built in other states. In New York, GE produces nuclear reactors and other components of the Trident submarine and the Los Angeles class nuclear attack submarine. It operates the Knolls Atomic Power Laboratory, the U.S. Department of Energy's reactor development and training facility. GE manufactures auto-pilot equipment and radar for the F-111 and F-4 aircraft as well as sonar equipment for the Navy.

Vital Statistics (1981)
NY rank: 2
NY contracts: $571 million
NY locations: Schenectady, Onondaga, Oneida, Broome
NY military work: Nuclear power systems for Trident and attack submarine
NY/US contracts: 19%
US rank: 4
Military dependency: 11%

3. Fairchild Industries, Inc.

Fairchild is another aerospace company that has its main offices on Long Island. It is not as dependent on the military as Grumman — military contracts constituted a little over a third of sales in 1981. The contracts go mostly for one airplane, the Air Force's A—10. The A—10 is designed for close air support of ground forces, particularly for use against tanks. It played a major role in the Rapid Deployment Force's recent exercises in Egypt. However, funds for production of the plane were cut back by the military and, as a result, Fairchild laid off 2500 workers in 1982. Representative Addabbo (D—Queens), from a nearby congressional district, managed to put additional money for the plane into the 1983 budget. The company is trying to sell the plane overseas. It also recently received a contract for the Air Force's new pilot training plane, the T—46A. [3]

Vital Statistics 1981
NY rank: 3
NY contracts: $426 million
NY locations: Nassau
NY military work: A—10 attack plane, T—46A trainer
NY/US contracts: 93%
US rank: 41
Military dependency: 34%

4. Sperry Corporation

Sperry Corporation produces computers, specialized farm equipment, heavy machinery and weapons. Almost half of its military business takes place on Long Island. Sperry receives over $100 million per year for the navigation system of the Trident submarine and other ballistic missile submarines. The company also does research and development of the Trident missile and builds the electronic combat control system of the FFG—7 guided missile frigate. Other military products include avionics, computers, and sonar. Military contracts are a key part of Sperry's business and are seen by the company as a growth industry.

Figure 4.3 A Sample of DoD Top 100 Contractors List

Washington—Following is a list of the top 100 defense contractors for Fiscal 1983, ended last Sept. 30. The top 100 companies received $89.578 billion, or 69.85% in Defense Dept. military prime contracts of $10,000 or more for research and development, services construction and supplies and equipment during Fiscal 1983. Military prime contracts totaled $128.242 billion.

Rank and Company	Breakdown $ Thousands	Company Total $ Thousands	% of Total
1. General Dynamics Corp.	6,804,679		
Datagraphix GmbH.	47		
Datagraphix Inc.	8,253		
Stromberg Carlson Corp.	5,328		
Total		**6,818,307**	**5.32**
2. McDonnell Douglas Corp.	6,134,947		
McDonnell Douglas Electronics Co.	6,320		
McDonnell Douglas Technical Services Co.	1,301		
Polhemus Navigation Sciences, Inc.	46		
Vitek Systems, Inc.	102		
Total		**6,142,716**	**4.79**
3. Rockwell International Corp.	4,544,214		
Collins International Service Co.	617		
Wescom Inc.	281		
Total		**4,545,112**	**3.54**
4. General Electric Co.	4,453,647		
Canadian General Electric Co., Ltd.	1,105		
General Electric Medical Systems	895		
Management & Technical Services Co.	62,368		
Total		**4,518,015**	**3.52**
5. Boeing Co.	4,021,366		
B. E. & C. Engineers, Inc.	838		
Boeing Computer Services, Inc.	38,678		
Boeing of Canada, Ltd.	63		
Boeing Services International, Inc.	84,240		
Boeing Vertol Co.	269,881		
Hydraulic Units, Inc.	7,684		
Total		**4,422,750**	**3.45**
6. Lockheed Corp.	2,063,135		
Lockheed California Co.	1,855		
Lockheed Electronics Co., Inc.	72,628		
Lockheed Engineering & Mgt. Svc. Co.	2,921		
Lockheed Missiles & Space Co., Inc.	1,516,074		
Lockheed Shipbuilding Construction	338,235		
Lockheed Support Systems, Inc.	7,812		
Murdock Machine & Engr. Co. of Texas	3,054		
Total		**4,005,714**	**3.12**
7. United Technologies Corp.	3,675,206		
American Computer & Electronics Co.	5,335		
Carrier International Corp.	1,087		
Essex Group, Inc.	3,173		
Inmont Corp.	25		
Norden Systems, Inc.	181,421		
Otis Elevator Co.	934		
Pratt & Whitney Aircraft of W. Va.	46		
United Technologies Research Ctr.	218		
Total		**3,867,445**	**3.02**

Rank and Company	Breakdown $ Thousands	Company Total $ Thousands	% of Total
8. Tenneco, Inc.			
Case (Jl) Co.	75,290		
Case Power & Equipment, Ltd.	237		
Monroe Auto Equipment Co.	3,221		
Newport News Shipbld. & Dry Dock Co.	3,683,357		
Packaging Corp. of America	30		
Total		**3,762,135**	**2.93**
9. Hughes Howard Medical Institute			
Hughes Aircraft Co.	3,151,308		
Hughes Communication Services, Inc.	55,000		
Santa Barbara Research Center	33,312		
Spectrolab, Inc.	295		
Total		**3,239,915**	**2.53**
10. Raytheon Co.	2,501,521		
Beech Aerospace Services	48,824		
Beech Aircraft Corp.	106,771		
Caloric Corp.	60		
Denver Beechcraft	242		
Electrical Installations, Ltd.	91		
Glenwood Range Co.	1,111		
Indiana Beechcraft, Inc.	304		
Iowa Mfg. Co. of Cedar Rapids, Iowa	325		
Machlett Laboratories, Inc.	195		
Raytheon Data Systems Co.	7,231		
Raytheon International Systems	248		
Raytheon Marine Co.	2,952		
Raytheon Ocean Systems Co.	200		
Raytheon Peninsula Systems Co.	5,614		
Raytheon Procurement Co., Inc.	2,718		
Raytheon Service Co.	43,830		
Raytheon Technical Assistance Co.	1,150		
Sedco Systems, Inc.	920		
Switchcraft, Inc.	37		
United Beechcraft, Inc.	94		
United Engineers & Constructors	3,889		
Total		**2,728,327**	**2.13**
11. Grumman Corp.	3,339		
Grumman Aerospace Corp.	2,291,662		
Grumman Data Systems Corp.	2,694		
Total		**2,297,695**	**1.79**
12. Martin Marietta Corp.	2,178,223		
Martin Marietta Aluminum, Inc.	133		
Martin Marietta Aluminum Sales, Inc.	93,583		
Total		**2,271,939**	**1.77**
13. Litton Industries, Inc.	29,433		
Beloit Power Systems	1,037		
Diehl Data Systems	3,119		
International Laser Systems, Inc.	3,632		
Itek Corp.	95,047		
Litton Industrial Products, Inc.	5,823		
Litton Microwave Cooking Products	258		
Litton Precision Prods International, Inc.	250		
Litton Systems, Inc.	2,029,883		
Monroe Business Equipment Co., Inc.	284		
Monroe Calculating Co.	133		
Monroe Systems for Business	33		
Total		**2,168,932**	**1.69**

Aviation Week & Space Technology, April 23, 1984

Chapter 5   Military Employment

Nationwide over 2.2 million people (mostly men) serve in the armed services. Another 2.6 million people are employed by private companies and work directly or indirectly on military projects for the DoD (800,000 work directly under DoD contracts). Another 1 million civilians are employed by the DoD and other federal agencies doing military work. These 5.8 million people represent about 5.2% of the entire workforce of the United States. [Statistical Abstract of the United States, Tables 581, 582, 591, 594, 624, DoD press releases, and Shipments to Federal Government Agencies, 1981.]

Many communities have much higher percentages of their workforce employed in one of these ways for the military. One good measure of military dependence is how many people in your community work directly for the military as (1) active-duty military personnel, (2) civilian employees of a military installation, or (3) employees of a company which produces military products or the components and raw materials that go into these products.

Sections 5.A., 5.B., and 5.C. show how to determine the number of people employed in these three ways. After the procedure description, we discuss important concepts you need to know in order to follow the procedure and a description of the source documents you need for the procedure. Section 5.D. discusses how to find out how many military employees are in each job category. Section 5.E. discusses how to work with labor unions and the kinds of information they can give you on military employees. And Section 5.F. talks about technical people (engineers, scientists, and technicians) and how you can find out more about these people and their special role in military production.

5.A. Active-Duty Military Personnel and Civilian Employment at Military Installations

DoD active duty military personnel are uniformed members of the armed forces. These jobs are found primarily at military bases. DoD civilian employees also work on bases, military training facilities, arsenals, and some are assigned to work as inspectors at the production plants of military industry contractors.

The number of military duty and DoD civilian employees in your county is available from several sources:

-- Write or call the local military bases and manufacturing facilities and ask for this information as well as a brochure describing the installation. Since they want to maintain good relations with the people in the community they will usually send you this. You can try asking for information on the number of people in each pay scale and/or job category, but they are less likely to have or be willing to send you this.

-- Write the Washington Headquarters Service (The Pentagon, Washington, DC 20301) for (a) the number of active duty military personnel and (b) the number of civilian employees of the DoD for your county in the most recent fiscal year. This is a special data request -- i.e., it does not come out of a standard publication -- so you should ask for a quote on the price also (which should not be much). The DoD will send you data broken down by: military or civilian, service, and town.

        -- The number of civilian employees at DoD facilities is reported in Manufacturing Activity in Government Establishments, 1982, or Tables 7 and 8 in Shipments to Federal Government Agencies in other years (both available from the Census Bureau). These reports list the number of employees by Standard Metropolitan Statistical Area (SMSA).

        -- This information may be listed in the Pentagon publications Atlas/State Data Abstract for the United States (L03) or Distribution of Personnel by State and by Selected Locations (M02) for your community.

        -- 1980 OBERS BEA Regional Projections lists the total number of Federal military employees by metropolitan areas, cities, etc. in 1969 and 1978.

5.B. Determining Direct Military Industry Employment

        This section will tell you how to estimate the number of employees in industry in your community who work directly on DoD contracts. These estimates are obtained from the three reports discussed below.

        Table 5 of Shipments to Federal Government Agencies lists the number of employees and value of shipments by SMSA (see Figure 5.1). Under the "To DoD" column for your SMSA is an estimate of employees working on military products. For example, in 1981, Shipments Table 5 lists 32,400 employees for shipments to the DoD in the San Jose SMSA (Santa Clara County). This is 12.5% of the 259,499 people employed in manufacturing in the county (from County Business Patterns, see Figure 5.2 for a sample page listing of this report).

        As described below, this is a conservative estimate since it includes only 92 SIC industries (out of 450); it excludes many subcontracts and purchases of off-the-shelf items and basic materials and services, and it excludes companies with shipments to the federal government less than $1 million. It also excludes military work done by the Department of Energy, NASA, etc.

        If you are investigating a single county and the SMSA in which it is located includes more than one county, you can derive an estimate of military employment by assuming that the ratio of military production to civilian production in the 92 defense-oriented industries is the same in your county as it is in the SMSA as a whole. This ratio can be determined from Table 5 of Shipments:

        1. Find the number for your SMSA under the "To DoD" column. Divide this number by the "Total Number of Employees" (for the 92 industries) for your SMSA. This is the ratio of military production to civilian production employees in your SMSA.

        2. Check to see which of the 92 industries in Shipments appear in County Business Patterns for your county. Compare the SIC codes (the names of the industries should match too) and list the number of employees for any industry that matches. (A column has been provided for this on Figure 5.3.) Add all these numbers. This is the total number of employees in defense-oriented industries in your county.

        3. Multiply the values you calculated in Steps 1. and 2. This is a rough estimate of the number of military employees in your county. An estimate of the total annual payroll for these employees could be made in this same way by adding the payroll numbers from County Business Patterns.

        For example, San Mateo County is just one of 5 counties which comprise the San Francisco-Oakland SMSA. The total number of employees listed under the "To DoD" column in Table 5 for the SMSA is 4,300. The total number of employees in the SMSA working in the 92 defense-oriented industries is 44,500. So in this SMSA as a whole in these 92 industries, 4,300 / 44,500 = 0.0966 = 9.66% of the employees work directly for the DoD on military production.

From County Business Patterns, 1981 we find that these 92 industries employ a total of 10,058 to 17,788 employees in San Mateo County (we only have a range due to the way the Census Bureau reports the data). We assume that 9.66% of these employees also work directly for the DoD: 10,058 to 17,788 x 0.966 = 972 to 1,719 people employed directly for the DoD. This is 2.5% to 4.4% of the total manufacturing employment in San Mateo County (39,080). We also see from this analysis that more than half of these people are employed by the electronics and communications industries -- SIC industries 3661, 3662, 3671, and 3674.

A Second Method

A second method of determining numbers of direct military employees is to aggregate the data from the company profiles you have prepared (see Section 4.A.) for all the companies in your community. This information is usually difficult to obtain for one company, so doing it for dozens of companies would probably be ridiculous. But it may be that one or two companies garner most of the military contracts in your community and this methodology is the best and most accurate for you. Also, if you are investigating a county which is not in an SMSA, this may be the only way to proceed.

In 1979 SRI International did a study for the Pentagon's Office of Economic Adjustment to determine the effect of defense spending on Santa Clara County (The Role of Defense in Santa Clara County's Economy). They reviewed the annual reports of the top 12 DoD prime contractors and interviewed them for information on how many employees were working on military equipment for the DoD. They then assumed that the ratio of DoD employment to total employment is constant for all industry in the county [p.66] and extrapolated the top 12 DoD companies' employment to estimate total DoD employment.

DoD Employment of the Top 12 Prime Contractors in Santa Clara

x   Total DoD Prime Contract Amounts in Santa Clara County
     DoD Prime Contract Amounts of the Top 12 Prime Contractors

=   Total DoD Employment in Santa Clara County

This method is probably pretty good (assuming that the companies could accurately estimate the number of their employees working on military products and assuming they reported these figures honestly). But it is probably much easier for SRI to get this information from the companies than it will be for you. You may have to make some pretty gross assumptions and use the data available from the Sales Marketing and Management magazine survey.

Some Important Information on Census Bureau Classifications

SIC Codes

Standard Industrial Classification (SIC) codes are numbers representing different industries by their chief products. The government uses these SIC codes to keep track of what is going on in the business world. Much of the government's statistical information is recorded and analyzed in this form. Businesses and trade magazines are increasingly recording company information by SIC codes.

The codes are organized hierarchically: a group of similar industries is headed by a 2-digit code, which is broken down into 3-digit subgroups. These are, in turn, divided into further subgroupings at the 4-digit, 5-digit, and 7-digit level. For example,

36   - Electrical and Electronic Equipment
366   - Communication Equipment
3662   - Radio and TV Communication Equipment
36625   - Search and detection systems and navigation and guidance
               systems and equipment
36625 13 - Underwater electronic countermeasures (jamming) equipment

The government compiles an incredible amount of information at the 2-digit level, but this is not very useful. Some good data is compiled at the 4-digit level, but more detailed information at the 5-digit and 7-digit level is almost impossible to find. Some of the 4-digit codes are obviously military related (3795 = Tanks and Tank Components, 3483 = Ammunition, Except for Small Arms), but most, like the example above, mix military with commercial production. Even at the 7-digit level, they may be mixed.

The first two digits of the SIC code represent the following:

01-09 Agriculture, Forestry, and Fishing
10-14 Mining
15-17 Construction
20-39 Manufacture
40-49 Transportation
50-51 Wholesale Trade
60-67 Finance, Insurance, and Real Estate
70-96 Services

Establishments

Census SIC data is usually recorded for each establishment. An **establishment** is a single physical location where business is conducted or industrial operations are performed. A company that is physically located all in one place may be considered as separate establishments if different divisions located there maintain separate accounting ledgers. So a company with facilities located in many different places or with different divisions at one location will be considered as many separate establishments.

Industry classification (SIC) of an establishment is based on the primary activity which is determined by its principal product or group of products. If several products (in different industrial classifications) are produced at one establishment, the principal product may not even represent 50% of the total output. Thus the reporting of products and employees by SIC code may be somewhat in error.

Sources of Information

Census Bureau Data on Direct Employment in Military Industry

Every contract for products and services with the federal government under a prime contract or a major subcontract to a prime contractor company is subject to renegotiation -- the total contract amount is renegotiated so that the company does not reap excessive profits (unfortunately, very few contracts are renegotiated). Every company therefore keeps a separate account of all of its prime contracts and subcontracts.

Each year the Bureau of the Census surveys these companies and estimates the amount of these shipments to various federal government agencies by SIC code and Standard Metropolitan Statistical Area (SMSA). Shipments to Federal Government Agencies (formerly Shipments of Defense-Oriented Industries) reports the results of this survey (see Figure 5.1). This report is issued about 11 months following the end of the calendar year for which it applies. For the most part, the data represent the value of finished goods or components produced to military specifications.

This sample survey covers only 92 of the approximately 450 4-digit SIC manufacturing industries. These 92 were determined to be those engaged most extensively in business with the Federal Government (prime contracts). The prime contract shipments figure for the industries surveyed are thought to account for the great bulk of all such Government contracts in manufacturing. But the subcontract data only covers those same 92 industries. It does not include those industries producing "basic materials" and "other components" -- usually important suppliers to prime military contractors and to their main subcontractors. Thus it probably reports only those people working **directly** producing equipment for the federal government and not those who work **indirectly** on these products (see Section 5.C. for more on this).

The amount of shipments and number of people employed making the products that are shipped are estimated for the Department of Defense (DoD), the Department of Energy (DoE), the National Aeronautics and Space Administration (NASA), and for "Other Agencies." Much of the work done for federal agencies other than the DoD may still be military related since it is mostly equipment which meets military specifications. In addition, all establishments with total federal government shipments under $1 million are classified in the "Other Agencies" category even if all their output went to the DoD. Still, in 1981, the "To DoD" category represented 76% of the total shipments to the federal government and 74% of the total employees. We have only considered the "To DoD" category in our analysis.

In 1981, of the total employees working in these 92 industries, 13.5% work on products that go to the DoD, 0.9% to DoE, 0.8% to NASA, and 3.2% to "Other Agencies." This is a sizeable percentage of all the people working in these basic industries.

It should also be noted that this data is derived from a sample survey. Only a limited number of companies are actually polled and they are asked for only limited information. An estimate is then made, based on these companies, of the total shipments and employment in each SIC industry and total shipments to each government agency. DoD employment is estimated by adjusting the total number of employees at each establishment by the proportion of that establishment's value of shipments that went to the DoD.

Columns 1 and 2 of Figure 5.3 are taken directly from Shipments to Federal Government Agencies, 1981 and show the total number of employees and the number estimated to work on products shipped to the DoD for each of the 92 SIC codes. Column 3 shows the percent of workers in each SIC code who worked directly on products shipped to the DoD.

Two Sources of SIC Employment Data by County

Every other year the Census Bureau prepares a document called County Business Patterns for each state in the United States and a summary for the entire U.S. For the state as a whole and for each county this report lists, by 4-digit SIC code, the number of employees, the total payroll, and the number of establishments in each of 9 size classes (see Figure 5.2). For any SIC code which has less than 50 employees, the data is consolidated into 3-digit SIC codes. Also, in accordance with Federal law governing the Census Bureau, data that may disclose the operations of an individual employer are not published (instead a range of values is given or a "D" is printed).

Oftentimes, for the county you are analyzing, there are one or two large employers which do a lot of military work, but since they are the only employers in that 4-digit SIC code, the Census data is missing. If the County has over 1,000 employees in that SIC code, you can get a fairly accurate estimate of employment from a survey done by Economic Information Systems (EIC) for Sales Marketing and Management Magazine (see the Reference section). They report, by 4-digit SIC code, the total employment, number of establishments, and total shipments for all counties with more than 1,000 employees.

For example, in Santa Clara County the Census Bureau reports there were two **establishments** working in SIC 3761, Guided Missiles and Space Vehicles in 1981. The number of employees is indicated by a "J" as the range from 10,000 to 24,999. The EIC survey indicates that in 1982, there was only one establishment and it had 18,500 employees. Furthermore, we learn that it had total shipments of $1,944,200,000 which represented 21.41% of the total output in this SIC code. We know, of course, that this establishment is Lockheed Missiles and Space Company's Sunnyvale facility and so we now have even a little bit more information on their operations.

The figures from SM&M magazine are not exactly the same and are probably not quite as accurate as those from the Census Bureau because of their more limited resources and their inability to compel industry with the force of law to give them information. Also, EIC adds a second, third, or fourth establishment to one address if a large establishment produces more than one product in significant volume.

5.C. Direct and Indirect Employment

Military spending creates jobs in military industry, but like all spending, it also supports other jobs: materials purchased by military industry companies are produced by other companies which hire many people and as all these workers use their paychecks to buy food, housing, transportation, and entertainment, they pay for the wages of even more workers.

In this book we use three different terms to indicate how jobs are created by military spending:

Direct jobs -- jobs at a company working directly on a military contract. Example: an engineer at Lockheed working on Trident missiles under a prime military contract issued by the DoD.

Indirect jobs -- jobs at a company that produces materials or machinery which is used by another company with military contracts. Example: a worker at a steel mill which produces steel which will be shipped to Lockheed for use in the Trident missiles.

Induced jobs -- jobs providing services or producing products needed by the people who work directly or indirectly for the military and their families. Example: a waitress who serves dinner to the Lockheed engineer or the steel mill worker or a seamstress who sews the clothes bought by the Lockheed engineer or the steel mill worker.

The number of jobs induced by military spending may be substantial in your community. Some estimate that two to three jobs are induced for every direct military job. But calculating the number of induced jobs is very difficult. In this book we do not attempt to determine the number of jobs induced by military spending even though this may be a major concern in the event of a contract cut back.

Indirect Jobs

CEP has analyzed the number of direct and indirect jobs which are created by $1 billion in military industry, civilian industry, and services, based on a detailed input-output model constructed by the Bureau of Labor Statistics [BLS 1979 Employment Requirements Table, Office of Economic Growth and Employment Projections, October 23, 1981]. The CEP results are shown in The Freeze Economy [CEC]. Almost every kind of civilian industry and service work provides more jobs per billion dollars than military industry provides.

For example, Complete Guided Missiles and Space Vehicles only produces 8,821 direct jobs per billion dollars and 20,715 total (direct plus indirect) jobs. The equivalent figures for Motor Vehicles are 9,041 and 30,394 and for Local Transit and Intercity Buses are 21,550 and 39,532.

Determining Direct and Indirect Military Industry Employment

This section will tell you how to estimate the number of employees in industry in your community who are directly or indirectly dependent on DoD contracts and the total amount of wages which goes to these employees. These estimates are based on the Defense Economic Impact Modeling System (DEIMS) model and from data in County Business Patterns.

1. In County Business Patterns (Table 2, first column) look up the number of employees working in your county for each industry by SIC code. Record that number in Column B of Figure 5.4. If a range is given, record either the mid-point or the range. If there is no listing for that 4-digit SIC code, then that industry is probably not very important in your county and you can assume the number is 0.

You may want to analyze only the manufacturing industry in your area, in which case ignore the Mining and Transportation sections at the beginning and end of Figure 5.4.

2. For each line in Figure 5.4, multiply Column B by the percent in Column A and place the result in Column C. This is an estimate of the number of employees directly or indirectly employed by the DoD in that industry in your community. If you recorded a range in Column B, make two calculations and report the range in Column C.

For example, in County Business Patterns, 1981 -- California under Santa Clara County we find that there are 75 people listed as employed in SIC industry 2448 Wood Pallets and Skids. We record this number in Column B of Figure 5.4. Column A says that 6.8% of the output from this industry goes to the DoD so we can assume that the equivalent of 0.068 x 75 = 5 people in Santa Clara County work directly or indirectly for the DoD manufacturing wooden pallets.

3. Add up all the numbers in Column C and record that number at the bottom. This is an estimate of the total number of direct and indirect military industry employees in your County. To help minimize addition errors when you are summing, you may want to write down the subtotals for each page in the space provided.

This analysis also gives an indication of which SIC industries have most of the military employment in your area (if you don't already know).

You can repeat this procedure for annual payroll. Use the figures given in Table 2, Column 3 of County Business Patterns. Since military workers frequently make more money than other workers, the percent of payroll going to military workers may be much higher than the percent of military workers.

This analysis assumes that defense expenditures in each industry are spread equally around the country, that is, we assume that if 57.0% of the Small Arms Ammunition industry (SIC 3482) goes to the DoD, then 57.0% of that industry that exists in your community also goes to the DoD. This may not be the case. The industry in your area may produce only commercial ammunition (0% to the DoD) or it may only supply ammunition to the military (100%). But without any better information (e.g., individual company data for all the local companies), this is probably a reasonable assumption.

Also we are assuming that the number of employees who can produce a given amount of output in each industry is the same everywhere. So if 500 employees work in the Small Arms Ammunition industry in your community, then 57.0% x 500 = 285 people can be assumed to be dependent on defense expenditures. But the industry in your community might be more automated than other communities or produce a particular kind of ammunition that requires very few work-hours for a large value of output and so only require 150 people to produce.

This analysis also only looks at the military equipment and services that go to the DoD. It does not include foreign military sales (FMS) or sales to the CIA, NASA, Department of Energy, or other agencies. For example, according to this analysis only 65.4% of Tanks and Tank Components (SIC 3795) goes to the DoD, though obviously, 100% of this industry's output is military. 33.8% of this industry goes to Foreign Military Sales (see Figure 5.5).

Note also that these numbers may completely overlook some important job categories which are not usually thought of as being military related, but, in your community, may be. Some SIC codes which might be heavily military-oriented in your area are:

    109   Mining of miscellaneous metal ores [uranium, etc.]
    162   Heavy construction, except highway [missile silos, etc.]
    737   Computer and data processing services
    739   Miscellaneous business services (including R&D labs, commercial testing
            labs, etc.)
    822   Colleges and universities
    892   Noncommercial research organizations

There may be others. Look through County Business Patterns to find other major SIC employers in your area and think about whether they might be military-related.

We performed this analysis of the manufacturing industry in our area and discovered that 15-20% of the people in manufacturing in Santa Clara County in 1981 worked directly or indirectly for the military. The figures for San Mateo County were 7-13%. It took about 3 hours to calculate these figures.

Sources of Information

Defense Economic Impact Modeling System (DEIMS)

The Pentagon has recently been concerned about whether industry has the capacity to keep up with the demands created by increased defense spending by the Federal government. They recognized that the Census survey (described above in Section 5.B.) did not consider the suppliers of basic materials and off-the-shelf components to the main defense industries (indirect contractors).

So they contracted with Data Resources, Inc. (DRI) to construct an Input-Output (I-O) model of the military procurement economy. This model is called the Defense Economic Impact Modeling System (DEIMS) [see Defense Economic Impact Modeling System: A New Concept in Economic Forecasting for Defense Expenditures]. The model is based on a detailed I-O table created in 1972 for the entire U.S. economy and currently being revised for 1977 [see the Input-Output Structure of the U.S. Economy, 1972 for more on this].

For every dollar of output produced by one industry, an I-O model indicates how much input is required from every other industry. For example, for every dollar of production in the Aircraft industry (SIC 3721), this model will indicate how many dollars of production are required by the the Radio and TV Communication Equipment industry (SIC 3662), the Aluminum Production and Refining industry (SIC 3334), etc. Since an industry like Radio and TV Communication Equipment in turn requires inputs from the glass, metal, and other industries, this model must be able to trace and accumulate all these inputs back to the original mining industry that extracted the raw materials from the ground. Input-output models do this.

DEIMS traces the flow of money from the DoD (and Foreign Military Sales) as it moves from prime military contractors through subcontractors back to the suppliers. The model thus includes all the direct and indirect sales and jobs produced by military spending. Using this model, the DoD can see what effect increased spending for one particular weapon system has on all the industries that supply parts and materials for that weapon (and for the factory that produces that weapon).

The DRI model has 400 categories for industry which roughly correspond to 4-digit SIC codes. It also has 161 skilled-labor (job classification) categories and 72 categories for strategic materials and minerals.

To construct and update the model, computer programs take information from the latest Five Year Defense Program available and allocate the cost of each weapon or project to one of 50 budget accounts (for example, Army Missiles Procurement, or Navy Reserve Military Construction). Then a special translation program allocates a portion of each of these 50 budget accounts to the 400 industrial sectors, 161 labor categories, and 72 strategic materials. For example, the Navy Aircraft Procurement budget account is currently estimated to spend 34.9% on SIC 3721 Aircraft, 21.7% on SIC 3662 Radio and Television Equipment, 9.75% on SIC 382 Measuring and Control Instruments, etc. The translator is based on the Department of Commerce Input-Output models and supplemented with special knowledge of the actual mix for particular weapons. Once the budget accounts are allocated to the appropriate SIC industries, the total amounts are summed for each of these industries.

The DEIMS model is based on numerous assumptions about the nature of the economy and how military money is actually spent as it moves through the economy. These assumptions may be fallacious or inaccurate, but there is really no way to know. Economists disagree on the reliability of any particular model. The Bureau of Industrial Economics created a similar, though not as extensive, model which they consider to be superior to the DEIMS model (see Sectoral Implications of Defense Expenditures). But since the DEIMS is the model the DoD uses, it is reasonable for us to use it too.

The DoD will send you two tables of information for any of the 400 industries and one table of information for any of the 161 job categories or 72 strategic materials. Each industry table reports the dollar amount of military production and sales, categorized in several ways, and total military employment in that industry. Each job category table gives the number of people employed in each major SIC industry group working on military products, and each strategic material table lists consumption by military industry. The information that is of most interest to us is the percentage of total production that goes (one way or another) to the DoD and to Foreign Military Sales (FMS) and the percentage of employees working for establishments in these two categories.

The DoD will send you a summary of the top 150 SIC industries ranked by their share of output which is estimated to go to the DoD in 1983. The industry ranked number 150 had 3.01% of its output ultimately going to the DoD. Column 1 of Figure 5.4 lists the percent share of output going to the DoD in 1983 taken from this summary table. The list is ordered according to SIC number. Figure 5.5 lists all the industries in which Foreign Military Sales represented more than 2% of total production.

Most of the rest of the information from the DEIMS model is not particularly useful to us. However, it is clear that the DEIMS model could be very useful for determining the impact of the cancellation of a particular weapon. Since each weapon is assigned to a particular budget account, its cancellation would cause that budget account to decrease which would then affect all the industries that get money from that account. The DEIMS model can predict the impact on all 400 industries and 161 job categories of this budget reduction. A Congressmember could ask the DoD to make special computer runs to determine what these impacts would be and by how much. The DoD also has a model that shows DoD spending impact by state.

5.D. Determining the Types of Occupations in Military Industry

In general, jobs in military industry break down into four basic categories:

(1) Production workers, which include: (a) the skilled category of craft and kindred workers, such as: metalworking craft workers (machinists, boilermakers, sheetmetal workers, tool and diemakers, etc.); mechanics, repairers and installers (aircraft mechanics, automechanics, air-conditioning, heating, and refrigeration mechanics, radio,

TV repairers, etc.); construction trades (carpenters, electricians, painters, plumbers, pipefitters, structural metalcraft workers, etc.); and several others; and (b) unskilled and semi-skilled operatives or factory workers (e.g. final assembly workers).

(2) Professional and Technical Workers, including several categories of engineers (civil, electrical, industrial, mechanical, metallurgical, chemical, aero-astronautic), scientists (chemists, physicists, mathematicians, biologists), computer specialists (computer scientists, programmers, systems analysts), technicians and drafters, social scientists, technical writers and editors, and various other professional and technical jobs.

(3) Managers, Officials, and Proprietors

(4) Clerical Workers

There are also several other types of workers, such as sales and services workers, and laborers, which are not ordinarily thought of as military related, who must be included.

Military spending for weapons mostly creates jobs for highly-skilled and highly-paid managers, engineers, scientists, technicians, and skilled craftspeople. Spending for weapons is therefore an employment program for those who need it least -- those groups with the lowest unemployment rate. Unskilled and semi-skilled workers generally represent a much lower proportion of the workforce than in civilian production. This places certain strains on the community whenever there is a change in production.

DEIMS lists the number of people in each job category employed directly and indirectly on military products by 4-digit SIC industry. See Section 5.C. for more on this model.

Information on job skills and occupations is very useful for military conversion planning. Some agency in every state keeps detailed information on the characteristics of the labor force for its planning and statistical reporting purposes. Usually this information is recorded for the whole state or for large metropolitan areas. Information for individual companies is usually proprietary. But if you can get information by detailed SIC codes and SMSA, you may get a good sense of what kind of occupations are employed in the military industry in your area.

For example, in California, the Employment Development Department (EDD) of the state government is charged with helping people find jobs and industry to find employees. EDD operates all the main state employment programs and publishes information for high school and college placement centers that tell which occupations have a lot of openings, so students may plan their education to maximize the chances of getting a good job (see, for example, Annual Planning Information, San Jose SMSA, 1983-84). As part of their record keeping, the EDD conducts surveys of industry and maintains monthly statistics on the number of people employed in various industries throughout the State. They pass this information on to the federal Department of Labor to be accumulated into national statistics of employment and unemployment.

In 1977, the EDD conducted an extensive survey of the occupations represented in each major (2- or 3-digit SIC) manufacturing industry. The results were published for California as a whole, the six largest SMSAs, and the Remainder of the State (see, for example, Occupational Employment in Manufacturing Industries, San Jose SMSA, 1977). This report is very useful to get a sense of the skills that people have in our community. It doesn't, of course, break down these job skills by military versus civilian spending, but by looking at those SIC codes which are known to be military related, we get some idea of what kind of skills are required.

Similar information is reported in Projections of Employment by Industry and Occupation, 1980-1985, San Jose SMSA. This report shows the number of people employed in 1980 and projected for 1985 for 375 occupations, but this data is only recorded for 9 major industry divisions. However, the San Jose EDD office has this same occupational information in a computer file for 2-digit SIC codes. This is still not very detailed, but it may be of use. This data is free for a limited number of requests.

Information on Individual Facilities

See Section 9.B for a discussion of how to determine the skills of military workers in a particular facility.

5.E. Labor Unions

There are about 23 million people organized in labor unions in the U.S. or somewhat less than 25% of those employed [Table 681 & 652, Statistical Abstract]. Approximately 35% of military workers are organized in trade unions [B.G. Lall, Prosperity Without Guns, Institute for World Order, New York, 1977].

Labor unions are an invaluable source of information, particularly in factories where they represent some or all of the workforce or where a union is attempting to organize the workers at a plant.

The labor movement is very diverse. Some unions are much more conservative than others. And they change: for example, the building trades, quite conservative on nuclear and military issues in the past, have been particularly hard hit by Reaganomics. Consequently, some local Building Trades Councils have begun to take progressive stands with respect to the arms race.

Two of the unions with the largest number of members in military work are the International Association of Machinists and Aerospace Workers (IAM) and the United Auto Workers (UAW). These unions have leaderships which have been sharply critical of the arms race. Some of the local chapters of these unions are much more conservative though. You must find out for yourself.

Forming effective working relationships with labor requires that you become aware of the major concerns of working people whom the unions represent. Union members may have some concern about the arms race and their participation in it, but layoffs, plant closings, work conditions, occupational health and safety, wages and benefits, job discrimination, the impact of technology, etc. may be even more important to them. The union may be facing these issues directly in their day-to-day negotiations and conflicts with management. It is important to find out what issues are most important to the unions in your local area in their own terms.

The AFL-CIO has local coordinating bodies called Central Labor Councils. These CLCs can tell you which plants in the local area are unionized, which unions represent each plant, a little about each of these unions, and contact names for each one so you can follow up with them. They can also give you general information about the state of labor organizing and job conditions in the area.

The local office for each union will usually know the number of employees at each of the companies where it represents the workers. It will know how many of the employees are unionized, their job classifications and skills, age, race, and sex breakdown, current health and safety issues, and the overall labor situation -- whether it is good for organizing, the history of strikes, the attitudes of management, and the history of the union. They may also know the history of employment at the company (boom and bust cycles, etc.) and how many skilled workers have been replaced by robots.

Rank and file union members working at a plant may have very good information. When you meet with union officials, also ask to meet with other concerned people who might be sympathetic to conversion.

Union or Central Labor Council newspapers may let you place an article or item in their newspaper describing your research needs. The people who work for these papers are usually very knowledgeable and may be able to give you good information too.

International offices of unions usually keep aggregate information on the union for states, nationwide, and worldwide and by industry. The union may have a state office with information on the union's state activities and lobbying efforts.

Unions which represent many military industry workers:

United Automobile, Aerospace, and Agricultural Implement Workers of America (UAW)
International Association of Machinists and Aerospace Workers (IAM)
United Steelworkers
United Electrical Workers (UEW)
International Union of Electrical Workers (IUE)
International Brotherhood of Electrical Workers (IBEW)
United Electrical, Radio and Machine Workers of America (UE)
Oil, Chemical, and Atomic Workers (OCAW) -- (Karen Silkwood's union)
Communications Workers of America (CWA)
Teamsters

A large percentage of unionized military workers are represented by the UAW and IAM.

Unions which have endorsed a Bi-lateral Nuclear Weapons Freeze include:

Amalgamated Clothing and Textile Workers Union (ACTWU)
American Federation of State, County, and Municipal Employees (AFSCME)
American Federation of Teachers (AFT)
Coalition of Black Trade Unionists (CBTU)
Communication Workers of America (CWA)
International Association of Machinists and Aerospace Workers (IAM)
Internation Chemical Workers Union (ICWU)
International Longshoremen's and Warehousemen's Union (ILWU)
National Association of Letter Carriers (NALC)
National Education Association (NEA)
National Union of Hospital and Health Care Employees (1199)
The Newspaper Guild
Screen Actors Guild (SAG)
Service Employees International Union (SEIU)
United Automobile, Aerospace, and Agricultural Implement Workers of America (UAW)
United Cement, Lime, Gypsum, and Allied Workers International Union (CLAGAW)
United Electrical, Radio and Machine Workers of America (UE)
United Farmworkers of America (UFW)
United Food and Commercial Workers (UFCWA)
California Labor Federation, AFL-CIO
Iowa Federation of Labor, AFL-CIO
Montana Labor Federation, AFL-CIO

Some other unions likely to be sympathetic:

American Federation of Government Employees (AFGE) -- employees at military bases
State employee unions such as the California State Employees Association (CSEA)

5.F. Scientists, Engineers, and Technicians

Only 3.8 million people (or 0.3% of the total labor force) are engineers, scientists, and scientific technicians. But it is estimated that 20-50% of these people work on military products [Military Expansion, Economic Decline, CEP, page 101]. In some areas, this percentage may be even higher.

This means that a very large number of technical professionals are concentrated in a relatively small number of large military aerospace and electronics firms. It is not unusual to find up to and sometimes more than half the workforce of a military plant composed of technical professionals and kindred workers. The aerospace industry is particularly known for this. Some 30-50% of the workers in some aerospace plants are engineers, scientists, and technicians [p. 103, Gansler, The Defense Industry].

Most technical professionals are unorganized and are less visible than unionized blue collar workers. Therefore you must generally relate to technical people on an individual basis. Yet some engineer's unions do exist at Boeing in Seattle, Washington, at Lockheed, Rockwell International, Aerospace, Corp., and McDonnell-Douglas in southern California, and at RCA and Westinghouse in New Jersey. These and other unions belong to a loose federation of technical unions called the Council of Engineers and Scientists Organizations (CESO). CESO covers over 50,000 workers.

Like organized labor, technical people are very diverse. Many are sympathetic to arms reductions and they personally would rather be working on other types of products. But like all workers, they need their jobs to support themselves and their families. They have special concerns related to their jobs: working conditions, job obsolesence, over-specialization, fear of job loss, a lack of control over what they work on, etc. All these issues may be paramount to them in their work situation.

Unlike organized labor, technical people are frequently very close to management. They may have some influence over the kind of contracts they work on and the direction their work takes. They may know a lot about what work is being done and where that work will lead.

Many technical people concerned about the arms race have formed organizations to address these issues. The national office may be able to put you in touch with technical people in your area. These people may work for military industry, or through their own personal and professional connections know people who work for these companies.

Computer Professionals for Social
  Responsibility
P.O. Box 717
Palo Alto, CA 94301
(415) 322-3778

High Technology Professionals for Peace
639 Massachusetts Ave. Room 316
Cambridge, MA 02139
(617) 497-0605

Union of Concerned Scientists
26 Church Street
Cambridge, MA 02238

IEEE Technology and Society Magazine
Editor: Norman Balabanian
Electrical Engineering Department
111 Link Hall
Syracuse University
Syracuse, NY 13210

Aerospace Engineers/Workers for Social
  Responsibility
P.O. Box 21471
Los Angeles, CA 90021

Federal of American Scientists (FAS)
Nuclear War Education Project
307 Massachusetts Ave., NE
Washington, DC 20002

Southern California Federation of
  Scientists
3425 McLaughlin Avenue
Los Angeles, CA 90066

Although they tend to be somewhat conservative, several trade and professional organizations have addressed the arms race and related issues. They include the American Association for the Advancement of Science (AAAS), the Society for the Social Implications of Technology of the Institute of Electrical and Electronics Engineers (SSIT/IEEE), and the American Society of Mechanical Engineers (ASME).

You may also be able to reach sympathetic technical people through other organizations they are likely to belong to: environmental, civic, or church groups. Student groups at colleges may also be a good source of information.

Some places you might look for more information:

    Trade organizations:
      Manufacturers Associations
      AEA (American Electronics Association)
      IEEE (Institute of Electrical and Electronic Engineers)
      ASME (American Society of Mechanical Engineers)
    Trade magazines (military magazines, trade organizations magazines, and business
        magazines)
    Chamber of Commerce
    State Employment Office (the Employment Development Department in California)
    Placement Services at colleges and elsewhere
    Temporary employment offices (in our area, many technical people "job shop" through
        temp agencies)

Figure 5.1   A Sample Page from <u>Shipments to Federal Government Agencies, 1981</u>

20

Table 5. Total Employment, Value Added, Value of Shipments, and

(Employment figures in thousands;

Line no.	Division, State, and Standard metropolitan statistical area[1]	Number of employees	Value added by manufacture	Total value of shipments and receipts	Government shipments			
					Total		Prime contracts	
					Employees	Value of shipments	Employees	Value of shipments
	Pacific--Continued							
191	California.........................	997.8	47,736.7	93,803.2	313.3	21,245.5	226.5	16,208.8
192	Anaheim-Santa Ana-Garden Grove................	214.2	8,715.4	13,678.5	38.4	2,581.9	27.4	1,863.3
193	Los Angeles-Long Beach................	336.6	18,920.7	40,802.4	136.5	11,350.8	101.6	8,797.4
194	Oxnard-Simi Valley-Ventura....................	9.0	474.6	713.3	2.2	166.5	1.3	101.8
195	Riverside-San Bernardino-Ontario..............	14.1	550.3	994.4	3.8	229.1	1.5	81.6
196	Sacramento................	6.3	214.9	399.2	2.3	208.2	1.8	164.2
197	San Diego........................	65.8	2,554.9	4,234.5	22.3	1,597.2	16.6	1,291.0
198	San Francisco-Oakland........................	44.5	3,393.5	10,354.2	6.5	613.2	3.0	378.4
199	San Jose..........................	199.9	9,443.8	15,690.0	40.6	3,537.0	30.1	2,826.0
200	Santa Barbara-Santa Maria-Lompoc..............	9.3	385.5	711.5	4.7	344.5	2.6	219.8
201	Santa Rosa........................	3.6	186.8	261.5	0.8	51.4	0.2	16.4
202	Vallejo-Fairfield-Napa........................	3.4	418.3	1,405.8	0.7	173.1	0.4	152.2
203	Alaska.........................	(D)	(D)	(D)	(D)	(D)	(D)	(D)
204	Hawaii.........................	(D)	(D)	(D)	(D)	(D)	(D)	(D)
205	Honolulu.........................	(D)	(D)	(D)	(D)	(D)	(D)	(D)

Data are preliminary estimates. See appendix C for a description of the methodology.

[1]Standard metropolitan statistical areas in more than one State are listed only once in the principle State. The SMSA total includes activities in all States for that SMSA. See appendix A for a description of the SMSA's.
[2]The standard error estimates are calculated from the unadjusted (reciprocal) government shipments that are reported on the MA-175. No adjustment has been made to the standard error for the ratio estimation to ASM levels. See appendix C for a description of the methodology.

21

Government Shipments, by Geographic Area and Agency: 1981—Continued

value figures in millions of dollars)

Government shipments--Continued										Standard error of estimate (percent) for total Government shipments[2]	Line no.
Subcontracts		To DOD		To NASA		To DOE		To other agencies			
Employees	Value of shipments	Employees	Value of shipments	Employees	Value of shipments	Employees	Value of shipments	Employees	Value of shipments		
86.8	5,031.6	227.5	15,825.1	25.3	2,056.4	5.7	382.4	54.8	2,981.6	2	191
11.1	718.6	30.5	2,059.5	2.7	180.6	0.3	26.8	5.0	315.1	4	192
34.8	2,553.3	95.9	7,947.2	18.1	1,638.2	2.9	231.8	19.6	1,533.6	1	193
0.9	64.7	1.9	143.5	(A)	1.4	-	-	0.3	21.6	18	194
2.3	147.5	2.8	181.5	0.3	16.5	(A)	0.2	0.6	30.9	19	195
0.6	44.1	2.0	182.6	0.3	21.3	(A)	0.3	(A)	4.0	1	196
5.7	306.1	16.9	1,285.4	1.3	98.4	1.3	93.5	2.9	119.8	19	197
3.5	234.8	4.3	463.5	(A)	5.5	(A)	0.8	2.1	143.4	12	198
10.5	710.9	32.4	2,948.1	1.1	101.6	0.4	20.7	6.8	466.6	2	199
2.0	124.7	3.8	290.1	0.3	21.5	-	-	0.5	32.9	12	200
0.5	35.0	0.7	45.8	(A)	2.0	(A)	1.3	(A)	2.3	1	201
0.3	20.9	0.6	167.4	-	-	(A)	(A)	(A)	5.7	18	202
(D)	-	(D)	(D)	-	-	-	-	(D)	(D)	(X)	203
(D)	(D)	(D)	(D)	-	-	-	-	(D)	(D)	(X)	204
(D)	(D)	(D)	(D)	-	-	-	-	(D)	(D)	(X)	205

Figure 5.2 A Sample Page from County Business Patterns

Table 2. Counties—Employees, Payroll, and Establishments, by Industry: 1981—Continued

(Excludes government employees, railroad employees, self-employed persons, etc.—see "General Explanation" for definitions and statement on reliability of data. Size class 1 to 4 includes establishments having payroll but no employees during mid-March pay period. "D" denotes figures withheld to avoid disclosure of operations of individual establishments, the other alphabetics indicate employment-size class—see footnote.)

SIC code	Industry	Number of employees for week including March 12	Payroll ($1,000) First Quarter	Payroll ($1,000) Annual	Total	1 to 4	5 to 9	10 to 19	20 to 49	50 to 99	100 to 249	250 to 499	500 to 999	1000 or more
	SANTA CLARA—Continued													
3398	Metal heat treating	60	334	1 378	6	1	2	3	·	·	·	·	·	·
34	Fabricated metal products	7 926	39 347	173 797	280	80	58	57	61	17	5	1	·	1
341	Metal cans and shipping containers	(E)	(D)	(D)	7	2	·	·	4	·	1	·	·	·
3411	Metal cans	(E)	(D)	(D)	5	·	·	·	4	·	1	·	·	·
342	Cutlery, hand tools, and hardware	248	624	2 742	13	5	2	3	1	2	·	·	·	·
3429	Hardware, nec	204	544	2 311	6	1	1	1	1	2	·	·	·	·
343	Plumbing and heating, except electric	114	290	958	5	1	1	·	3	·	·	·	·	·
3433	Heating equipment, except electric	114	290	958	5	1	1	·	3	·	·	·	·	·
344	Fabricated structural metal products	1 539	6 739	36 843	94	29	17	23	18	6	1	·	·	·
3441	Fabricated structural metal	262	1 381	11 812	14	4	5	1	2	2	·	·	·	·
3442	Metal doors, sash, and trim	73	318	1 264	4	·	1	2	1	·	·	·	·	·
3444	Sheet metal work	922	3 751	17 478	56	15	7	18	13	3	·	·	·	·
3446	Architectural metal work	76	345	1 778	9	4	2	2	1	·	·	·	·	·
3448	Prefabricated metal buildings	(B)	(D)	(D)	1	·	·	·	·	1	·	·	·	·
3449	Miscellaneous metal work	(C)	(D)	(D)	2	1	·	·	·	·	1	·	·	·
345	Screw machine products, bolts, etc.	96	461	1 553	7	1	2	3	1	·	·	·	·	·
3451	Screw machine products	(B)	(D)	(D)	5	·	2	2	1	·	·	·	·	·
346	Metal forgings and stampings	928	4 393	18 725	35	7	8	6	9	3	2	·	·	·
3469	Metal stampings, nec	(F)	(D)	(D)	34	7	8	6	8	3	2	·	·	·
347	Metal services, nec	1 649	6 926	27 752	71	25	13	15	12	4	1	1	·	·
3471	Plating and polishing	991	4 637	17 522	50	19	10	11	8	1	·	1	·	·
3479	Metal coating and allied services	658	2 290	10 230	21	6	3	4	4	3	1	·	·	·
348	Ordnance and accessories, nec	(G)	(D)	(D)	4	2	1	·	·	·	·	·	·	1
3489	Ordnance and accessories, nec	(G)	(D)	(D)	2	·	1	·	·	·	·	·	·	1
349	Misc. fabricated metal products	775	3 456	14 248	42	7	13	7	13	2	·	·	·	·
3494	Valves and pipe fittings	216	1 009	4 224	9	1	2	1	4	1	·	·	·	·
3495	Wire springs	(B)	(D)	(D)	2	·	·	·	2	·	·	·	·	·
3496	Misc. fabricated wire products	87	310	1 517	7	1	4	1	1	·	·	·	·	·
3499	Fabricated metal products, nec	305	1 333	5 277	18	3	5	4	5	1	·	·	·	·
35	Machinery, except electrical	68 620	386 976	1 701 902	635	227	105	113	87	35	28	13	12	15
352	Farm and garden machinery	(B)	(D)	(D)	5	1	1	2	1	·	·	·	·	·
3523	Farm machinery and equipment	(B)	(D)	(D)	5	1	1	2	1	·	·	·	·	·
353	Construction and related machinery	715	3 925	14 762	13	6	3	1	1	1	·	·	1	·
3531	Construction machinery	(B)	(D)	(D)	2	1	·	·	·	1	·	·	·	·
3535	Conveyors and conveying equipment	(F)	(D)	(D)	8	3	3	1	·	·	·	·	1	·
354	Metalworking machinery	710	4 006	16 939	57	19	14	12	11	1	·	·	·	·
3541	Machine tools, metal cutting types	146	702	3 695	9	1	4	1	3	·	·	·	·	·
3544	Special dies, tools, jigs & fixtures	432	2 595	10 246	34	12	8	7	6	1	·	·	·	·
3545	Machine tool accessories	(B)	(D)	(D)	7	4	1	·	2	·	·	·	·	·
355	Special industry machinery	1 388	7 000	26 887	26	6	6	3	3	3	4	1	·	·
3551	Food products machinery	(E)	(D)	(D)	11	1	3	3	1	2	1	·	·	·
3555	Printing trades machinery	(C)	(D)	(D)	1	·	·	·	·	·	1	·	·	·
3559	Special industry machinery, nec	818	4 039	14 669	11	3	2	·	2	1	2	1	·	·
356	General industrial machinery	2 565	14 577	54 197	24	2	4	8	·	4	3	2	1	·
3561	Pumps and pumping equipment	(F)	(D)	(D)	2	·	·	·	·	·	1	·	1	·
3563	Air and gas compressors	(E)	(D)	(D)	2	·	1	·	·	·	·	1	·	·
3564	Blowers and fans	(C)	(D)	(D)	3	·	·	1	·	2	·	·	·	·
3569	General industrial machinery, nec	1 229	8 029	23 663	9	·	1	3	·	2	2	1	·	·
357	Office and computing machines	58 863	338 643	1 506 679	144	30	10	12	22	17	18	10	10	15
3572	Typewriters	(B)	(D)	(D)	1	·	·	·	·	1	·	·	·	·
3573	Electronic computing equipment	56 497	325 799	1 449 773	134	29	10	11	21	14	17	9	9	14
3574	Calculating and accounting machines	(G)	(D)	(D)	4	1	·	·	·	1	·	1	1	·
3579	Office machines, nec	(G)	(D)	(D)	5	·	·	1	1	1	1	·	·	1
358	Refrigeration and service machinery	454	1 755	8 102	18	3	1	9	2	2	1	·	·	·
3589	Service industry machinery, nec	407	1 598	7 498	14	1	1	7	2	2	1	·	·	·
359	Misc. machinery, except electrical	3 848	16 761	72 988	344	157	65	66	47	7	2	·	·	·
3599	Machinery, except electrical, nec	(H)	(D)	(D)	343	156	65	66	47	7	2	·	·	·
36	Electric and electronic equipment	84 153	429 126	1 821 687	544	125	55	81	105	67	55	24	13	19
361	Electric distributing equipment	668	3 077	13 966	11	·	2	2	5	·	1	1	·	·
3612	Transformers	(E)	(D)	(D)	5	·	2	·	2	·	·	1	·	·
3613	Switchgear and switchboard apparatus	(C)	(D)	(D)	5	·	·	1	3	·	1	·	·	·
362	Electrical industrial apparatus	939	4 013	16 488	19	6	3	3	3	1	2	1	·	·
3621	Motors and generators	(E)	(D)	(D)	2	·	·	1	·	·	·	1	·	·
3622	Industrial controls	(F)	(D)	(D)	15	5	3	2	2	1	2	·	·	·
364	Electric lighting and wiring equipment	689	2 814	11 114	14	2	1	4	2	2	3	·	·	·
3641	Electric lamps	(B)	(D)	(D)	3	1	·	1	·	1	·	·	·	·
3643	Current-carrying wiring devices	200	574	2 459	5	1	·	3	·	·	1	·	·	·
3644	Noncurrent-carrying wiring devices	(C)	(D)	(D)	2	·	·	·	1	1	·	·	·	·
3648	Lighting equipment, nec	(C)	(D)	(D)	3	·	1	·	1	·	1	·	·	·
365	Radio and tv receiving equipment	193	920	3 804	9	3	1	3	1	·	1	·	·	·
3651	Radio and tv receiving sets	188	912	3 706	6	·	1	3	1	·	1	·	·	·
366	Communication equipment	18 784	105 234	432 979	105	24	10	11	14	20	14	1	6	5
3661	Telephone and telegraph apparatus	2 665	12 911	48 219	14	2	1	2	3	3	·	·	3	·
3662	Radio and tv communication equipment	16 111	92 281	383 594	84	16	8	9	11	17	14	1	3	5
367	Electronic components and accessories	60 730	303 275	1 299 029	343	78	32	52	72	41	28	19	7	14
3671	Electron tubes, receiving type	8 353	47 067	201 536	6	·	·	·	2	·	·	1	1	2
3673	Electron tubes, transmitting	(C)	(D)	(D)	3	·	·	1	1	·	1	·	·	·
3674	Semiconductors and related devices	34 775	174 053	735 221	108	24	11	11	15	10	13	10	4	10
3677	Electronic coils and transformers	(F)	(D)	(D)	7	1	·	·	4	1	·	1	·	·
3679	Electronic components, nec	16 273	75 088	323 569	193	38	20	35	46	28	15	8	1	2
369	Misc. electrical equipment & supplies	2 060	9 502	42 471	34	5	5	6	8	2	6	2	·	·
3691	Storage batteries	336	1 589	5 417	4	·	1	1	·	·	2	·	·	·
3693	X-ray apparatus and tubes	932	4 884	23 391	9	2	·	1	1	1	3	1	·	·

A:0–19; B:20–99; C:100–249; E:250–499; F:500–999; G:1,000–2,499; H:2,500–4,999; I:5,000–9,999; J:10,000–24,999; K:25,000–49,999; L:50,000–99,999; M:100,000 or more.

Figure 5.3 Military Employment by SIC Industry

SIC Code	Industry	Notes	Census Bureau [1]			Number of Employees in Your County
			Number of Employees 1981 Total (000)	for DoD (000)	Share to DoD 1981 (%)	
28	Chemicals and allied products					28
2813	Industrial gases		7.3	S	S	2813
2819	Industrial inorganic chemicals, nec		95.5	1.7	1.8	2819
2873	Nitrogenous fertilizers		11.0	S	S	2873
2874	Phosphatic fertilizers		14.2	0.0	0.0	2874
2892	Explosives		13.1	5.6	42.7	2892
29	Petroleum and coal products					29
291	Petroleum refining	[2]	107.3	1.7	1.6	291
2992	Lubricating oils and greases	[3]	9.4	0.1	1.1	2992
30	Rubber & miscellaneous plastics products					30
304	Rubber and plastic hose and belting	[2]	30.3	0.2	0.7	304
306	Fabricated rubber products, nec	[2][3]	89.1	3.4	3.8	306
32	Stone, clay, glass, & concrete products					32
3293	Gaskets, packets, and sealing devices		31.2	S	S	3293
33	Primary metal industries					33
3324	Steel investment foundries		16.9	1.4	8.3	3324
3325	Steel foundries, nec		56.1	0.8	1.4	3325
3339	Primary nonferrous metals, nec		10.2	0.1	1.0	3339
3351	Copper rolling and drawing		29.2	0.1	0.3	3351
3353	Aluminum sheet, plate, and foil		31.4	0.6	1.9	3353
3354	Aluminum extruded products		29.1	S	S	3354
3355	Aluminum rolling and drawing, nec		5.5	A	0.0	3355
3356	Nonferrous rolling and drawing, nec		20.2	0.5	2.5	3356
3357	Nonferrous wire drawing and insulating		63.6	1.5	2.4	3357
3361	Aluminum foundries		57.3	1.2	2.1	3361
3369	Nonferrous foundries, nec		18.0	S	S	3369
34	Fabricated metal products					34
3441	Fabricated structural metal		98.0	4.3	4.4	3441
3443	Fabricated plate work (boiler shops)		131.2	1.6	1.2	3443
3451	Screw machine products		51.6	S	S	3451
3452	Bolts, nuts, rivets, and washers		59.3	1.0	1.7	3452
3462	Iron and steel forgings		41.3	1.3	3.1	3462
3463	Nonferrous forgings		10.3	2.6	25.2	3463
3482	Small arms ammunition		9.4	2.7	28.7	3482
3483	Ammunition, except for small arms, nec		21.2	19.0	89.6	3483
3484	Small arms		19.6	3.6	18.4	3484
3489	Ordnance and accessories, nec		28.9	9.9	34.3	3489
3494	Valves and pipe fittings	[4]	117.3	2.3	2.0	3494
3499	Fabricated metal products, nec		64.0	S	S	3499

Figure 5.3 Military Employment by SIC Industry (continued)

SIC Code	Industry	Notes	Census Bureau [1]			Number of Employees in Your County
			Number of Employees 1981 Total (000)	Share for DoD (000)	to DoD 1981 (%)	
35	Machinery, except electrical					35
3511	Turbines and turbine generator sets		35.8	2.0	5.6	3511
3519	Internal combustion engines, nec		78.4	3.5	4.5	3519
3531	Construction machinery		146.2	1.8	1.2	3531
3536	Hoists, cranes, and monorails		14.6	S	S	3536
3537	Industrial trucks and tractors		21.9	S	S	3537
3541	Machine tools, metal cutting types		78.7	0.3	0.4	3541
3542	Machine tools, metal forming types		22.0	S	S	3542
3561	Pumps and pumping equipment		72.2	2.8	3.9	3561
3562	Ball and roller bearings		48.9	0.7	1.4	3562
3563	Air and gas compressors		32.5	0.7	2.2	3563
3566	Speed changers, drives, and gears		26.2	S	S	3566
3568	Power transmission equipment, nec		31.4	S	S	3568
3569	General industrial machinery, nec		57.3	S	S	3569
3573	Electronic computing equipment		314.9	12.4	3.9	3573
3574	Calculating and accounting machines		15.1	0.4	2.6	3574
3579	Office machines, nec		52.4	S	S	3579
3592	Carburetors, pistons, rings, valves		31.3	S	S	3592
3599	Machinery, except electrical, nec		268.3	5.6	2.1	3599
36	Electrical and electronic equipment					36
3612	Transformers		42.4	S	S	3612
3613	Switchgear and switchboard apparatus		66.2	1.2	1.8	3613
3621	Motors and generators	[4]	94.1	4.8	5.1	3621
3622	Industrial controls		67.6	S	S	3622
3643	Current-carrying wiring devices		51.5	S	S	3643
3644	Noncurrent-carrying wiring devices		28.3	S	S	3644
3661	Telephone and telegraph apparatus		165.6	1.8	1.1	3661
3662	Radio and TV communication equipment		420.0	192.4	45.8	3662
3671	Electron tubes, all types	[5]	39.4	6.3	16.0	3671
3674	Semiconductors and related devices		165.6	4.2	2.5	3674
3675	Electronic capacitors		26.1	0.2	0.8	3675
3676	Electronic resistors		20.4	0.1	0.5	3676
3677	Electronic coils and transformers		19.4	S	S	3677
3678	Electronic connectors	[4]	37.0	2.2	5.9	3678
3679	Electronic components, nec		185.3	9.2	5.0	3679
3691	Storage batteries		24.1	1.7	7.1	3691
3692	Primary batteries, dry and wet	[4]	11.8	1.0	8.5	3692
3693	X-ray apparatus and tubes		34.8	S	S	3693
3694	Engine electrical equipment		55.7	S	S	3694
3699	Electrical equipment and supplies, nec		25.4	S	S	3699

Figure 5.3 Military Employment by SIC Industry (continued)

SIC Code	Industry	Notes	Census Bureau [1]			Number of Employees in Your County	
			Number of Employees 1981		Share to DoD 1981		
			Total (000)	for DoD (000)	(%)		
37	Transportation equipment						37
3713	Truck and bus bodies		35.5	S	S		3713
3715	Truck trailers		21.1	S	S		3715
3721	Aircraft		284.6	112.9	39.7		3721
3724	Aircraft engines and engine parts		137.6	56.1	40.8		3724
3728	Aircraft equipment, nec		173.7	68.8	39.6		3728
3731	Shipbuilding and repairing		177.9	78.0	43.8		3731
3761	Guided missiles and space vehicles		113.5	73.3	64.6		3761
3764	Space propulsion units and parts		26.4	18.2	68.9		3764
3769	Space vehicle equipment, nec		6.1	1.1	18.0		3769
3795	Tanks and tank components		11.0	8.0	72.7		3795
38	Instruments and related products						38
381	Engineering & scientific instruments	[2]	43.8	4.4	10.0		381
3823	Process control instruments		50.0	0.8	1.6		3823
3824	Fluid meters and counting machines		14.3	S	S		3824
3825	Instruments to measure electricity		93.3	9.5	10.2		3825
3829	Measuring and controlling devices, nec		36.2	1.7	4.7		3829
383	Optical instruments and lenses	[2]	40.1	7.0	17.5		383
3842	Surgical appliances and supplies	[4]	61.8	0.4	0.6		3842
3843	Dental equipment and supplies		17.4	A	0.0		3843
385	Ophthalmic goods	[2]	27.4	S	S		385
386	Photographic equipment and supplies	[2]	113.6	1.9	1.7		386
387	Watches, clocks, and watchcases	[2]	20.9	0.3	1.4		387
88	Miscellaneous industries	[6]	45.8	8.2	17.9		88
	Total						

Figure 5.3 Military Employment by SIC Industry (continued)

Notes:

nec = not elsewhere classified

S = "Data supressed because they did not meet publication standards. This includes cells
      where the total value of government shipments is less than $20 million or the
      standard error is 20% or greater."

A = Less than 100 employees.

[1] Census Bureau employment data is derived from a survey of plants in 92 of the
     approximately 450 4-digit SIC manufacturing industries which engage most
     extensively with the Federal Government. It is believed these industries provide
     the vast bulk of Federal procurement. DoD employment is estimated by adjusting the
     total average number of employees at each establishment in 1981 by the proportion
     of that establishment's **value of shipments** that went to the DoD. The data contains
     some, but not all, subcontracts. Because the employment figures are rounded to the
     nearest 100, the percent share of employment to the DoD may be off by as much as
     1%. Table 3, Shipments to Federal Government Agencies 1981, MA-175(81)-1, Bureau
     of the Census.

[2] Several 3-digit codes have no subsets and are therefore equivalent to the 4-digit
     codes:

          291   2911   383   3832
          304   3041   385   3851
          306   3069   386   3861
          381   3811   387   3873

[3] The values of DoD shipments for SIC 2992 and 3069 were derived by subtracting the
     value of another industry from the total for that 2-digit SIC group. These values
     may therefore not be very accurate.

[4] There is no data listed for 1981, so this is 1980 data (revised) as shown in Table 4,
     Shipments to Federal Government Agencies 1981, MA-175(81)-1, Bureau of the Census.

[5] In 1977, SIC codes 3671, 3672, and 3673 were combined into 3671. However, the old
     categories are still used sometimes.

[6] Represents nonmanufacturing facilities of the manufacturing canvassed and selected
     nonprofit research corporations working on government contracts.

Figure 5.4 Worksheet for Calculating the Share of Direct and Indirect DoD Employment
in a County by 4-Digit SIC Code in 1983

County: _____

SIC Code	Industry	Notes	DEIMS Est. Share to DoD 1983 (%) A [1]	Employees on March 12 [2] [3] Total Number B	Total DoD C	
MINING						
10	Metal mining		_____	_____	_____	10
101	Iron ore mining	[4]	! 9.3 !	_____	! _____	! 101
102	Copper ore mining		! 12.1 !	_____	! _____	! 102
106	Ferroalloy ores, except vanadium	[4]	! 9.3 !	_____	! _____	! 106
14	Nonmetallic minerals, except fuels		_____	_____	_____	14
147	Chemical and fertilizer mineral mining		! 3.3 !	_____	! _____	! 147
MANUFACTURING						
22	Textile mill products		_____	_____	_____	22
224	Narrow fabric mills		! 4.9 !	_____	! _____	! 224
23	Apparel and other textile products		_____	_____	_____	23
2393	Textile bags	[4]	! 6.2 !	_____	! _____	! 2393
2394	Canvas and related products	[4]	! 6.2 !	_____	! _____	! 2394
2395	Pleating and stitching	[4]	! 6.2 !	_____	! _____	! 2395
2396	Automotive and apparel trimmings	[4]	! 6.2 !	_____	! _____	! 2396
2397	Schiffli machine embroideries	[4]	! 6.2 !	_____	! _____	! 2397
2399	Fabricated textile products, nec	[4]	! 6.2 !	_____	! _____	! 2399
24	Lumber and wood products		_____	_____	_____	24
2441	Nailed wood boxes and shook	[4]	! 10.0 !	_____	! _____	! 2441
2448	Wood pallets and skids		! 6.8 !	_____	! _____	! 2448
2449	Wood containers, nec	[4]	! 10.0 !	_____	! _____	! 2449
25	Furniture and fixtures		_____	_____	_____	25
2515	Metal and household furniture		! 5.8 !	_____	! _____	! 2515
2517	Wood TV and radio cabinets		! 5.8 !	_____	! _____	! 2517
2522	Metal office furniture		! 3.5 !	_____	! _____	! 2522
26	Paper and allied products		_____	_____	_____	26
2642	Envelopes		! 4.4 !	_____	! _____	! 2642
27	Printing and publishing		_____	_____	_____	27
274	Miscellaneous publishing	[5]	! 3.5 !	_____	! _____	! 274
276	Manifold business forms	[5]	! 6.1 !	_____	! _____	! 276

Page Total   ! _____ !

Figure 5.4 Indirect DoD Employment Worksheet (continued)

SIC Code	Industry	Notes	!DEIMS ! Est. !Share !to DoD! 1983 ! (%) ! A [1]	Employees on March 12 [2] [3]		
				Total ! Number ! B	Total DoD C	
28	Chemicals and allied products					28
2812	Alkalies and chlorine	[4]	! 7.9 !	!	!	2812
2813	Industrial gases	[4]	! 7.9 !	!	!	2813
2816	Inorganic pigments	[4]	! 7.9 !	!	!	2816
2819	Industrial inorganic chemicals, nec	[4][6]	! 7.9 !	!	!	2819
2821	Plastics materials and resins		! 5.1 !	!	!	2821
285	Paints and allied products	[5]	! 4.7 !	!	!	285
2861	Gum and wood chemicals		! 3.1 !	!	!	2861
2865	Cyclic crudes and intermediates	[4]	! 7.9 !	!	!	2865
2869	Industrial organic chemicals, nec	[4]	! 7.9 !	!	!	2869
2892	Explosives		! 41.4 !	!	!	2892
2893	Printing ink		! 3.1 !	!	!	2893
2895	Carbon black		! 3.0 !	!	!	2895
2899	Chemical preparations, nec		! 5.0 !	!	!	2899
29	Petroleum and coal products					29
291	Petroleum refining	[4] [5]	! 5.0 !	!	!	291
2992	Lubricating oils and greases	[4]	! 5.0 !	!	!	2992
2999	Petroleum and coal products, nec	[4]	! 5.0 !	!	!	2999
30	Rubber and miscellaneous plastics products					30
303	Reclaimed rubber	[5]	! 3.1 !	!	!	303
306	Fabricated rubber products, nec	[5]	! 4.9 !	!	!	306
307	Miscellaneous plastic products	[5]	! 4.0 !	!	!	307
31	Leather and leather products					31
313	Footwear cut stock	[5]	! 14.3 !	!	!	313
32	Stone, clay, glass, and concrete products					32
321	Flat glass	[4] [5]	! 4.2 !	!	!	321
3229	Pressed and blown glass, nec	[4]	! 4.2 !	!	!	3229
323	Products of purchased glass	[4] [5]	! 4.2 !	!	!	323
324	Cement, hydraulic	[5]	! 4.0 !	!	!	324
325	Structural clay products		! 3.2 !	!	!	325
326	Pottery and related products		! 3.3 !	!	!	326
3274	Lime		! 6.0 !	!	!	3274
3291	Abrasive products		! 5.5 !	!	!	3291
3292	Asbestos products	[4]	! 3.9 !	!	!	3292

Page Total   !_____!

Figure 5.4 Indirect DoD Employment Worksheet (continued)

SIC Code	Industry	Notes	!DEIMS ! Est. !Share !to DoD! 1983 ! (%) A [1]	Employees on March 12 [2] [3] Total Number B	Total DoD C	
32 (continued)						
3293	Gaskets, packets, and sealing devices	[4]	3.9			3293
3295	Minerals, ground or treated		8.4			3295
3297	Nonclay refractories		3.0			3297
3299	Nonmetallic mineral products, nec		13.0			3299
33	Primary metal industries					33
3312	Blast furnaces and steel mills		8.6			3312
3313	Electrometallurgical products		9.3			3313
3315	Steel wire and related products		3.0			3315
3316	Cold finishing of steel shapes		11.5			3316
3317	Steel pipe and tubes		7.0			3317
332	Iron and steel foundries		6.7			332
3331	Primary copper		10.3			3331
3332	Lead smelting and refining		8.8			3332
3333	Zinc smelting and refining		11.6			3333
3334	Aluminum production and refining	[6]	9.4			3334
3339	Primary nonferrous metals, nec		8.5			3339
334	Secondary nonferrous metals	[5]	11.8			334
3351	Copper rolling and drawing		9.2			3351
3353	Aluminum sheet, plate, and foil	[4]	9.7			3353
3354	Aluminum extruded products	[4]	9.7			3354
3355	Aluminum rolling and drawing, nec	[4]	9.7			3355
3356	Nonferrous rolling and drawing, nec		13.4			3356
3357	Nonferrous wire drawing and insulating		7.0			3357
3361	Aluminum foundries		13.6			3361
3362	Brass, bronze, and copper castings		9.6			3362
3369	Nonferrous foundries, nec		17.5			3369
3398	Metal heat treating		12.9			3398
3399	Primary metal products, nec		16.4			3399
34	Fabricated metal products					34
3412	Metal barrels, drums, and pails		5.6			3412
3423	Hand and edge tools, nec		4.4			3423
3425	Hand saws and saw blades		3.8			3425
3429	Hardware, nec		4.1			3429
3432	Plumbing fittings and brass goods		5.9			3432
3433	Heating equipment, except electric		5.2			3433

Page Total

Figure 5.4 Indirect DoD Employment Worksheet (continued)

SIC Code	Industry	Notes	DEIMS Est. Share to DoD 1983 (%) A [1]	Employees on March 12 [2] [3]	
				Total Number B	Total DoD C
34	**(continued)**				
3441	Fabricated structural metal		4.7		3441
3443	Fabricated plate work (boiler shops)		7.8		3443
3444	Sheet metal work		3.4		3444
3446	Architectural metal work		4.9		3446
3451	Screw machine products	[4]	11.3		3451
3452	Bolts, nuts, rivets, and washers	[4]	11.3		3452
3462	Iron and steel forgings		11.5		3462
3463	Nonferrous forgings		31.3		3463
3465	Automotive stampings	[4]	6.2		3465
3466	Crowns and closures	[4]	6.2		3466
3469	Metal stampings, nec	[4]	6.2		3469
3471	Plating and polishing		18.8		3471
3479	Metal coating and allied services		10.5		3479
3482	Small arms ammunition		57.0		3482
3483	Ammunition, except for small arms, nec		75.6		3483
3484	Small arms		8.1		3484
3489	Ordnance and accessories, nec		76.3		3489
3493	Steel springs, except wire		3.1		3493
3494	Valves and pipe fittings	[4]	3.5		3494
3495	Wire springs	[4]	5.2		3495
3496	Misc. fabricated wire products	[4]	5.2		3496
3498	Fabricated pipe and fittings	[4]	3.5		3498
3499	Fabricated metal products, nec		7.0		3499
35	**Machinery, except electrical**				35
3511	Turbines and turbine generator sets		18.4		3511
3519	Internal combustion engines, nec		6.0		3519
3534	Elevators and moving stairways		4.0		3534
3535	Conveyors and conveying equipment		3.8		3535
3536	Hoists, cranes, and monorails		6.0		3536
3537	Industrial trucks and tractors		24.3		3537
3541	Machine tools, metal cutting types		13.8		3541
3542	Machine tools, metal forming types		9.0		3542
3544	Special dies, tools, jigs, & fixtures	[4]	9.4		3544
3545	Machine tool accessories	[4]	9.4		3545
3546	Power driven hand tools		5.6		3546
3549	Metalworking machinery, nec		8.4		3549
3559	Special industry machinery, nec		3.7		3559

Page Total

Figure 5.4 Indirect DoD Employment Worksheet (continued)

SIC Code	Industry	Notes	DEIMS Est. Share to DoD 1983 (%) A [1]	Employees on March 12 [2] [3] Total Number B	Total DoD C	
35	(continued)					
3561	Pumps and pumping equipment	[4]	4.5			3561
3562	Ball and roller bearings		9.1			3562
3563	Air and gas compressors	[4]	4.5			3563
3564	Blowers and fans		5.7			3564
3565	Industrial patterns		9.0			3565
3566	Speed changers, drives, and gears	[4]	9.6			3566
3568	Power transmission equipment, nec	[4]	9.6			3568
3569	General industrial machinery, nec		4.8			3569
3573	Electronic computing equipment		10.6			3573
3586	Measuring and dispensing pumps		3.3			3586
3592	Carburetors, pistons, rings, valves	[4]	11.9			3592
3599	Machinery, except electrical, nec	[4]	11.9			3599
36	Electrical and electronic equipment					36
3612	Transformers		4.2			3612
3613	Switchgear and switchboard apparatus		3.4			3613
3621	Motors and generators		7.2			3621
3622	Industrial controls		8.6			3622
3623	Welding apparatus, electric		6.3			3623
3624	Carbon and graphite products		8.9			3624
3629	Electrical industrial apparatus, nec		10.9			3629
3643	Current-carrying wiring devices	[4]	9.6			3643
3644	Noncurrent-carrying wiring devices	[4]	9.6			3644
3661	Telephone and telegraph apparatus		4.7			3661
3662	Radio and TV communication equipment		47.3			3662
3671-3	Electron tubes, all types	[7]	15.1			3671-3
3674	Semiconductors and related devices		18.4			3674
3675	Electronic capacitors	[4]	23.8			3675
3676	Electronic resistors	[4]	23.8			3676
3677	Electronic coils and transformers	[4]	23.8			3677
3678	Electronic connectors	[4]	23.8			3678
3679	Electronic components, nec	[4]	23.8			3679
3692	Primary batteries, dry and wet		3.2			3692
3694	Engine electrical equipment		5.1			3694
37	Transportation equipment					37
3713	Truck and bus bodies		2.8			3713
3714	Motor vehicle parts and accessories		3.5			3714

Page Total

Figure 5.4 Indirect DoD Employment Worksheet (continued)

SIC Code	Industry	Notes	DEIMS Est. Share to DoD 1983 (%) A [1]	Employees on March 12 [2] [3]		
				Total Number B	Total DoD C	
37	**(continued)**					
3721	Aircraft		51.7			3721
3724	Aircraft engines and engine parts	[4]	49.0			3724
3728	Aircraft equipment, nec	[4]	48.8			3728
3731	Shipbuilding and repairing		69.9			3731
3761	Guided missiles and space vehicles		55.2			3761
3764	Space propulsion units and parts	[4]	49.0			3764
3769	Space vehicle equipment, nec	[4]	48.8			3769
3795	Tanks and tank components		65.4			3795
38	**Instruments and related products**					38
381	Engineering and scientific instruments	[5]	41.7			381
3822	Environmental controls	[4]	24.6			3822
3823	Process control instruments	[4]	24.6			3823
3824	Fluid meters and counting machines	[4]	24.6			3824
3825	Instruments to measure electricity		43.9			3825
3829	Measuring and controlling devices, nec	[4]	24.6			3829
383	Optical instruments and lenses	[5]	13.5			383
3841	Surgical and medical instruments		3.6			3841
3842	Surgical appliances and supplies		9.7			3842
387	Watches, clocks, and watchcases	[5]	8.7			387
	Total Manufacturing					
	Percent to DoD				%	

SIC Code	Industry	Notes	A	B	C	
TRANSPORTATION AND OTHER PUBLIC UTILITIES						
44	Water transportation		8.4			44
45	Air transportation		6.3			45
46	Pipelines, except natural gas		5.1			46
83	Social services		4.2			83
	TOTAL					
	Percent to DoD				%	

Figure 5.4 Indirect DoD Employment Worksheet (continued)

Notes:

nec = not elsewhere classified

[1] The Defense Economic Impact Modeling System (DEIMS) estimates the percent of output from each of 400 industries that ultimately goes to the Department of Defense based on an input-output model of the U.S. economy. The DEIMS model is based on **value of output** rather than employment, but here it is assumed that employment is proportional to value of output. Defense Economic Impact Modeling System: A New Concept in Economic Forecasting for Defense Expenditures, July 1983, Office of the Under Secretary of Defense for Research and Engineering.

[2] Obtain the information to put in Column B from County Business Patterns (most recent year available), Bureau of the Census, for your state. If a range is given, either list the range or take an average value. Multiply Column B by the percentage in Column A to get a value for Column C.
    If you use data for any year other than 1983, the results you obtain will be slightly inaccurate. Since the military budget was much greater in 1983 than in previous years, it is a good assumption that therewas **more** military employment in 1983.

[3] You may want to perform this same calculation for the amount of the employees' **annual payroll** that comes from the DoD. The total annual payroll for each SIC industry is also listed in County Business Patterns. The **annual** payroll data is in the third column after the SIC code listing. If no amount is given, multiply the number of employees by $10,000 for a conservatively low estimate.

[4] The DEIMS model lumps several SIC industries together. Here we assume that each SIC industry in that grouping has the same DoD share of output as the group as a whole. The groups that are lumped together are:

SIC Code				Group Description
101	106			Iron and ferroalloy ores mining
2393	2394	2395	2396	Fabric textile products, nec
2397	2399			
2812	2813	2816	2819	Inorganic and organic chemicals
2865	2869	(except 28195)		
2441	2449			Wood containers
2991	2992	2999		Petroleum refining and related products
3211	3229	3231		Glass and products except containers
3292	3293			Asbestos products and sealing devices
3353	3354	3355		Aluminum rolling and drawing
3451	3452			Screw machine products
3465	3466	3469		Metal stampings
3494	3498			Pipe valves and pipe fittings
3495	3496			Miscellaneous fabricated wire products
3544	3545			Special dies and machine tool accessories
3561	3563			Pumps and compressors
3592	3599			Miscellaneous machinery
3643	3644			Wiring devices
3675	3676	3677	3679	Electronic components
3724	3764			Aircraft and missile engines and parts
3728	3769			Aircraft and missile equipment, n.e.c.
3822	3823	3824	3829	Measuring and control instruments

Figure 5.4 Indirect DoD Employment Worksheet Notes (continued)

[5] Several 3-digit codes have no subsets and are therefore equivalent to the 4-digit codes:

274	2741	321	3211
276	2761	323	3231
285	2851	324	3241
291	2911	334	3341
303	3031	381	3811
306	3069	383	3832
307	3079	387	3873
313	3131		

[6] SIC 2819 does not include SIC 28195 Aluminum Oxide (Alumina). It is instead included in SIC 3334.

[7] In 1977, SIC codes 3671, 3672, and 3673 were combined into 3671. However, the old categories are still used sometimes.

Some SIC groups were not included in this table because they were too unwieldy or could not be easily used:

SIC Codes	Group Description	1983 DoD Share
103-105, part of 108, 109	Metal ores mining, n.e.c.	8.2%
1111, part of 1112, 1211, part of 1213	Coal mining	3.5
131, 132, part of 138	Crude petroleum and natural gas	4.9
Part of 15-17, part of 138	Maintenance & repair, other	4.4
Part of 15-17	New military facilities	100.0
Part of 16-17	New railroads	3.9
40, 474, part of 4789	Railroads & rail-related services	4.2
42, part of 4789	Motor freight	5.2
Part of 47	Transportation service, n.e.c.	6.3
491, part of 493	Electric utilities	3.1
Part of 70	Hotels and lodging places	7.5
732-739, part of 76	Misc. business services	6.0
81, part of 89	Misc. professional services	3.7
84, 86, 8922	Nonprofit organizations	3.2

Figure 5.5 Percent of Output to Foreign Military Sales

Figure 5.4 only considers the percent of industry output which eventually goes to the DoD. In addition to the sales to the DoD and its contractors, a lot of military output goes to other countries as **Foreign Military Sales (FMS)**. The DEIMS also models these sales. For several industries more than 3% of the total output goes to FMS:

1983

SIC Code	Industry	Percent to FMS		Percent to DoD		Percent Total Military
2892	Explosives	2.2	+	41.4	=	43.6
3361	Aluminum foundries	3.2	+	13.6	=	16.8
3369	Nonferrous foundries, nec	4.6	+	17.5	=	22.1
3399	Primary metal products, nec	3.8	+	16.4	=	20.2
3463	Nonferrous forgings	8.0	+	31.1	=	39.1
3483	Ammunition, except for small arms, nec	24.1	+	75.6	=	99.7
3484	Small arms	9.0	+	57.0	=	66.0
3489	Ordnance and accessories, nec	23.7	+	76.3	=	100.0
3511	Turbines and turbine generator sets	3.7	+	18.4	=	22.1
3537	Industrial trucks and tractors	2.2	+	24.3	=	26.5
3662	Radio and TV communication equipment	13.2	+	47.3	=	60.5
3671	Electron tubes, all types	3.0	+	15.1	=	18.1
3674	Semiconductors and related devices	4.1	+	18.4	=	22.5
3675	Electronic capacitors	5.3	+	23.8	=	29.1
3676	Electronic resistors	5.3	+	23.8	=	29.1
3677	Electronic coils and transformers	5.3	+	23.8	=	29.1
3678	Electronic connectors	5.3	+	23.8	=	29.1
3679	Electronic components, nec	5.3	+	23.8	=	29.1
3721	Aircraft	13.2	+	51.7	=	64.9
3724	Aircraft engines and engine parts	14.6	+	49.0	=	63.6
3728	Aircraft equipment, nec	8.0	+	48.5	=	56.5
3731	Shipbuilding and repairing	5.1	+	69.9	=	75.0
3761	Guided missiles and space vehicles	9.9	+	55.2	=	65.1
3764	Space propulsion units and parts	14.6	+	49.0	=	63.6
3769	Space vehicle equipment, nec	8.0	+	48.5	=	56.5
3795	Tanks and tank components	33.8	+	65.4	=	99.2
3811	Engineering and scientific instruments	7.5	+	41.7	=	49.2
3822	Environmental controls	10.0	+	24.6	=	34.6
3823	Process control instruments	10.0	+	24.6	=	34.6
3824	Fluid meters and counting machines	10.0	+	24.6	=	34.6
3829	Measuring and controlling devices, nec	10.0	+	24.6	=	34.6
3832	Optical instruments and lenses	3.4	+	13.5	=	16.9

It is surprising that more than half of the output from several large and significant industries in the United States goes to the military, either to the DoD or to Foreign Military Sales: 60% of the Radio and TV Communication Equipment industry, 65% of the Aircraft industry, 75% of the Shipbuilding and Repair industry, and 49% of the Engineering and Scientific Instruments industry. These are large and significant industries in the United States but not ones that are usually considered military industries.

Chapter 6　　Local Economic and Budget Impacts

Whether your community receives large military contracts or not, it still has a very large impact on the local economy and local government.

6.A.　The Effects of Military Spending on Local Communities

Negative:

-- Tax money spent on the military represents a large drain on the economy. Over 50% of individual income taxes go to the military and military spending now represents about 6% of the total U.S. Gross National Product. Large amounts of work and resources are diverted into products which cannot be bought by consumers or used in any socially useful way. As the military budget has grown, municipal and county budgets have lost much of their Federal funding. Local taxes must be increased to compensate for this loss. Benefits to individuals (like AFDC) have also been cut.

The money spent on the military could otherwise be used for education, economic development, mass transit, environmental protection, and human services. Or, rather than switching the money from the military to these other services, federal taxes could be lowered for most people, allowing them to buy more products and services and thus bolster the economy, invest their money in industry and thus rebuild the industrial base of the country, or contribute their excess money to people in need.

-- Because military spending ties up large amounts of capital, it is difficult to obtain money for other uses except at very high interest rates. Local employment and small business development may be stunted by a lack of capital for research, equipment, facilities, and the rebuilding of the local infrastructure.

-- Government-owned production facilities, whether operated by the government or by a private contractor, don't pay property taxes. If these facilities represent a large portion of the industry in an area, the other companies must pay significantly higher property taxes to provide the same amount of funding for local services. Other companies thus subsidize the government facility.

-- Federal contracts are exempted from local or state sales taxes. In some areas, the industrial sales tax represents an important source of funding for the community.

-- Federal contracts encourage labor-displacing production and information technologies to improve productivity (output per worker hour). Federal contracts may also have a role in shaping local wage rates, working conditions, and labor-management relations. All these things may affect local labor conditions and employment.

Positive:

-- Military contractors pay local taxes on their own facilities. They also provide jobs (frequently high-paying), enabling their employees to also pay local taxes.

-- Salaries for locally based military personnel, veterans benefits, and military retirement pay provide a direct cash infusion into the local economy, enabling these people to require less from local government and also to pay local taxes.

6.B. Relative Flow of Tax Money Into and Out of Your Community

The Pentagon Tax

One of the main arguments used in communities across the U.S. to defend continued military spending is its purported stimulation of the local economy. Large amounts of military money flowing into a community create jobs and provide taxes for local government. However, for most communities this apparent economic benefit is more than offset by the economic drain of what is called the **Pentagon tax**. The Pentagon tax represents the amount of money a community pays in taxes to support the Department of Defense. Since the DoD budget is large, this tax is also quite large for any community. [Note the way the Pentagon Tax is defined: it only covers expenditures by the Department of Defense and ignores military money spent by the DoE, NASA, and other agencies.]

James Anderson, of Employment Research Associates, has calculated the Pentagon Tax for local communities and the money returned to each community in prime military contracts. He has calculated this by 1980 Congressional District (Bankrupting America) and by Standard Metropolitan Statistical Area (Bankrupting American Cities). These studies use 1980 base year data and extrapolate the results to 1982 and 1983 respectively (see Figures 6.1 and 6.2). For each community these studies list the total net gain or loss of money from the military and the net gain or loss per family. These studies are quite impressive and provide a good starting point for countering the economic arguments that favor greater military spending. Note the danger in using this data though: you must be careful not to get caught arguing that your community has been deprived of its fair share of military spending, but rather argue that military spending should be cut back overall and other kinds of funding which your community needs should be increased and fairly allocated.

Anderson employed the following methodology: The total DoD budget expenditure amount for the entire country was obtained for the appropriate year from the DoD. In order to pay for this military spending, taxes must be collected from us all. This tax amount is called the **tax burden** by the Tax Foundation, Inc. This Pentagon tax burden was allocated to each state in accord with a special distribution computed each year by the Tax Foundation (Facts and Figures on Government Finance in the table called "Allocation of the Federal Tax Burden by State," Table 134). This distribution is calculated to reflect the actual origin of Federal taxes rather than the point of collection. The DoD tax burden for each state was in turn allocated to each county or SMSA in accord with its proportion of state population and its ratio of per capita income to the average for the state. This allocation is fairly rough, but trying to calculate a more precise amount would be very difficult.

The Pentagon tax burden was then compared with total Pentagon expenditures in the community. The net tax drain is equal to the Pentagon tax burden for that community minus total Pentagon expenditures for that community. 1980 was used as the base year because data on DoD expenditures was available from the Community Services Administration (CSA) in Geographic Distribution of Federal Funds, 1980. (This study was defunded by the Reagan Administration after 1980.) Since part of prime military contracts are subcontracted out to companies in other communities, this analysis may not accurately reflect the true extent of Pentagon spending in any particular community. But subcontract data is not available so this is the best analysis that can be done.

If you would like to perform this calculation for your particular city or county, we can send you a rough draft of a detailed methodology paper prepared by Tom Webster of New York Public Interest Research Center (NYPIRC). Now, data on Federal procurements by County is available from the Federal Procurement Data System (FPDS) (see Section 2.H.). Data on Federal assistance awards is available from the Federal Assistance Award Data System (FAADS) (see below). Community Action Agencies, County Commissioners' offices, and State Information Reception Offices (SIRO) may also be able to give you this information. And your Congressmember should be able to track down everything you need to do your own analysis.

Federal Assistance Award Data System (FAADS)

A list of all the federal assistance grants to individuals, companies, and local and state government from federal programs listed in Catalog of Federal Domestic Assistance is maintained by the Department of Commerce. This list is maintained on a computer file called the Federal Assistance Award Data System (FAADS). These awards represent most of the non-military federal money distributed to communities. The part of the list applicable to each state is given to the state government for their use and distribution.

For example, in California, requests for this information can be made to the Governor's Office of Planning and Research, 1400 10th Street, Sacramento, CA 95814 (916) 323-7480. They will send you free quarterly information for any county or city. Their printouts include a code number for the federal program granting the award, the name, city, and zip code of the recipient, the federal share and total amount of the award, the start and end date for the work, and a 10-20 word description of the work. The California listing format is very bulky allowing only four awards per page so one three-month listing of awards for Santa Clara County is spread out over 130 pages. This makes it very difficult to scan the listings for a particular contract, total amounts by agency, etc.

California Study

The State of California prepared a report called The Effect of Increased Military Spending in California. This report details the net job consequences of an inflow of military money into California and the loss resulting from cutbacks in other areas of the Federal budget. See the description of this report in the References section.

Peace Budgets

Jobs with Peace (JwP) is a nationwide campaign which advocates a major shift in national priorities -- away from military spending and programs of foreign military intervention, and into the rebuilding of socially productive industries and into education, health care, and transportation.

One of the major activities of the Jobs with Peace campaign has been to get referenda on local ballots asking the electorate to vote yes or no on the following question:

> Shall the City Council call upon the U.S. Congress to make more federal funds
> available for local jobs and programs -- in quality education, public
> transportation, energy-efficient housing, improved health care, and other
> essential services -- by reducing the amount of our tax dollars spent on nuclear
> weapons and programs of foreign military intervention?

So far, 81 cities and towns have approved Jobs with Peace referenda and 40 city and County councils and four State legislatures have passed JwP resolutions. The campaign has also focused on producing "Peace Budgets," which demonstrate in easy-to-read form the local impact of the military budget and propose positive alternatives.

These budgets detail the local impact of federal budget cuts, the Pentagon tax drain, and the job losses to individuals. These budgets consider the effect of a Nuclear Weapons Freeze and reductions in military waste and programs of foreign intervention, and calculate the funds saved in the local community. The budget describes the jobs and services which could be developed with civilian use of these funds. Unions, religious groups, and community organizations have participated in formulating these budgets and in distributing them widely in the community through their organizations, as well as by the city itself.

One good example of this, the <u>Boston Peace Budget</u>, suggests cuts in the military budget and increases in social services funding and shows how these changes would affect Boston (see Figure 6.3). This presentation brings home how military spending affects our daily lives and how a change in our military posture could significantly benefit us.

.Up-to-date information on federal social programs is available from a number of organizations in Washington. Each year the U.S. Conference of Mayors, 1620 Eye Street, NW, Washington, D.C. 20006, produces a response to the Administration's budget proposals as soon as they are released in late January or early February -- the response is titled "The Federal Budget and the Cities." During the Reagan years, a number of groups have cooperated in producing manuals reviewing the Administration's various proposals. Manuals will be produced by the Coalition on Block Grants and Human Needs, 1000 Wisconsin Avenue, NW, Washington, D.C. 20007, and the Fair Budget Action Campaign, P.O. Box 2735, Washington, D.C. 20013. The Fair Budget Action Campaign can also put you in touch with your local budget action group or coalition. The Center for Community Change, 1000 Wisconsin Avenue, NW, Washington, D.C. 20007, produces a very useful multi-issue newsletter and acts as a clearinghouse for information.

Mendocino County Study

Another approach was recently taken by activists in one rural California community. Don Lipmanson and David Colfax of the Mendocino Jobs with Peace Campaign recently prepared an excellent report called <u>Down the Federal Drain: The Impact of Military Spending on Mendocino County</u>, 8 pages, $2.00. They sought to make two comparisons. First, they determined the total inflow of federal dollars into the County for all agencies and compared that to the net outflow of all Federal taxes from Mendocino County (see Figure 6.4, Table 1) and found a significant and growing net outflow from the County.

Second, they performed the same kind of analysis as in <u>Bankrupting America</u>: they compared the total amount of money that left the County destined for use by the U.S. military (the Pentagon tax plus half the DoE budget plus one-fourth the NASA budget plus 10% of the federal debt, the part accrued during the Vietnam War) with the total returned to the County in military contracts, salaries, retirement benefits, and operating expenses for local military installations (see Figure 6.4, Table 2).

For their area, it was particularly useful to make both these comparisons to expose two prevalent myths:

(1) "One popular view, sometimes expounded by elected officials, is that Mendocino County, being poor and economically depressed, is a beneficiary of federal funds -- that the County receives more in federal program services and contract dollars than its citizens, businesses, and industries pay in federal taxes each year. This view -- which is in fact absolutely false -- serves the purpose of dampening criticism of federal programs and their administration." [page 1] "Contrary to the conventional view, Mendocino County, with one of the highest unemployment rates in the nation, is being drained of millions of dollars every year. And matters are getting worse." [page 2]

(2) "Where do these federal tax dollars go? Not to improve education elsewhere, or to create jobs or provide housing in areas even more severely depressed than here. Since 1980 these funds have been used **to support an expanding military budget.**" [page 3]

They also compared the net drain of Federal monies with the meager $40 million County Budget to indicate that a change in the Federal budget could substantially help local communities. "As the military takes an increasingly larger portion of the taxes Mendocino County residents and businesses send to Washington, the quality of life in the County inevitably declines. In 1983 more Mendocino County tax dollars will be spent for the military than for any local domestic sector, including local health and human services" [page 4]. They expose the great need in the County for (a) local health, social welfare, and education programs, (b) local economic development programs to offset the long-term decline in the wood products industry, and (c) maintenance of the many roads in the County necessary to sustain the timber and tourist industries.

Their methodology was similar to that used by James Anderson. They obtained up-to-date information on Federal spending in Mendocino County from the General Accounting Office (GAO) via local Congressman Doug Bosco's office. The GAO gave them computer printouts listing expenditures by Federal agency and program for almost all the civilian programs funded in the County. For the data from the Department of Transportation (DoT) and the Department of Energy (DoE) which the GAO couldn't supply, Bosco's office got the information directly from these departments. Bosco's office also obtained an estimate of the total salaries of locally employed federal workers from the GAO and operating expenses for local military installations from the DoD.

Military prime contract data came from Prime Contract Awards over $10,000 by State, County, Contractor and Place (P11) (now replaced by ST25). They calculated local military retirement expenditures by assuming that the County share would be proportional to the total for California based on population. The California total amount is listed in Estimated Expenditures for States and Selected Areas (F02).

Data on the County Budget came from County officials. In a letter to us, Don Lipmanson urges: "A study of the local effects of the arms race should not fail to inventory the cutbacks in local spending for vital municipal and county services, amenities, and economic development programs, which can be shown to result from militarizing the economy. These cuts concretely influence individual lives; focusing on them helps balance the abstract approach of a budgetary analysis and clarifies the cause/effect link between excessive military spending and human hardship.

"Researchers should consult with officials and clients from as many local government departments and service agencies as possible. Such contacts help identify the scope/scale/severity of service cutbacks, the promising projects forsaken for lack of funds; they also permit verification of federal figures on local expenditures.

"The research ought to examine which classes of people are the main victims of underfunding of local government. Advocacy groups which intervene in the local political process will be able to pinpoint the harmful effects of federal cuts. Organizations to be consulted for this purpose include labor union locals and central labor councils, welfare and tenants' rights groups, PTA's, seniors'/womens'/minority groups. Single working women, minorities, and the elderly are usually the first to suffer from local service reductions. But the recent bankruptcy of the School District in San Jose, California, a city with a booming military supply economy, indicates the need to avoid assuming that the middle class automatically benefits from military expansion. The prosperity of military contractors needs to be distinguished from the socio-economic situation of the local population as a whole."

According to Bankrupting America, fully 70% of the Congressional Districts in the United States, like Mendocino County, incur a net loss of tax money whenever the Pentagon budget goes up. If you live in an area like this, a study like the Mendocino County study should be very useful.

6.C. Other Effects of Local Military Spending

Because of its high-tech nature, most of the jobs created now in military production are for people trained in high-technology fields. In areas with massive military contracting, this may cause a shortage of high-paid technical and management people and a glut of unskilled and semi-skilled workers. Military spending has become an employment program for the wrong people -- that group with the lowest unemployment rate. Wages offered to managers, engineers, and technicians may be very high in order to attract these workers, while the wages for lower skilled workers remain low. This results in a stratification of the workforce with the higher-paid people getting richer while the earnings of lower-paid workers remain constant.

In Silicon Valley, as the industry has grown rapidly, the higher-paid workers have managed to find housing nearby only by paying exorbitant prices while the lower-paid workers have been forced to live 20-50 miles away from work and commute for hours each day on crowded freeways. Services and schools in the rich areas are excellent, but just barely adequate in the poorer areas.

There are specific compliance laws designed to make Federal contractors model employers -- to encourage other companies to follow suit. But often they are no better than other employers (and sometimes worse). Because military contractors are often large employers in a community and can threaten to lay off their workers and move to another, more favorable (to them) area, they wield a lot of political power. Sometimes they use this power to get reduced property tax assessments or other concessions from the local government. They may pay shabby wages and provide poor working conditions.

Government-owned, contractor-operated facilities (GOCOs) are exempt from local and state property taxes. They are also not required to meet the same Occupational Health and Safety Administration (OSHA) or Environmental Protection Agency (EPA) requirements as commercial companies. Instead they must (supposedly) meet comparable regulations issued by the DoD and DoE. But enforcement of the regulations is often more lax. Secrecy, which surrounds such weapons plants, often prevents local community organizations and workers from criticizing the toxic discharges and unsafe working conditions there.

It would seem that government-operated facilities should serve as models of what good employers should be. But instead, these facilities are often as bad or worse than private industry in how they treat their employees. Like any large employer, controlled by outside forces, the government engages in such practices as work speed-ups, increasing automation and robotization ("increasing productivity"), and union busting. When one facility performs at less than the rate they expect (sweat shop conditions), they set up other facilities in other communities to compete for the same contracts (parallel production). They may threaten people's jobs (job blackmail) and eventually move production somewhere else (runaway shops). They usually do no planning for retraining or relocating of laid-off workers.

Under cost-plus contracts, military companies may deliberately slow down production to incur cost overruns. This results in bored employees who feel useless.

The Highlander Center in Tennessee has extensive experience investigating these kinds of practices. See their research guide How to Research Your Local Military Contractor for more information.

There are, of course, many other social, political, environmental, moral, and spiritual effects of military spending, but we cannot consider them all here.

Figure 6.1 A Sample Page from Bankrupting America

The Pentagon Tax Gain or Loss by Congressional District Fiscal Year 1980

CONGRESSIONAL DISTRICT	PENTAGON EXPENDITURES ($ MILLIONS)	PENTAGON TAX BURDEN ($ MILLIONS)	NET GAIN OR LOSS ($ MILLIONS)	NET GAIN OR LOSS PER FAMILY
Alabama				
Heflin-D, Denton-R	$2,092.0	$1,841.5	+$250.5	
1 Edwards-R	242.0	252.0	−10.0	−$100
2 Dickinson-R	640.3	256.8	+383.5	+2,600
3 Nichols-D	318.2	234.4	+83.8	+600
4 Bevill-D	100.6	233.6	−133.0	−900
5 Flippo-D	561.7	296.2	+265.5	+1,800
6 Smith-R	123.5	335.9	−212.4	−1,400
7 Shelby-D	105.7	263.1	−157.4	−1,100
Alaska				
Stevens-R, Murkowski-R ..	762.3	410.8	+351.5	
1 Young-R	762.3	410.5	+351.5	+2,400
Arizona				
DeConcini-D, Goldwater-R .	1,648.4	1,402.3	+246.1	
1 Rhodes-R	404.6	352.0	+52.6	+300
2 Udall-D	615.6	344.6	+271.0	+1,800
3 Stump-D	342.3	322.5	+19.8	+100
4 Rudd-R	285.9	383.2	−97.3	−600
Arkansas				
Pryor-D, Bumpers-D	610.2	977.4	−367.2	
1 Alexander-D	100.0	212.6	−112.6	−800
2 Bethune-R	238.2	285.2	−47.0	−300
3 Schmidt-R	123.9	249.0	−125.1	−800
4 Anthony-D	147.4	230.7	−83.3	−600
California				
Hayakawa-R, Cranston-D	22,571.7	16,445.7	+6,126.0	
1 Chapple-R	163.4	315.5	−152.1	−1,000
2 Clausen-R	75.2	322.0	−246.8	−1,700
3 Matsui-D	743.0	376.0	+367.0	+2,500
4 Fazio-D	929.3	315.1	+614.2	+4,100
5 J. Burton-D	245.5	532.8	−287.3	−1,900
6 P. Burton-D	343.8	387.0	−43.2	−300
7 Miller-D	105.8	421.5	−315.7	−2,100
8 Dellums-D	360.3	431.8	−71.5	−500
9 Stark-D	379.9	393.5	−13.6	−100
10 Edwards-D	683.7	335.4	+348.3	+2,300
11 Lantos-D	259.1	441.0	−181.9	−1,200
12 McCloskey-R	1,024.5	473.5	+551.0	+3,700
13 Mineta,D	1,143.6	444.8	+698.8	+4,700
14 Shumway-R	156.8	312.9	−156.1	−1,000
15 Coelho-D	164.2	282.6	−118.4	−800
16 Panetta-D	495.4	326.2	+169.2	+1,100
17 Pashayan-R	494.9	284.9	+210.0	+1,400
18 Thomas-R	570.9	293.7	+277.2	+1,900
19 Lagomarsino-R	1,018.9	367.5	+651.4	+4,400
20 Goldwater-R	567.6	451.7	+115.9	+800
21 Fiedler-R	442.2	378.6	+63.6	+400
22 Moorhead-R	510.2	491.5	+18.7	+100
23 Bellenson-D	612.3	644.1	−31.8	−200
24 Waxman-D	510.2	320.5	+189.7	+1,300
25 Roybal-D	374.2	337.3	+36.9	+200
26 Rousselot-R	476.2	431.8	+44.4	+300
27 Dornan-R	544.3	600.5	−56.2	−400
28 Dixon-D	442.2	371.4	+70.8	+500
29 Hawkins-D	374.2	245.5	+128.7	+900
30 Danielson-D	442.2	329.7	+112.5	+800
31 Dymally-D	374.2	382.8	−8.6	−100
32 Anderson-D	510.2	340.4	+169.8	+1,100
33 Grisham-R	374.2	373.7	+.5	+*
34 Lungren-R	511.4	443.3	+68.1	+500
35 Dreier-R	476.5	365.6	+110.9	+700
36 Brown-D	404.1	276.1	+128.0	+900
37 Lewis-R	496.1	322.4	+173.7	+1,100
38 Patterson-D	597.9	341.9	+256.0	+1,700
39 Dannemeyer-R	637.1	410.8	+226.3	+1,500
40 Badham-R	744.8	431.4	+313.4	+2,100
41 Lowery-R	1,191.7	418.0	+773.7	+5,200
42 Hunter-R	1,028.5	301.0	+727.5	+4,900
43 Burgener-R	922.7	396.2	+526.5	+3,500
Connecticut				
Weicker-R, Dodd-D	$4,239.3	$2,478.9	+$1,760.4	
1 Cotter-D	1,383.9	422.7	+961.2	+$6,500
2 Gejdenson-D	843.5	350.8	+492.7	+3,300
3 DeNardis-R	127.8	388.8	−261.0	−1,800
4 McKinney-R	667.0	507.8	+159.2	+1,100
5 Ratchford-D	317.2	418.1	−100.9	−700
6 Moffett-D	906.1	392.9	+513.2	+3,400
D.C.	2,348.0	552.4	+1,795.6	+9,500
Delaware				
Roth-R, Biden-D	409.4	425.0	−15.6	
1 Evans-R	409.4	425.0	−15.6	−100
Florida				
Chiles-D, Hawkins-R	5,105.3	5,425.3	−320.0	
1 Hutto-D	1,097.3	293.0	+804.3	+5,400
2 Fuqua-D	121.3	268.7	−147.4	−1,000
3 Bennett-D	548.7	315.8	+232.9	+1,600
4 Chappel-D	291.7	332.0	−40.3	−300
5 McCollum-R	369.5	312.9	+56.6	+400
6 Young-R	286.7	388.1	−101.4	−700
7 Gibbons-D	392.0	334.6	+57.4	+400
8 Ireland-D	94.1	332.0	−237.9	−1,600
9 Nelson-D	1,019.7	388.8	+630.9	+4,200
10 Bafalis-R	159.9	347.2	−187.3	−1,300
11 Mica-D	296.2	453.6	−157.4	−1,100
12 Shaw-R	78.3	447.4	−369.1	−2,500
13 Lehman-D	100.5	381.9	−281.4	−1,900
14 Pepper-D	107.5	401.8	−294.3	−2,000
15 Fascell-D	142.4	426.8	−284.4	−1,800
Georgia				
Nunn-D, Mattingly-R	2,953.8	2,677.2	+276.6	
1 Ginn-D	537.0	228.9	+308.1	+2,100
2 Hatcher-D	180.5	204.3	−23.8	−200
3 Brinkley-D	772.2	243.1	+529.1	+3,600
4 Levitas-D	93.8	385.2	−291.4	−2,000
5 Fowler-D	44.7	360.6	−315.9	−2,200
6 Gingrich-R	217.2	283.5	−66.3	−400
7 McDonald-D	452.3	302.5	+149.8	+1,000
8 Evans-D	62.0	221.1	−159.1	−1,100
9 Jenkins-D	71.4	243.1	−171.7	−1,100
10 Barnard-D	408.9	234.0	+174.9	+1,200
Hawaii				
Matsunaga-D, Inouye-D ...	1,648.3	623.3	+1,025.0	
1 Haftel-D	982.3	358.7	+623.6	+4,200
2 Akaka-D	666.0	269.9	+396.1	+2,700
Idaho				
McClure-R, Symms-R	360.6	467.5	−106.9	
1 Craig-R	68.7	238.9	−170.2	−1,100
2 Hansen-R	292.3	228.6	+63.7	+400
Illinois				
Percy-R, Dixon-D	2,306.2	8,725.7	−6,419.5	
1 Washington-D	48.7	303.2	−254.5	−1,700
2 Savage-D	52.6	348.7	−296.1	−2,000
3 Russo-D	55.2	391.9	−336.7	−2,300
4 Derwinski-R	57.2	415.9	−358.7	−2,400
5 Fary-D	50.0	306.9	−256.9	−1,700
6 Hyde-R	62.6	445.4	−382.8	−2,600
7 Collins-D	46.7	264.3	−217.6	−1,500
8 Rostenkowski-D	50.0	322.5	−272.5	−1,800
9 Yates-D	61.8	494.1	−432.3	−2,900
10 Porter-R	68.4	581.7	−513.3	−3,400
11 Annunzio-D	57.2	422.5	−365.3	−2,500
12 Crane-R	187.2	473.4	−286.2	−1,900
13 McClory-R	280.7	371.2	−90.5	−600
14 Erlenborn-R	88.4	446.5	−358.1	−2,400
15 Corcoran-R	20.1	331.9	−311.8	−2,100
16 Martin-R	95.7	336.3	−240.6	−1,600

Figure 6.2 A Sample Page from Bankrupting American Cities

The Pentagon Tax Burden and Expenditures by Metropolitan Area, Fiscal Year 1983

METROPOLITAN AREA	PROJECTED FY 1983 MILITARY EXPENDITURES ($ MILLIONS)	FY 1983 PENTAGON TAX BURDEN ($ MILLIONS)	NET GAIN OR LOSS ($ MILLIONS)	NET GAIN OR LOSS PER FAMILY
Alabama	$3,159.4	$2,781.1	+$378.3	
Anniston	266.7	82.0	+184.7	+$5,600
Birmingham	256.6	762.5	−505.9	−2,100
Florence	11.9	96.5	−84.6	−2,300
Gadsden	40.3	69.9	−29.6	−1,000
Huntsville	814.3	232.4	+581.9	+6,800
Mobile	352.9	323.8	+29.1	+200
Montgomery	526.5	212.3	+314.1	+4,200
Tuscaloosa	31.6	92.7	−61.1	−1,700
Alaska	1,151.3	620.4	+530.9	
Anchorage	686.6	301.6	+385.0	+7,100
Arizona	2,489.5	2,117.8	+371.7	
Phoenix	1,388.7	1,210.6	+178.1	+500
Tucson	631.6	399.6	+232.0	+1,700
Arkansas	921.5	1,476.1	−554.6	
Fayetteville	36.4	120.2	−83.8	−1,800
Fort Smith	67.4	132.3	−64.9	−1,200
Little Rock	322.6	350.4	−27.8	−300
Pine Bluff	50.3	63.0	−12.7	−500
California	34,088.5	24,836.8	+9,251.7	
Anaheim	2,960.7	2,018.9	+941.8	+1,800
Bakersfield	757.1	338.1	+419.0	+3,900
Fresno	66.3	454.6	−388.3	−2,800
Los Angeles	10,271.8	8,480.1	+1,791.7	+900
Modesto	30.1	220.0	−189.9	−2,700
Oxnard	796.8	417.9	+378.9	+2,734
Riverside	1,466.4	1,127.1	+339.3	+900
Sacramento	1,526.8	913.8	+613.0	+2,200
Salinas	689.7	304.5	+385.2	+4,700
San Diego	4,931.1	1,631.8	+3,299.3	+6,600
San Francisco	2,921.8	4,442.8	−1,521.0	−1,600
San Jose	3,925.4	1,471.4	+2,454.0	+6,800
Santa Barbara	1,172.1	326.8	+845.3	+9,900
Santa Cruz	23.3	150.4	−127.1	−2,500
Santa Rosa	72.2	253.1	−180.9	−2,300
Stockton	169.8	323.2	−153.4	−1,700
Vallejo	1,061.8	286.8	+775.0	+8,900
Colorado	2,680.1	2,716.8	−36.7	
Colorado Springs	1,130.6	245.0	+885.6	+10,200
Denver	1,237.9	163.3	+1,074.6	+2,500
Fort Collins	31.4	101.2	−69.8	−1,900
Greeley	6.3	92.4	−86.1	−2,600
Pueblo	34.0	109.3	−75.3	−2,100
Connecticut	6,402.3	3,743.7	+2,658.6	
Bridgeport	1,549.8	1,233.3	+316.5	+2,700
Hartford	3,378.4	1,201.5	+2,176.9	+12,100
New Haven	160.7	817.6	−656.9	−5,400
New London	147.9	234.4	−86.5	−1,100
Delaware	618.3	641.8	−23.5	
Wilmington	382.5	599.3	−216.8	−1,400
Florida	7,710.2	8,193.5	−483.3	
Bradenton	23.9	108.1	−84.2	−2,300
Daytona Beach	125.0	176.7	−51.7	−814
Fort Lauderdale	160.8	975.5	−814.7	−3,200

METROPOLITAN AREA	PROJECTED FY 1983 MILITARY EXPENDITURES ($ MILLIONS)	FY 1983 PENTAGON TAX BURDEN ($ MILLIONS)	NET GAIN OR LOSS ($ MILLIONS)	NET GAIN OR LOSS PER FAMILY
Florida continued...				
Fort Myers	$43.3	$137.6	−$94.3	−$1,900
Gainesville	36.7	94.8	−58.1	−1,600
Jacksonville	1,103.1	608.5	+494.6	+2,400
Lakeland	44.6	221.2	−176.6	−2,100
Melbourne	752.2	199.0	+553.2	+8,000
Miami	451.0	1,622.7	−1,171.7	−2,700
Orlando	1,254.2	518.9	+735.3	+4,200
Panama City	272.6	62.2	+210.4	+7,700
Pensacola	700.9	190.3	+510.6	+6,300
Sarasota	42.6	211.9	−169.3	−3,400
Tallahassee	67.8	98.2	−30.4	−700
Tampa	1,076.6	1,228.4	−151.8	−400
West Palm Beach	445.5	552.6	−107.1	−800
Georgia	4,460.9	4,043.2	+417.7	
Albany	127.5	71.4	+56.1	+1,800
Atlanta	1,213.3	1,891.0	−677.7	−1,200
Augusta	1,018.0	239.7	+778.3	+9,200
Columbus	624.3	175.5	+448.8	+6,600
Macon	747.9	200.3	+547.6	+7,700
Savannah	228.3	179.7	+48.6	+800
Hawaii	2,489.3	941.3	+1,548.0	
Honolulu	2,424.1	831.5	+1,592.6	+7,500
Idaho	544.6	706.0	−161.4	
Boise City	70.8	159.2	−88.4	−2,100
Illinois	3,482.9	13,177.8	−9,694.9	
Bloomington	9.5	116.9	−107.4	−3,100
Champaign	316.1	153.3	+162.8	+3,300
Chicago	1,841.7	8,857.2	−7,015.5	−3,400
Decatur	9.8	140.0	−130.2	−3,500
Kankakee	4.4	96.1	−91.7	−3,200
Peoria	88.3	428.0	−339.7	−3,200
Rockford	134.0	284.7	−150.7	−1,900
Springfield	39.7	217.9	−178.2	−3,200
Indiana	2,816.0	5,241.3	−2,425.3	
Anderson	10.9	132.9	−122.0	−3,000
Bloomington	15.3	60.6	−45.3	−1,700
Evansville	54.2	292.1	−237.9	−2,800
Fort Wayne	396.0	381.9	+14.1	+100
Gary	223.5	636.0	−412.5	−2,200
Indianapolis	1,086.8	1,203.4	−116.6	−300
Kokomo	10.3	112.5	−102.2	−3,300
Lafayette	15.3	98.0	−82.7	−2,400
Muncie	7.9	104.7	−96.8	−2,500
South Bend	357.6	272.9	+84.7	+1,000
Terre Haute	91.8	148.5	−56.7	−1,100
Iowa	642.5	2,823.8	−2,181.3	
Cedar Rapids	216.4	187.0	+29.4	+600
Davenport	386.2	430.6	−44.4	−400
Des Moines	69.8	383.4	−313.6	−3,200
Dubuque	32.9	96.1	−63.2	−2,200
Sioux City	18.7	123.7	−105.0	−2,900
Waterloo	45.8	−143.0	−97.2	−2,400

Figure 6.3 A Sample Peace Budget for Boston from Jobs with Peace

Proposed savings in the military budget

1983 savings

Freeze the nuclear arms race.
(Eliminate funding for the MX missile, Trident program, B-1 bomber, cruise missiles, Pershing II missiles, and warhead production.) .... $20.94 billion

Stop planning for foreign intervention.
(Eliminate funding for the Rapid Deployment Force, new aircraft carriers and support cruisers, and the reactivation of WWII battleships. Reduce funding for overseas bases.) .... $15.58 billion

Reduce funding for ineffective and extravagant weapons.
(Cut back funding for SSN nuclear subs, XM-1 tank, F/A-18, F-14, and F-15 aircraft, and chemical weapons. Eliminate funding for the Patriot missile, the ABM, and anti-satellite programs.) .... $ 6.78 billion

TOTAL SAVINGS: $43.30 billion

SAVINGS FOR BOSTON: $117 million

These figures represent only the most obvious cuts that can be made without harming America's security. The Boston Study Group, made up of several defense analysts, has calculated that the U.S. could have a strong defense for about $105 billion in current dollars. It would be non-interventionary and would give us an invulnerable nuclear deterrent, as well as the ability to protect western Europe and preserve the freedom of the seas. If the U.S. had this reduced defense commitment now, we could save about $140 billion in 1983 alone! Boston's share would be $380 million.

The Boston Peace Budget

The following budget examines what Boston can do if the $117 million in unnecessary military spending is invested in vital social programs in 1983.

Jobs and Training
Provide training and find jobs for 6,000 adults ($8.4 million); Fund 3,000 summer jobs for youth ($5.8 million); Provide public service jobs for 1,300 adults ($9.8 million). .... $24.0 million

Housing
Restore federal aid to 1981 levels for Community Development Block Grants, Urban Development Action Grants, rental subsidies, and low-interest loans to repair existing housing ($13.8 million); Expand Neighborhood Housing Service ($800,000); Build new public housing for 200 households ($12.4 million); Insulate 1,000 homes ($3 million) . $30.0 million

Health Care
Restore federal aid to 1981 levels for mental health and drug and alcohol rehabilitation ($590,000); Keep seven threatened neighborhood health centers open ($2.1 million); Restore Boston City Hospital funding cuts ($10 million); Create a new mental health clinic and a new community residence ($580,000) .... $13.3 million

Education
Restore federal aid to 1981 levels for vocational education and programs for educationally deprived, bilingual, and handicapped students ($4.4 million); Restore the Kindergarten I program ($2.8 million); Rehire 500 teachers laid off by Proposition 2½ ($12.7 million) .... $19.9 million

Human Services
Restore federal aid to 1981 levels for Food Stamps and programs for Women, Infants, Children (WIC) and the elderly ($1 million); Restore AFDC benefits to 2,000 women and children ($8.1 million); Provide daycare funding for 1,000 children—500 at full subsidy, 500 at half subsidy ($3.7 million) .... $12.8 million

Transportation
Restore federal aid to 1981 levels for operation of the MBTA... $8.0 million

Public Safety
Rehire 100 police officers and 100 firefighters laid off by Proposition 2½ .... $4.8 million

Public Improvements
Make capital improvements to parks and public works .... $4.2 million

TOTAL: $117 million

Figure 6.4 A Sample of Tables from <u>Down the Federal Drain: The Impact of Military Spending on Mendocino County</u> by Mendocino Jobs with Peace

---

TABLE 1. Flow of Tax Dollars and Federal Expenditures
(in millions of dollars)

	1980	1982	1983
Federal taxes paid by Mendocino County residents, businesses, and industries[2]	$150	$200	$225
Total federal expenditures in Mendocino County[3]	104	125	127
Net loss of Mendocino County tax dollars	$ 46	$ 75	$ 98

Where do these federal tax dollars go? Not to improve education elsewhere, or to create jobs or provide housing in areas even more severely depressed than here. Since 1980 these funds have been used **to support an expanding military budget.** In 1980, Mendocino County sent $36 million to Washington to be spent on the military; in 1983 this will increase to $57 million, or about $850 for every man, woman and child in Mendocino County.[4] Of the $57 million County residents pay for military programs, only about $5.5 million — less than 10% — comes back into the County, mainly in the form of payments to retired military personnel and support for the Pt. Arena Radar Station.

TABLE 2. Mendocino County Share of Military Expenditures

	1980	1982	1983
Amount contributed by County Taxpayers to Military Expenditures (in millions)	$ 36	$ 48	$ 57
Per Capita	537	716	850

As Table 2 shows, the increase in local contributions to military programs over the past three years has increased 58%. Allowing for inflation of 25% since 1980, there has been **a real increase in local contributions to military programs of 33% in only three years.** Thus there has been a substantial increase in the tax dollars being drained from the County each year to pay for military programs, the production of new nuclear weapons systems, and military aid to foreign countries.

Chapter 7   Determining the Military Dependency of Your Community

Now that you have gathered a lot of information about the military work being done in your community, you can estimate just how dependent your community is on military spending. This chapter explains military dependency and various ways to measure it.

7.A.   Types of Dependency

There are several ways that your community can be dependent on the military:

-- Large numbers or a large percentage of people are employed through military contracts or at military bases, either directly or indirectly.

-- Large numbers or a large percentage of people with particular skills (usually engineers or technicians) are employed by the military.

-- Local governments rely on the taxes paid by military contractors for a large part of their finances.

Dependency can be measured in many ways: percent of the workforce employed working on military products, percent of the wages paid to these workers (since military industry wages are frequently higher than civilian wages, this may be a much higher figure than the percent of the workforce), percent of technical or skilled workers who work on military products, percent of total sales (or value added) to the military from the local area, percent of profits made on military industry sales versus civilian industry sales, and percent of taxes paid by military contractors. You may want to report these values as percentages or as a dollar figure per resident, per worker, per company, or in some other way. And it is interesting to see how dependency changes over time.

In the next section, we show how to calculate these values.

7.B.   Determining Military Dependence

Table 7.1. shows the various kinds of dependency you might want to calculate and lists the values necessary to make these calculations. It also indicates where in this book these values are determined.

When using this table, decide what area you will be looking at: the whole State, a County, a City, an SMSA, a Congressional District, or a single company. You may want to look at these figures only as they apply to a particular weapon system. Or you may only want to look at one particular type of worker: aerospace engineers for example. Don't feel that you have to fill out the whole table. Perhaps you just want one single value (e.g., Percent of Manufacturing Employees Working Directly for the DoD on Prime Contracts) which you can then quote in all your leaflets, etc. Just ignore all the rest!

Also, don't feel limited by this table. These were just the values for which we could easily give a calculation recipe. You might have other ideas: for instance, the number of chemists working directly on military products in your County as a percentage of all chemists. For this calculation you need to look in various places. Perhaps your State employment office has information on the total number of chemists in your County and you can estimate the number who work on military projects by calling the main military companies or by some other way. Be creative!

Note, when you are making calculations of military employment dependency that unemployed people are not included in military production. An unemployed person trained to produce military goods or services, and seeking employment with a military contractor, is just as dependent on military contracts as a person who is employed performing that same kind of work.

Also note that Section 4.A. explains how to determine what percent of an individual company's business is military and that calculation is not repeated here.

Furthermore, all of these values may have one or more of the following problems:

-- Since industry sales include the whole value of the final product including the value of the materials and sub-components which are bought and included in this product, this is not as good a measure of the amount of work done in your community as the value added figure. If you know that the raw inputs represent a very small percentage of the final product, then these two numbers will be very similar and you don't need to worry about this. Employment is a good measure of the amount of work done, but it is frequently difficult to determine the number of people working on military products if the company makes both military and civilian products.

-- Prime military contract data for your community includes money which is used to pay for subcontract work performed by companies in other areas. You might assume that the amount of subcontract work that leaves the community is equal to the amount of subcontract work which comes into your community from prime contractors in other areas. This is a good assumption if there is a lot of diverse industry in your community. It may not be true if one or two large military contractors dominate your community.

-- Much of this data is collected over different time periods: for example, it may be collected by Calendar Year (most Census data) or by Fiscal Year (all Federal government spending). Companies may have their own fiscal year. Sometimes you will be forced to use data recorded for different years. Be aware of all the assumptions you make when you do this.

-- The data collected may not be exactly comparable. For example, Census Bureau employment data is collected in different ways and covers slightly different categories than the data collected by the Department of Labor.

-- Much of the data reported is based on sample polls of a small percentage of the whole field. Therefore it has a built-in uncertainty. All data has errors and other uncertainties which makes it suspect. Just because it is numerical doesn't mean it is accurate. As computer users say, "garbage in -- garbage out."

7.C. Sources of Information for Other Items

Total Population
    1980 Census of Population and Housing
    State Statistical Abstract

Total Workforce
    1980 Census of Population and Housing
    State Statistical Abstract

Total Employment
    1980 Census of Population and Housing
    State Statistical Abstract
    Total County Employment is found at the beginning of each County listing in County Business Patterns.   Total State Employment is listed in the front of this report.

Total Manufacturing Employment
    Listed after SIC 1799 in County Business Patterns.

Total Manufacturing Sales or Value Added (military and civilian)
    Census of Manufactures, 1977

Total Sales or Value Added (military and civilian)
    Census of Manufactures, 1977

Total Payroll
    County Business Patterns

Total Taxes
    Check with the City or County Tax Assessors Office

Total Taxes from Military Firms
    Check with the City or County Tax Assessors Office

Also take a look at:

    Earnings and Employment

    Sales Marketing and Management Magazine

Figure 7.1 A Worksheet for Determining Military Dependence

VALUE	DESCRIPTION	SECTION LOCATION
_____	Direct Armed Service Personnel (Number of people in the armed services)	[5.A.]
_____	Direct Civilian Employment by the Military (Number of civilians employed at military bases, etc.)	[5.A.]
_____	Direct DoD Industry Employment (in Manufacturing)	[5.B.]
_____	Total (direct and indirect) DoD Industry Employment	[5.C.]
_____	Total DoD Industry Employment in Manufacturing (This only looks at manufacturing industry and leaves out Transportation, Utilities, etc.)	[5.C.]
_____	Total Direct Military Employment (The sum of Armed Service Personnel, Civilian Employees, and Direct DoD Industry Employment)	
_____	Total Military Employment (The sum of Armed Service Personnel, Civilian Employees, and Total DoD Industry Employment)	
_____	Payroll for Total DoD Industry Employment	[5.C.]
_____	Total Prime DoD Contracts	[2.A.]
_____	Total Prime Contracts from DoE and NASA	[2.F.]
_____	Total Prime Military Contracts from DoD, DoE, NASA (The sum of the two numbers directly above)	
_____	Total National Defense Spending in 1980	[2.G.]
_____	Total Population	[7.C.]
_____	Total Workforce	[7.C.]
_____	Total Employment	[7.C.]
_____	Total Manufacturing Employment	[7.C.]
_____	Total Manufacturing Sales or Value-Added (military and civilian)	[7.C.]
_____	Total Sales or Value-Added (military and civilian)	[7.C.]

Here are some other values that are difficult to obtain:

Total Taxes	[4.E., 7.C.]
Total Taxes from Military Firms	[4.E., 7.C.]
Total DoD Contracts (prime plus subcontracts)	[2.A., 2.F.]
Average Profit Rate of Military Contractors	[4.C., Appendix 2]
Average Profit Rate of All Industry	[4.C., Appendix 2]

Figure 7.1 (continued)

There are several important measures of military dependence you can derive from these numbers:

Employment

_____ Percent of Manufacturing Employees Working Directly for the DoD

$$= \frac{\text{Direct DoD Industry Employment (in Manufacturing)}}{\text{Total Manufacturing Employment}} \times 100$$

_____ Percent of Total (direct and indirect) Industry Employees Working for the DoD

$$= \frac{\text{Total (direct and indirect) DoD Industry Employment}}{\text{Total Employment} \quad \text{or} \quad \text{Total Workforce}} \times 100$$

_____ Percent of Total (direct and indirect) Industry Employees in Manufacturing Working for the DoD

$$= \frac{\text{Total DoD Industry Employment in Manufacturing}}{\text{Total Employment} \quad \text{or} \quad \text{Total Workforce}} \times 100$$

_____ Percent of the Workforce or Percent of Total Employment Working Directly for the DoD

$$= \frac{\text{Total Direct Military Employment}}{\text{Total Employment} \quad \text{or} \quad \text{Total Workforce}} \times 100$$

_____ Percent of the Workforce or Percent of Total Employment Working Directly or Indirectly for the DoD

$$= \frac{\text{Total Military Employment}}{\text{Total Employment} \quad \text{or} \quad \text{Total Workforce}} \times 100$$

Payroll

_____ Percent of the Total Manufacturing Industry Payroll Going to Employees Who Work for the DoD

$$= \frac{\text{Payroll for DoD Industry Employment in Manufacturing}}{\text{Total Payroll for Manufacturing Industry}} \times 100$$

_____ Percent of the Total Industry Payroll Going to Employees Who Work for the DoD

$$= \frac{\text{Payroll for DoD Industry Employment in Manufacturing}}{\text{Total Payroll}} \times 100$$

Figure 7.1 (continued)

Sales

_____ Percent of Total Sales or Value-Added Represented by Prime DoD Contracts

$$= \frac{\text{Total Prime DoD Contracts}}{\text{Total Sales or Value-Added (military and civilian)}} \times 100$$

_____ Percent of Manufacturing Sales or Value-Added Represented by Prime DoD Contracts

$$= \frac{\text{Total Prime DoD Contracts}}{\text{Total Manufacturing Sales or Value-Added (military and civilian)}} \times 100$$

_____ Percent of Total Sales or Value-Added Represented by Prime Military Contracts from the DoD, DoE, and NASA

$$= \frac{\text{Total Prime Military Contracts from DoD, DoE, NASA}}{\text{Total Sales or Value-Added (military and civilian)}} \times 100$$

_____ Percent of Manufacturing Sales or Value-Added Represented by Prime Military Contracts from the DoD, DoE, and NASA

$$= \frac{\text{Total Prime Military Contracts from DoD, DoE, NASA}}{\text{Total Manufacturing Sales or Value-Added (military and civilian)}} \times 100$$

Taxes

_____ Percent of Total Taxes Paid by Military Companies

$$= \frac{\text{Total Taxes from Military Firms}}{\text{Total Taxes}} \times 100$$

Chapter 8   Effects of Buildups and Cutbacks

Military spending levels in this country are greatly related to the political climate and to the political maneuvering which goes on in Congress. When groups such as the Committee on the Present Danger and the military industry lobbies gain currency, the military budget goes up. When there are strong social movements (such as the Freeze) demanding diplomacy and arms cutbacks, the military budget goes up more slowly. As individual weapons are attacked for being too expensive or ineffective, or as individual companies are accused of defrauding the government for the work they have done, particular contracts may get cut. And of course, every contract eventually runs out.

When a company receives a big contract it will hire thousands of employees. But then, if the contract ends or is cancelled and no other comparable contracts are granted, the company will lay off these many workers. For example, at the end of the Vietnam War in the early 1970s, a major slump in the aerospace industry occurred during which thousands of people, including thousands of aerospace engineers with specialized skills, and attractive salaries were laid off. Many of these workers found no employment until the military once again embarked on massive jet aircraft and missile production in the mid-1970s. When the current military buildup is over, there will likely be a big bust. These cutoffs and the resulting layoffs may occur very quickly. For example, orders for the B-1B Bomber will drop from 48 to 0 in 1987, leaving 50-60,000 jobs in jeopardy. No contingency plans have been made for these workers or their local community as it is buffetted by this boom and bust cycle.

Of course, this problem is not limited to military production. The civilian market can also be volatile, but usually growth and decline of sales occurs a little more slowly.

8.A. Buildups

Usually, when local industry receives more military contracts, it is seen as a great benefit to the community. The particular company receiving the contracts prospers, more money comes into the community, and more people are hired. However, because of the nature of military contracts, there are many potential pitfalls from their increase. Based on our own experience in Silicon Valley the following may occur:

-- As military equipment becomes more technologically sophisticated, military contracts tend to require a larger number of engineers, scientists, and skilled technicians than commercial industry. More contracts may create a demand for these occupations greater than the community can meet. Lower-skilled workers may not be hired at all, while this high-skill labor shortage entices skilled professionals to move in from other places around the country. The overall unemployment rate is not appreciably lowered.

-- With their higher wages (and thus greater spending power) military employees can bid up the cost of the available housing, creating a shortage while bidding up the cost, which then prices many current residents out of the market.

-- Lower-paid workers must then move further away from the industry resulting in transportation problems. Communities with the industry facilities may make out quite well, but those where the lower-skilled workers live may have constricted tax bases and poor city services.

These problems are highlighted when extremely rapid growth occurs due to the granting of very large contracts.

Other problems which may come from increased military production include:

-- The Pentagon has tried to increase the productivity of military industry. Specifically, they have allowed costs of capital equipment (frequently computer-controlled machines and robots) to be included in contract costs (the DoD pays for the automation). This frequently leads to job loss in the local community. Productivity (output per worker) goes up, but employment goes down.

-- Some people refuse to work on military products on moral grounds. As more and more industry in the area is diverted to military production, the jobs available to these socially-conscious people decrease. They may be forced to work on these products simply because those are the only jobs available.

8.B. Cutbacks

Every contract eventually runs out and the hiring and increased production that accompanied the buildup may be followed by layoffs and a business slump. Of course, the company will attempt to attract more contracts to replace the expiring one, but they may not be able to do this. If the company has promised more than it can deliver (a common problem) or if the weapon system is poorly conceived (equally common), as this comes to light, there will be efforts in Congress to cut off funding.

An affected company usually points out the negative consequences on the local economy and how many jobs will be lost if the contract is cancelled. It often tells the employees directly and encourage them to lobby Congress for continuation of the contract (rather than to plan for conversion to commercial production).

The company may also threaten to move to another state or a foreign country whether or not its contracts are in jeopardy in order to get tax concessions from the local government (job blackmail).

On the other hand, some companies will be very reluctant to admit that the loss of the contract will have any consequences because they want to assure investors their company is still as financially healthy as ever and therefore their stock is still worth as much. In this case it may be difficult to get information.

When a request is made to delete funding for a project, there may be Congressional hearings held to detail the importance of the weapon, how many jobs are dependent on the contract, what work each company is doing and how much money it received last year for the weapon system, etc. If so, the transcripts of these hearings are invaluable.

Call up each company and ask them what impact this contract loss will have on the local economy. The PR person will hopefully talk your ear off telling you how important this contract is, the hardship its loss will have on the employees at the plant, etc.

The union, if there is one, can tell you a lot about the effect the cutback will have on union members (see Section 5.E. for more on working with unions).

8.C.   A Nuclear Freeze

The National Nuclear Weapons Freeze Campaign proposes a bi-lateral freeze by the United States and the Union of Soviet Socialist Republics (USSR) on the testing production, and deployment of nuclear weapons and all missiles and new aircraft which have nuclear weapons as their sole or main payload. The weapons affected by this Freeze are listed below. If this Freeze were negotiated today, the United States would immediately stop production and deployment of several weapon systems. Furthermore, research and development for several future nuclear missile systems could be halted. This would, of course, have a major effect on the companies working on these systems, their employees, and the communities in which they are located.

It is expected that 350,000 jobs would be directly affected by a Freeze [The Economic Consequences of a Nuclear Weapons Freeze, CEP]. The Freeze Economy [CEC] has an excellent description of the effects a Freeze would have on the country. It lists the major contractors on these weapon systems and their locations as well as all the nuclear warhead research and production sites.

The research outlined in Chapter 3 and 4 should give you a good idea of the Freeze-related work going on in your community. The New York Public Interest Research Center (NYPIRC) listed all the contractors in New York State (in 1981) with prime contracts on Freeze (and other nuclear) weapons (see Figure 3.2).

U.S. Weapon Systems Affected by a Nuclear Freeze

Systems Directly Halted by a Freeze:

        MX Missile
        B-1B Bomber
        Trident I Submarine-launched Ballistic Missile (SLBM)
        Air-launched Cruise Missile (ALCM)
        Sea-launched Cruise Missile (SLCM
        Ground-launched Cruise Missile (GLCM)
        Pershing II Missile

Systems Halted after 1987 by a Freeze:

        Trident II Missile D-5 (now in R&D)
        Stealth Bomber (now in R&D)
        Midgetman Missile (just beginning R&D)

Systems Which Might be Reduced or Eliminated Once a Freeze Takes Effect:

        Ballistic Missile Defense (BMD)
        Strategic Air Defense
        Command, Control, Communications, and Intelligence (C3I)
        Trident Submarine

Chapter 9   Economic Conversion Planning

Any serious reduction in the arms budget, such as that resulting from a Nuclear Weapons Freeze, will cause significant economic dislocation in many sectors of the economy and many regions of the country. Millions of workers and their communities and businesses throughout the nation are dependent on sustained military spending for their livelihoods. Economic conversion provides a response to this potential disruption.

Substantial barriers confront military-dependent firms and communities seeking to convert or diversify into commercially-viable civilian activity. This is due in part to the peculiar nature of military production and the military market which are substantially different from what goes on in the civilian sector. Also, the general decline of the U.S. industrial and economic base and the decline of U.S. industry competitiveness (hastened by the military economy) further limits effective civilian options for military enterprises.

An antidote to this "military addiction syndrome" is economic conversion. Without economic conversion programs in place, and a perception that conversion alternatives are politically and economically viable, the fear of potential dislocation due to arms cuts will remain a major stumbling block to winning Congressional votes for substantial reductions in military spending. As long as people fear that military cutbacks might cause them to lose their jobs or seriously impact their businesses, they will find it difficult to support arms reductions.

Economic conversion must therefore be established as part of overall national programs and policies and promoted and instituted at the regional and local community and plant levels at the same time.

Macro-Economic Conversion

In its broadest sense, economic conversion refers to the transitional process by which the massive quantities of capital, labor, and resources currently employed in military activity are redirected towards meeting non-military related social needs. Obviously, conversion must be linked to large-scale reductions in the arms race and to a re-ordering of Federal budget priorities. It must also be tied to the formation of a broad new industrial policy that focuses on the revitalization of the nation's civilian technological and industrial base as well as its public infrastructure. This new industrial policy must include (1) new incentives and special subsidies for creating effective market demand in the economy for new socially needed products and services such as mass transit and alternative energy equipment and (2) a new civilian-oriented Federal science and technology research and development (R&D) policy and budget.

Conversion legislation is a key element of macro-economic conversion policy (see Chapter 10). In general, conversion legislation attempts to set up mechanisms for protecting workers, businesses, and communities from the worst impacts of sudden cutbacks in military programs and activities, and establish the means for advance planning for converting plants and bases to alternative uses. These mechanisms would be coordinated and facilitated through national and regional government offices, but planned and implemented at the local level, with participation of the workforce, managements, and the community.

Micro-Level (Local) Conversion

Economic conversion, when applied to the local or company level, can be defined as "a planning process aimed at developing alternative uses of the workforce and facilities currently engaged in military production in advance of changes in military policy which may shut down or slow down work at particular military facilities." [Bill Hartung, The Economic Consequences of a Nuclear Weapons Freeze, Council on Economic Priorities]

Conversion is not the same as diversification. Increasingly, military firms are attempting to avoid the economic instability that often comes from being dependent on large Pentagon contracts. Many are taking steps to spread their financial risk across a number of product lines, civilian as well as military, often through mergers and acquisitions. Such diversification may or may not enhance the ability of a contractor to convert its military production operations to commercial ventures. Economic conversion requires a conscious commitment to ending military production, revamping existing production facilities, and retraining the workforce. Without this commitment, diversification may only dilute the share of military sales.

There are different requirements, limitations, and possibilities for conversion for the five different kinds of military facilities:

    -- military weapons production plants (aerospace; ordnance; shipbuilding; radio, electronics, and communications; and missiles)

    -- military logistical and material resource suppliers (oil, clothing, food, metals, etc.)

    -- research and development facilities (government laboratories, government-owned and -operated laboratories such as Lawrence Livermore and Los Alamos Labs, universities, independent think-tanks)

    -- military bases

    -- small subcontractors and businesses (which are directly or indirectly dependent on the business generated by large contractors or military bases)

9.A Types of Local Conversion Activities

There are several examples of individual, localized conversion activities which have occurred or are still going on. These activities take a variety of forms, which are illustrated in Figure 9.1.

Figure 9.1 shows a number of examples of successful **military base conversions** which have been carried out under the auspices of the DoD's Office of Economic Adjustment. But as you can see from the figure, since World War II, there have only been a few known successful **corporate-initiated conversions**. There are, however several notable examples of unsuccessful attempts by major military companies to convert to commercial products. These examples illustrate why conversion planning must occur in advance of real cuts and why it is critical to include substantial retraining programs for managers and technical workers to enable them to function effectively in the civilian marketplace.

Community, labor, or public-interest groups have initiated most of the conversion planning activities in industry. They are of two types: conversion studies and alternate use planning projects. **Conversion studies** are generally theoretical exercises, which may or may not involve participation of the workforce at the facilities in question. They attempt to look at the possibilities for skill and technology transfer from military facilities to alternative civilian, socially-needed uses. **Alternate use planning** projects are either worker-initiated or involve the direct participation of workforce representatives with management in actual efforts to convert existing facilities to alternative uses.

In the future, we plan to develop detailed descriptions of conversion planning options. Sections 9.B. through 9.E. present only the rudiments of some of the key elements of local conversion planning. A list of references on conversion is provided in the Reference section.

9.B. Capacity Assessment: Skills, Plant, Equipment, and Technology

The first step in any kind of conversion planning is to make an assessment of the overall and specific capacities of the facilities being studied: composition, size, and skills of the workforce; plant space and layout; equipment, machinery, and tools; technology and processes; production organization and management; marketing organization and experience.

Workforce

See Section 5.D. for a listing of the types of occupations in military industry.

The composition and size of the overall workforce and its categories will naturally vary from location to location and industry to industry. For example, although production workers represent the largest portion, engineers and scientists comprise a significant percentage of the workforce at most aerospace plants (ranging from 30-50%), which is far greater than that in most manufacturing industries. Similarly, at research facilities, such as Lawrence Livermore Labs or Draper Labs, technical professionals make up an even larger portion of the workforce with few or sometimes no production workers. At shipyards or ordnance factories, on the other hand, the technical workforce may be much smaller or practically non-existent. In making an assessment of the workforce, therefore, these considerations must be kept in mind.

The best sources of information concerning production jobs and skills at a facility are trade unions, where they exist (see Section 5.E. for more information on working with unions). Unions usually have a roster of their employed (and sometimes unemployed) workers, with a breakdown by job classifications and pay scales. In addition, there are usually job description manuals associated with union-company collective bargaining agreements. For example, a study by the St. Louis Economic Conversion Project (SLECP) used Factory Job Descriptions: IAMW District 837 and McDonnell Douglas Corporation, St. Louis. The Center for Economic Conversion (CEC) in its Creating Solar Jobs study drew upon the Agreement between Lockheed Missiles and Space Company and the International Association of Machinists and Aerospace Workers (November 11, 1974). Chart A, Figure 9.2 shows SLECP's listing of union jobs at McDonnell Douglas.

Non-union job classifications and descriptions are harder to determine. SLECP found that the McDonnell Douglas telephone directory indicated job classifications at the plant. In conjunction with the Dictionary of Occupational Titles (DOT), a publication of the Department of Labor, they were able to identify the occupational titles applicable to McDonnell Douglas, St. Louis engineers (shown in Chart B, Figure 9.2) and the non-union, non-engineer jobs. The DOT titles, the SLECP study discovered, matched well with actual McDonnell Douglas plant job descriptions in some cases, but not well in others. Overall, however, it was a particularly useful tool for those production workers, engineers, and managers not covered by job description manuals.

Employees may be able to get company documents describing the workforce and job classifications. The Public Relations department at many companies may be willing to give you general information on the workforce. The Employment or Personnel department may give you this information and the particular skills you would need to work there, especially if they thought you were a prospective employee.

In 1978, the University of California Nuclear Weapons Labs Conversion Project did a study of the possibilities of converting the Lawrence Livermore National Labs to alternative production in the energy field. They requested and received a detailed computer print-out of every employee at Livermore (operated by the University of California at Berkeley) with her or his job category and salary. This information was available because all non-proprietary information collected by the state is in the public-domain.

Plant Equipment and Technology

Plant capacity includes: floorspace, buildings, outdoor work areas, location and access (near roads, railway links, water ports, etc.), and other features. **Equipment** includes machine tools (lathes, mills, grinders, etc.), and all other types of production facilities and equipment used in the plant. An assessment would include identifying the types, numbers, condition, and values of the different categories of tools and equipment. In addition, the assessment should identify the types of engineering and R&D facilities and laboratories at the plant.

A more detailed assessment of a facility's capabilities might identify the kinds of **technological processes** employed: i.e., continuous processes, fabrication (forging, forming, stamping, machining, cutting, electronics wiring), assembly, testing, special chemical, mechanical, and electronic processes and techniques, etc. It could also be important to determine the materials, components, and subassemblies utilized in the production process, including their sources of supply.

A listing of the past and current products (and services) produced at the facility will enable you to evaluate the production experience of the firm and its potential for transferring this expertise to new production.

This information may be more difficult to obtain than that about jobs and skills. Some of it may be considered proprietary by the company, or even classified. To help gather the needed information to develop their alternate-use plan, the Lucas Aerospace Workers Shop Stewards Committee sent a questionnaire to all 13,000 Lucas workers, asking them to analyze their own skills and machinery, as well as to propose alternative products (see Figure 9.3).

Other potential sources are unions, public corporate documents such as annual reports and 10-K reports, company public relations offices, internal company documents, and company employees.

Management and Marketing Organization and Experience

Both management organization and marketing in the military sector (as well as engineering design) are substantially different than in civilian industries. An assessment of the management and marketing organizations -- their structure and experience -- are important in the development of a viable plan for producing and marketing of alternative products. It is also valuable to know the company's current production and marketing strategy.

Some sources of this information are public corporate documents and data files on corporations, unions, internal company documents, and company employees. The Data Center, Oakland, California and the Corporate Data Center, New York are examples of institutions with extensive files on major corporations available to the public (see the Resource Center section for more on these organizations).

9.C. Product Selection

After assessing the current capacity of the firm, it is necessary to identify and evaluate a range of potentially viable alternative products, services, or activities which can be produced or undertaken at the facility. The principal steps involved are:

Selecting the Appropriate Criteria for Evaluating the Alternative Product Ideas

The Lucas Workers were concerned primarily with the social usefulness of the product alternatives, whether they could be produced at their plants, and the creation of jobs. In a current project of CEC -- working with the UAW Local 148 to explore alternative products at the McDonnell Douglas plant in Long Beach, California (the MDC Project) -- eight criteria were identified. These are shown in Figure 9.4.

Generating Alternative Product Ideas

The workforce at a facility can be a source of many product ideas based on their experience and knowledge of production activity, facilities, and equipment as the Lucas Workers showed. See Figure 9.5 for an example of the types of products they identified. The IAM also recently polled its membership for ideas for new products through a survey in their national newspaper The Machinist (May, 1983). Not only does this get ideas and information from the people who know the most about the production at the plant, but it encourages them to begin to consider the possibility of conversion and their participation in planning this conversion.

Potential ideas may also be identified through studies of trade and technical magazines and by asking experts at universities and in other industries.

A number of alternative product ideas have already been identified through previous conversion studies and planning projects. Figure 9.1 alludes to the various product ideas being considered in different conversion planning projects and studies. Figure 9.6 lists alternate product ideas compiled in another study. A list of alternative R&D ideas compiled by the United Nations is shown in The Arms Drain, Job Risk, and Industrial Decline by Tim Webb.

The McDonnell Douglas Project in Long Beach has identified a different kind of production option in its planning. It may be possible to lease or subcontract some of the available production capability at the facility to other firms who have already invested in the design and marketing of a new product. This may be more viable than the company taking on the risks and costs of designing, manufacturing, and marketing a product from scratch. For example, the MDC Project is trying to get the company to become a subcontractor for final assembly of rail car vehicles (rapid transit and light rail vehicles) manufactured by another firm, to be used ultimately in new mass transit systems in the Los Angeles County area.

Product Evaluation

Each product idea should be evaluated according to the selected criteria. Certain considerations, such as the products' marketability and potential profitability, are especially important. Workers and community activists engaged in a conversion planning project or study can do preliminary feasibility studies themselves. Buyout: A Guide for Workers Facing Plant Closings, a manual put out by the California Office of Economic Policy, Planning, and Research, contains guidelines that can aide worker/community researchers in doing these preliminary analyses. A set of preliminary product feasibility study guidelines has also been developed by the MDC Project.

However, more extensive studies require assistance from consultants and specialists.

The main components of a detailed product evaluation report is shown in Figure 9.7. There are a growing number of consultant groups and individuals engaged in working with communities and unions in local economic and industrial revitalization efforts. State and county economic development agencies may also be sources of technical assistance for conversion planning. Expertise and research assistance can be obtained, as well, from local colleges and universities (for example, from business, management, urban planning, and engineering schools). The MDC Project has utilized the help of consultants and student researchers in its work with excellent results.

9.D. Capacity Matching

Given an alternative or a range of alternative products or services, there next needs to be a detailed assessment of how well the existing capabilities of the plant facilities match the production requirements for the new activities. This is actually the last step in the product evaluation process.

The production requirements, skills, equipment, plant space, processes, etc., must be assessed for the prospective alternative products. Then these requirements must be matched to the actual capacity of the military industry facility being studied. A full discussion of the methodology for doing this analysis is beyond the scope of this workbook. Examples of the capacity matching process are given in the conversion studies listed in Figure 9.1.

9.E. Implementation

Once alternative products have been identified and evaluated, there remains the difficult process of developing and implementing a workable plan for converting the facility to the new activity. Most conversion studies leave out this step; they merely illustrate the feasibility of converting the facility in question to alternative uses. Conversion planning projects, however, must consider a number of crucial questions to bring their proposals for alternate use to fruition.

Who should be involved in the conversion planning effort? Should a community/worker organization be set up and if so how should it function? Just as important, a strategy must be developed for approaching the management of the facility with the alternate-use proposal. Should the project attempt to set up a cooperative labor-management planning and problem solving process, or attempt to push management's acceptance through collective bargaining? When is the best time to approach management -- before, during, or after the completion of the proposal? In addition, what role can and should local and state government bodies play in the process? How can they facilitate the process?

There may be disadvantages in approaching management before plans are well formulated, but fully developing a proposal without management cooperation may be very difficult and time consuming. It may encourage an adversarial relationship which could be counter-productive in the long run.

Other concerns that need to be addressed include: What kind of management, marketing, and ownership structures are necessary to make the new product enterprise viable? What kind of financing is needed, and how can it be secured? What retraining programs are needed for the different categories of workers and managers at the plant?

Figure 9.1 Economic Conversion Efforts and Studies

1. Corporate-Initiated Conversions and Diversifications

Following are a few known examples:

Kaman Corporation, Bloomfield, Connecticut
> Formerly a prime contractor for military turbine-powered helicopters, began converting in 1965 to successful production of acoustic guitars, borrowing heavily from its helicopter technology base. Also, now entering into alternative energy field with windmill prototypes.

Acurex Corporation, Mountain View, California
> Successful diversification and conversion of a portion of its systems engineering skills to advanced large-scale industrial applications.

Varian Associates, Palo Alto, California
> Diversification into energy field, redirecting its military scientific and engineering talents and its long experience in advance electronics devices, to produce efficient photovoltaic cells.

Boeing-Vertol
> Unsuccessful attempt to enter into the light-rail vehicle market.

Grumman Corporation
> Unsuccessful attempt to enter into production of buses.

2. Military Base Conversions

Since 1961, the Office of Economic Adjustment (OEA) a Department of Defense (DoD) agency under the interagency Economic Adjustment Committee (EAC) has obtained economic assistance for over 200 communities that have faced base reductions and shutdowns. Successful examples include:

> Clinton County Air Force Base, Ohio, 1971-73
> Fort Wolters, Mineral Wells, Texas, 1974-77
> Glynco Naval Air Station, Brunswick, Georgia, 1974-76
> Laredo Air Force Base, Topeka, Kansas
> Hunters Point Naval Shipyard, San Francisco, California, 1973-76
> Brooklyn Air Force Base, Mobile, Alabama, 1965-69

3. Conversion Studies

St. Louis Economic Conversion Project's (SLECP) study of job skills transfer from military to non-military production at McDonnell Douglas Corporation, St. Louis, Missouri (1981).

Converting the Workforce: Where the Jobs Would Be, Marion Anderson, Employment Research Associates (1979), broad study of jobs conversion from military industry to alternative industries (windmills, industrial solar, photovoltaics, heat engines, gasohol, railroads, education, miscellaneous professional services, fishing vessels).

Figure 9.1 Economic Conversion Efforts and Studies (continued)

National Center for Economic Alternatives study "Jobs for People: Planning for Conversion to New Industries" (1979) identifies a number of areas in the civilian economy needing investment to which current military expenditures could be reallocated

Shaping Alternatives for Lawrence Livermore Laboratory: A Preliminary Analysis, University of California Nuclear Weapons Labs Conversion Project (1979).

Creating Solar Jobs: Options for Military Workers and Communities, Mid-Peninsula Conversion Project study (1978) of the feasibility of transferring jobs and technology at Lockheed Missiles and Space Company, Sunnyvale, California to alternative energy technology products.

4. Conversion Planning Projects

Lucas Aerospace Workers Corporate Plan. In 1975 the Lucas Combine Shop Stewards Committee representing a workforce of 13,000 at Lucas Aerospace Corp., Britain's largest military firm, drew up a detailed plan for converting jobs from military to socially-useful production. It included proposals for 150 new products and a number of proposals for re-organizing Lucas Production.

The McDonnell Douglas Project. The Center for Economic Conversion (CEC), Mountain View, California is working with the UAW Local 148 at McDonnell Douglas-Long Beach, California; State representatives; and the Los Angeles Coalition Against Plant Shutdowns to develop an alternative products plan to utilize idle plant capacity, create new jobs, and counter proposed new military production. Product ideas being investigated include: rail transit vehicles, commuter aircraft, cogeneration equipment, and power wheelchairs.

South Shore Conversion Committee. SSCC works with the shipbuilders union at General Dynamics' Quincy Shipyards, Massachusetts to develop a plan to produce alternative products such as ocean thermal energy conversion plants, toxic waste incinerators, and sludge treatment ships.

Atomic Reclamation and Conversion Project sponsored by OCAW Local 3-689, Piketon, Ohio to explore "site conversions" of three government-owned enrichment plants in Piketon, Ohio; Paducah, Kentucky; and Oak Ridge, Tennessee to alternative uses such as toxic waste treatment or alternative energy technologies.

Greater London Council and Greater London Enterprise Board are involved in an ambitious program of defense conversion and alternative product and technology development for the Greater London metropolitan area.

Figure 9.2 Union and Engineering Job Categories at McDonnell Douglas, St. Louis, Missouri

CHART A Union Jobs at McDonnell Douglas, St. Louis

CLASSIFICATION POPULATION
IAMAW 837 as of 12/30/80

CLASSIFICATION TITLE	QUANTITY
Anodizer	39
Builder, jig and fixture	342
Builder, mock-up and tooling	131
Builder, plastic tooling	112
Carpenter, maintenance	71
Crater packer	116
Die finisher, form block	33
Engraver	2
Expediter	506
Extrusion hand former	31
Fitter, metal all around	12
Fitter, metal S & B	21
Furniture mover	26
Grinder, precision parts	13
Grinder, precision tool & cutter	212
Heat treater, dural	8
Heat treater, steel	5
Heat treater, tool room	6
Inspector, detail	71
Inspector, experimental	0
Inspector, final assembly	40
Inspector, flight and service	81
Inspector, jig and fixture	19
Inspector, magnetic part	13
Inspector, material review	28
Inspector, metrology	33
Inspector, model, form block and pattern	8
Inspector, process	32
Inspector, radio and electrical	65
Inspector, receiving & shipping	66
Inspector, sub-assembly	129
Inspector, tool and cutter	16
Inspector, tool and die	11
Laborer	206
Machine and equipment operator, maintenance	101
Machine and hand sewer	18
Machinist, all around	178
Material receiver	77
Material receiver, all around	4

CLASSIFICATION TITLE	QUANTITY
Mechanic, aircraft experimental	234
Mechanic, aircraft production	224
Mechanic, automotive	18
Mechanic, building maintenance	74
Mechanic, electrical and electronics	186
Mechanic, electrical & radio	494
Mechanic, field and service	205
Mechanic, machine repair	150
Mechanic, machine repair	150
Mechanic, office equipment	5
Mechanic, tape and cable	50
Molder, form dies	3
Office custodian	76
Oiler, maintenance	26
Operator, borematic	6
Operator, chemical milling	71
Operator, drill press and special machines	60
Operator, drill press radial	5
Operator, drop hammer	8
Operator, engine lathe	43
Operator, hydraulic press	58
Operator, jig borer	43
Operator, milling machine	612
Operator, planer and shaper	8
Operator, power brake	18
Operator, power hammer	2
Operator, power roll	7
Operator, power shear	10
Operator, punch press	16
Operator, router drill shaper and saws	101
Operator, tumbling machine	10
Operator, turret lathe	82
Painter, maintenance	58
Painter, sign	5
Painter, spray	139
Pipefitter, maintenance	69

CLASSIFICATION TITLE	QUANTITY
Plastic mechanic, all around	19
Plastic worker	43
Plater, precision	14
Sand blaster	7
Sheet metal assembler and riveter	1,487
Sheet metal worker	121
Sheet metal worker, all around	45
Stockkeeper, finished parts	132
Store keeper	147
Sub-assembler, precision	202
Sweeper janitor	171
Template maker	10
Tool and die maker	96
Tool crib attendant	88
Tool & parts control specialist	210
Tool storage attendant	35
Trucker, interdepartmental	1
Welder, aluminum and gas	1
Welder, combination aluminum	0
Welder, combination steel	5
Welder, heli arc-aluminum	17
Welder, heli arc-steel	15
Welder, maintenance	17
Welder, resistance	3
Welder, tooling	26
Welder, utility	273

FIELD GRADES
CLASSIFICATION TITLE

CLASSIFICATION TITLE	QUANTITY
Builder, mock-up and tooling	0
Inspector, experimental	0
Inspector, flight and service	24
Inspector, radio; electrical and electronics	0
Mechanic, aircraft experimental	57
Mechanic, aircraft production	0
Mechanic, electrical & electronics	12
Mechanic, electrical and radio	0
Mechanic, field and service	0
Sheet metal assembler & riveter	0

CHART B McDonnell Douglas St. Louis Engineers

OCCUPATIONAL TITLES (DOT) APPLICABLE
TO MDC AEROSPACE (NON-UNION)

AEROSPACE/AIRCRAFT INDUSTRY
Aerodynamics engineer
Aeronautical test engineer
Avionics technician
Calibration laboratory technician*
Standards laboratory technician
Cost analysis engineer
Value engineer
Aeronautical research engineer
Corporation pilot
Engineering clerk*
Engineering development technician
Engineering document control clerk*
Field service engineer
Field service representative
Flight test data transcriber
Laboratory test mechanic
Material planner
Radio operator, ground
Sales engineer, aeronautical products
Service liaison representative
Stress analyst
Test pilot

ELECTRONICS INDUSTRY

Calibration laboratory technician*
Component tester
Electronics tester II
Electronics assembler
Electronics technician, automated process
Electronics tester I
Engineering clerk*
Engineering document control clerk*
Etcher, printed circuits
Field engineer
Technical representative
Laser technician
Photographer, photoengraver
Supervisor, electronics

OCCUPATIONS AT MDC THAT DO NOT SEEM TO
APPEAR IN THE DOT (NON-UNION)

Loads engineer
Weight engineer
Structural dynamics engineer
Guidance and control engineer
Propulsion engineer
Thermodynamics engineer
Reliability engineer
Design engineer
Avionics engineer
Ground support equipment engineer
Operations analysis engineer
Product support analyst

*appears in both Aircraft/Aerospace
and Electronics job titles

Figure 9.3 Lucas Shop Stewards Corporate Plan Questionnaire

Factory

A. (1) Size: square feet of floor space
(2) Other space: car parks, perimeters, land, etc.
(3) Total space.
B. (1) Age and condition of buildings
(2) Suitability of buildings for modern production
C. (1) Location and access, e.g., near motorway, main road or railway link.
(2) Other services, e.g. Telex, computer, gas,etc.

Workforce

A. Total number employed.
B. (1) Total number hourly paid
(2) Number skilled.
(3) Number semi-skilled
(4) Number unskilled.
C. (1) Total number of staff
(2) Number of design, development, etc.
(3) Number of other technical staff, e.g., Production engineering, contracts, technical sales
(4) Number of administrative staff.
(5) Number of supervisory staff.
D. (1) General availability of labour
(2) Availability of skilled labour
(3) Availability of design and other technical staff.

Equipment

A. (1) Total number of machine tools
(2) Breakdown into groups, e.g., lathes, mills, N.C. machines, etc.
B. Other production facilities, e.g., Heat treatment, Plating, welding, etc.
C. Details of equipment, e.g. age, value, condition

Products

A. (1) List present product range
(2) List subcontract work out and No. hours
(3) List subcontract work in and no. hours
(4) Hourly rate for manufacturers
B. List new products made in past
C. (1) List new products under development
(2) Any other new products outside aircraft work which your plant could design, develop, and manufacture.
(3) Any socially useful products which your plant could design, develop, and manufacture.

Running the Plant

A. (1) How could the plant be run by the workforce?
(2) Could existing 'line' managers still be used?
(3) Have you got a joint staff/works Committee?
(4) Have you set up a local Corporate Planning Committee?

Figure 9.4 Product Selection Criteria Developed by the McDonnell Douglas Project
(Long Beach, California)

Marketability: The size, nature, and scope of existing and projected future market demand for the product; the extent to which the product can be produced competitively at the existing site.

Engineering/Manufacturing Viability: The extent to which the product can be manufactured competitively using existing plant, equipment, technology, materials, and skills; the amount of retooling and new research and development that will be necessary.

Job Transferability: The extent to which job skills are transferrable in the production of the new product and the amount of retraining or relocation of the existing workforce that will be necessary.

Profitability: The extent to which the product will yield a reasonable profit.

Social Utility: The extent to which the product fulfills a social need.

Quality of Work: The impacts that the production of the product will have on the existing quality of the work environment.

Environmental Impact: The extent to which the product and the production process are environmentally safe.

Local Sourcing: The extent to which local and domestic suppliers of materials, equipment, and components will be capable of supplying these essential factors in the production of the product.

Figure 9.5 Lucas Alternative Product Proposals

The product proposals

1. **Oceanic equipment** — for use in the exploration and extraction of natural gas, collection of mineral-bearing nodules from the sea bed, and submarine agriculture.
2. **Telecheiric machines** — electro-mechanical extensions to the human body, remotely controlled by the operator, for use in dangerous environments.
3. **Transport systems** — lightweight road/rail vehicles; hybrid internal combustion/ battery-powered vehicles, combining the best characteristics of both; airships.
4. **Braking systems** — safe systems for both road and rail vehicles.
5. **Alternative energy sources** — wind generators; solar collectors, producing electrical output or direct heating; tidally-driven turbines.
6. **Medical equipment** — portable life support systems for ambulances; kidney machines; aids for the disabled; sight-substituting aids for the blind.
7. **Auxiliary power units** — interchangeably driven by petrol, diesel or methane, and able to operate as a pump, compressor or generator.
8. **Micro-processors** — electronic devices for continuously monitoring and controlling the operation of large machines.
9. **Ballscrews** — used for converting rotating to linear motion, or *vice versa*, with wide applications to machine tools and other products in the plan.

Figure 9.6 Alternative Products for Aerospace and Related Industry

Alternative Products for Aerospace and Related Industry

A LIST OF PRODUCTS IDENTIFIED AS BEING SUITABLE FOR MANUFACTURE IN THE CONVERTED DEFENCE INDUSTRIES

This is not an exhaustive list; some products are of more importance than others; inclusion does not imply automatic possibility of direct conversion.

for the AEROSPACE AND RELATED MILITARY INDUSTRIES

Aircraft
Short to medium range civil aircraft seating up to 200.
Civil helicopters to service North Sea oil installations.
Short take-off and landing passenger and freight aircraft.
Helium airships for air freight.
Robot helicopter for crop spraying.

Marine Vessels
Jet propulsion of ships.
Submerged production systems.
Micro-processors for submersibles.
Marine agriculture.

Transport
Retarder brake systems for trains and coaches.
Development of other brake systems for all vehicles.
Speed/distance related warning systems.
Battery cars.
New rolling stock.
Monorail development.
Hybrid engines containing internal combustion engine, generator, batteries, electric motor.

Energy
Nuclear material disposal.
Integrated energy systems.
Components for low-energy heating, e.g., solar heating.
Fuel cell power plants.
Standby power units for the computer industry.
Power packs for oil pumping.
Processing plants, e.g., sewage, proteins from fine chemicals, ethylene recovery from oil, etc.
Barrage schemes (tidal power).
Extended application of gas-turbine system.

Medical
Pacemakers and renal dialysis machines.
Medical electronic equipment, including hospital communications, computers in hospitals, etc.
Personalized machinery for the disabled.
Telecheiric machines.

Building
Industrial soundproofing.
Prefabricated parts for building.

Mechanical Engineering
Ball screws and machine tools to produce them.
Computer controlled servo-hydraulically operated machine tools.
Other digitally controlled machine tools.

Motors
Linear motors operating pumps and compressors.
High-speed motors.

Other
Electronic libraries.
Self-teaching devices.
Mechanized agricultural equipment.
Test facilities for manufactured products.

Source: SENSE ABOUT DEFENCE, THE REPORT OF THE LABOUR PARTY DEFENCE STUDY GROUP, London: Quartet Books, 1977.

Figure 9.7   Components of a Detailed New Product Evaluation

Description of the Product
- What the product is and does
- What social need it fulfills

Market Analysis
- Existing and projected future demand for the product
- Existing and projected future supply of the product
- Nature of competition and competitive factors in product/industry

Manufacturing/Engineering Feasibility and Material Requirements
- Physical capital and skill requirements of new products
- Transferability of existing plant, equipment, technology, and labor skills
- Need for maintenance, modernization, regulation compliance, new equipment, research and development, and retraining of production workers, engineers, and managers
- Whether inputs are available at a competitive price from reliable sources and from local or domestic sources
- Nature of product distribution channels required and available

Financial and Competitive Analysis
- Existing and projected economics of product and plant
- Plant strengths and weaknesses (based upon market and cost analyses)
- Feasibility of improving operating margins, profitability, cash flow
- Whether plant will be able to compete

Employment Impacts of New Product
- Market, physical, technological, and organizational constraints on employment
- Projected employment requirements by occupational classification
- Potential wage and salary impacts
- Impacts on the quality of the work environment

[Source: "New Product Development for Idle Plant Utilization: A Profile of the McDonnell Douglas Project" (Internal Document), 1983]

Chapter 10   Using the Results of Your Work

10.A. Educating the General Public

If you have used some or all of the analyses outlined in this workbook, you will have generated quite a bit of interesting and important information. The challenge now is to put this data to effective use.

The great majority of people in your community, even those concerned about peace and disarmament issues, will probably have little awareness of the nature and extent, not to mention the impact, of military spending in your area. The point of doing this research is to become well-informed about local military spending and to share this information with others. The result, hopefully, is an expanded and active peace movement.

You can get the word out to the general public in various ways. Most of them are very straightforward, but we encourage you to be creative in your educational outreach. Your educational activities may include: publishing your results and conclusions in a report and circulating it widely; developing flyers and other handouts highlighting the findings; writing op-ed pieces or letters-to-the-editor on this topic; holding a press conference for local media representatives; appearing on radio and television talk shows; giving talks before various groups (church groups, service clubs, college classes, etc.); creating a slide show featuring the results of your research and suggested alternatives; holding demonstrations at local defense plants; lobbying public officials about their stands on military spending; and organizing groups which will continue to raise the issue of economic impacts of military spending and promote conversion to civilian production.

Publishing Research Results

One very good way to get your results out to people is to publish the information in a newspaper or on leaflets. We publish a summary of all the important research we do in our bi-monthly newspaper, the Plowshare Press. In the fall of 1984, we hope to publish a description of the Top 100 contractors in Santa Clara Valley and what they produce. We plan to present the information in a format similar to that in NYPIRC's study Production for Destruction and the CEP study The Defense Department's Top 100. Another study you might want to look at to give you ideas on how to present your information is Projected Impact of a Freeze on Connecticut by the Economic Task Force of the Connecticut Freeze.

The Plowshare Press is mailed out to MPCP supporters (members) and handed out to people who come into our office. We also hand out some issues at plant gates, at bus stops and train stations during commute hours, and at large public events and rallies. We leave stacks of them at local college campuses and at sympathetic bookstores, etc. We also pass them on to sympathetic newspaper reporters.

Military workers who read the paper sometimes call us for more information. Some have told us what military work they do and have given us insights and information about their employers. Others help us with research or arrange for us to speak to organizations to which they belong.

News Media

When you have compiled some incisive data which you believe will be of interest to the news media, write a press release describing the data, where you got the information, how you compiled it, and why it is important. Send it with a summary of the information to the local media. Sympathetic reporters may then call you to ask for more information. You can mail it or drop it off in person, making it possible for them to interview you. For the less sympathetic, you must call them to ask if they received the press release and if they would like more information or an interview. This personal contact is essential since most reporters are overworked (and therefore write stories on whatever interests them and whatever is easiest) and they may not understand the value of this information and the possible implications of the research. By talking directly with them, you put a "bug in their ear" and may also convince them that you know what you are talking about.

While working on this workbook, we received ten calls from news reporters asking for information on defense contractors and how to get more information. When we complete our study of Santa Clara Valley, we hope to have all the newspapers and major radio stations run stories on the military dependency of our community.

10.B. Constituency Organizing

Public education activities can catalyze efforts to involve various constituencies in promoting conversion to a peace economy. The most likely groups are labor unions, church groups, peace organizations, and people from the technical community. The business community is also a critical group, but difficult to reach. Somewhat different strategies must be developed for each constituency.

Many churches have concerns about the ethical and social implications of the current massive military buildup. Helping members perceive the economic underpinnings of the arms race and its local manifestations is likely to attract a number of them to the economic conversion movement. Ideally ecumenical coalitions of religious groups will form around this issue.

While the peace community is a "natural" constituency in which to promote economic conversion, adherents may encounter some surprising resistance. Many peace activists assume that conversion will be an inevitable by-product of military budget cuts. They need to be educated about the role that conversion planning can play in reducing Congressional resistance to cuts in weapon systems and in preventing the dislocation of thousands of workers once cuts are made.

Job creation and preservation is obviously of primary concern to people in the labor movement. The job-saving aspect of conversion planning has helped secure the support of many national union leaders. Still, many defense workers have legitimate concerns about the ability of conversion to generate civilian jobs which are comparable in terms of pay and benefits to their present ones. Ideally, labor representatives should be actively involved in conversion planning endeavors in order to identify viable alternative products for the enterprises in which they work.

Historically, the business community has been staunchly in favor of high levels of military spending and resistant to economic conversion, citing national defense needs and management prerogatives in determining products. A small but growing number of business leaders are expressing doubts about the size of the military buildup and the negative impacts it has on our economy. The findings of local economic impact studies can serve as a vehicle for establishing a dialogue with concerned business and civic leaders. Since economic conversion would ideally be a democratic planning process involving blue collar workers, technical personnel, and management, it is essential to seek out potential allies in the business community and gain their support and involvement.

10.C. Conversion Legislation

Conversion legislation will probably not be adopted until there is a substantial constituency of people who support and advocate it. Such a constituency can be developed through the organizing activities outlined above. Supportive elected officials who can sponsor such legislation are essential to this process.

Conversion legislation can be implemented at the national, state, and local levels. Federal legislation would undoubtedly have the most impact, but state legislation is most likely to be influenced by local activists. Below we list the most important aspects of conversion legislation which could be implemented on the state level. Finally, we present an overview of specific national legislation currently being considered.

There are two primary emphases of conversion legislation: protecting workers and communities from the adverse impacts of defense spending cuts and initiating planning processes to insure a transition to civilian production. What follows is an outline of some of the approaches possible in these two areas.

Protecting Workers and Communities

-- Provide funds for supplementary unemployment and health benefits for laid-off defense workers.

-- Provide funds for retraining laid-off (or dissatisfied) defense workers.

-- Provide funds for re-employing or relocating laid-off defense workers.

-- Assist business, labor organizations, and local units of government affected by military spending cuts.

-- Develop a reserve fund to support the above forms of assistance.

Promoting Conversion Planning

-- Encourage or mandate defense contractors and local governments to prepare economic conversion (alternate-use) plans and set up labor-management committees to plan the production of non-military socially-useful products.

-- Publish an economic conversion handbook with guidelines on how to undertake conversion.

-- Develop economic conversion pilot projects in select companies and industries.

-- Authorize or mandate counties to create economic impact committees to assess the impact of military production and develop recommendations for diversification and conversion.

-- Develop a statewide plan for reducing military dependency, converting the defense sector to peaceful work, and achieving full employment.

-- Facilitate investment in civilian growth industries through the use of tax incentives, loan guarantees, etc. (for example, establish a "community development finance corporation").

Other steps which states can take to facilitate the conversion to civilian production include:

-- Hold hearings and conduct official studies which assess the effects of military spending upon the state's economy, consider potential economic dislocation caused by fluctuations in military spending, and develop strategies to cope with these dislocations.

-- Implement methods for discouraging all or some types of military production. (For example, legislation proposed in Washington State would establish a business and occupations tax on the sales/profits of contractors producing nuclear weapons.)

-- Establish a governmental agency to promote economic conversion within the state (for example, a "conversion planning commission") or add this function to the duties of an existing state agency.

National Legislation

On the national level, comprehensive conversion legislation has been introduced over the years by New York Representative Ted Weiss and others, but has not fared very well in Congress. In 1984, Rep. Nicholas Mavroules (D-MA) introduced a more limited version called the "Economic Conversion Act." The bill contains four main provisions:

-- The Defense Department must give a one-year advance notification of any plan to close a base or terminate a contract worth $10 million or more. (The great majority of all military contracts are less than this amount.)

-- The local government unit most directly affected may apply for a $250,000 Federal grant for job retraining and planning for alternative production.

-- The Defense Department must make weekly assistance payments to workers affected by the base closing or contract termination. The assistance amounts to as much as $25,000 a year minus any other employment compensation. This is a controversial aspect of the bill, but should be acceptable because the assistance is tied to job retraining.

-- Funding will come from Defense Department unobligated funds -- money previously obligated to the cancelled contract. So no new appropriation funds are needed.

For political reasons, the Mavroules bill leaves out several good provisions and therefore has some weaknesses:

-- Responsiblity for administering this program is given completely to the DoD.

-- No provision is made for direct worker participation in conversion planning and on-going alternate-use planning is not included.

10.D. Converting to a Peace-Oriented Economy

Implementing economic conversion is certainly not an easy task, but it is clearly necessary if we are to reduce our dependence upon military spending as a stimulus to the economy. In order to achieve economic conversion we need a national commitment to building a peace economy. This commitment may take years to develop, and it will happen only if thousands of people in hundreds of communities devote themselves to working for a smooth transition away from our military-dominated economy. The information generated through the research outlined in this workbook could be an excellent starting point for building a conversion movement.

References

Below are listed the references mentioned in the body of the text and others you may find useful. However, it is not a complete list of references by any means. See the section below and the references under the category called Research Guides for more ideas on other sources.

The references used in this workbook are followed by a Chapter and Section number in brackets like this ➡[3.B.] indicating the places where the reference is discussed and used. Often there is a more complete description of the reference in the body of the text. In this case, the bracketed value is printed in bold ➡[3.B., **3.C.**]

References marked with a ▶ are good resources and cost very little for the amount of information they provide. You should probably buy these reports or obtain copies from one of the Resource Centers. References for California are listed to give you an idea of analagous resources which might be available in your state. The sources for obtaining each Federal government document are shown after the cost figure and are indicated by the abbreviations listed below.

Federal Government References

The S/N number is the GPO stock number (or the stock number of the source indicated). Prices are those listed in the publication or the quoted price as of the fall of 1983 or winter 1984. Check with the source for current prices. Library of Congress call numbers are listed in the form: C3.134/5:982. The letter "C" stands for the issuing agency, in this case the Department of Commerce and the 3.134/5:982 is a unique number identifying the series and particular document.

Popular government documents are available from the Government Printing Office (see the address below), but more obscure government documents are only available from the Department or Agency that publishes it. We have indicated where to obtain each reference. Most useful government documents are also available for viewing and copying in a Government Depository (library). These are located all across the United States. Call your local librarian for the location of the nearest one.

DIOR   Directorate for Information Operations and Reports (DIOR)
            Department of Defense
            Washington Headquarters Services
            Washington, DC 20301

▶ Catalog of DIOR Reports, 36 pages, issued annually in February, free.
            This catalog lists reports on statistical data available on the military (see
            the section below called **Prime Contracts**). Many of these are quite expensive so
            for those that aren't too long, it may be cheaper to get a photocopy from NARMIC
            or CEC (MPCP).

GPO   Superintendent of Documents
Government Printing Office (GPO)
Washington, DC 20402
(202) 783-3238
(8:00 AM to 4:30 PM, Eastern Time)

These two GPO documents have information for ordering other reports:

U.S. Government Books, 60 pages, issued periodically, free.
This catalog lists all the popular books available from the GPO.

Subject Bibliography: Statistical Publications, SB-273, most recent version, free.
This publication lists all the statistical publications available from the GPO.
There are also Subject Bibliographies for many other subjects. Ask for a list
of all the Subject Bibliographies.

CBO   Office of Intergovernmental Relations
Congressional Budget Office
House Office Building
Annex #2
2nd and D Streets, SW
Washington, DC 20515

The CBO puts out a series of budget issue papers, dealing with the federal budget as
a whole and with the effects of particular weapons programs. CBO will put you on its
mailing list to receive any or all of its categories of reports for free. For an
order form listing the available categories of reports write to the address above.

GAO   U.S. General Accounting Office
Document Handling and Information Services Facility
P.O. Box 6015
Gaithersburg, MD 20877
(202) 275-6241

The General Accounting Office investigates problems in the operation of the
government (fraud, inefficiency, etc.), often at the request of a Congressmember, and writes reports of 1 to 200 pages of their findings. If a report
covers a contractor in your area it may be of use. Sometimes they investigate
the various options for upcoming legislation. One copy of each report is free
on request.

Monthly List of GAO Reports, about 12 pages each, free (ask to be put on the
distribution list).

NTIS   National Technical Information Service (NTIS)
Springfield, VA 22161
(703) 557-4650

Government Reports Announcements and Index.
This presents an abstract of all the non-classified reports published by the
government and its contractors. It is indexed by keyword, personal author,
contract number, and NTIS report number. [3.E.]

OEA   President's Economic Adjustment Committee
            Office of Economic Adjustment
            Office of the Assistant Secretary of Defense
            (Manpower, Reserve Affairs and Logistics)
            The Pentagon
            Washington, DC 20301

DUSD   Data User Services Division
            Customer Services (Publications)
            Bureau of the Census
            Washington, DC 20233

BIE   Bureau of Industrial Economics
            Department of Commerce
            Washington, DC
            (202) 377-4356

BEA   Bureau of Economic Analysis (BE-51)
            Department of Commerce
            Washington, DC 20230

State Government Publications

Each state has an office responsible for collecting employment data for relay to the Bureau of Labor. In addition, your state may publish other useful information on the military or on employment effects. Federal Government Depositories (libraries) may have many of the state publications or you may have to go to the state capitol or a large city library.

For California there are several good resources which we have listed to give you an idea of what might be available in your state. We have listed the publication applicable to the San Jose SMSA (Santa Clara County), but most of these reports are available for every SMSA in California.

Other Places to Look

Most of the Resource Centers publish useful information. It is worthwhile to get on their mailing lists (usually by subscribing to their newsletters) to see what good new things they have to offer. New government reports are published all the time. There are several indices which help you learn of new reports. Most good government documents libraries will have the following:

American Statistics Index (ASI) is published yearly with monthly updates. It is "a comprehensive guide and index to the statistical publications of the U.S. Government." Since almost any government document with numbers in it pertaining to military spending is considered a statistical publication, it is listed in ASI. ASI therefore has a fairly complete list of publications of interest.

Statistical Reference Index (SRI) has the same format as ASI but lists publications from business organizations, associations, commercial publishers, (large) independent research organizations, state governments, and university research centers.

CIS/Index, published by the Congressional Information Service, has a similar indexing service for all Federal government hearings, reports, etc.

OUTLINE OF THE REFERENCES LISTED BELOW

References on Military Contracts and Purchasing Offices

Prime Contracts

Commerce Business Daily, published Monday through Friday except Federal holidays, about 32 pages/day printed in tiny print, Government Printing Office, $100/year for 2nd class mailing, GPO.
> This is a daily list of U.S. Government procurement invitations, contract awards over $25,000 (over $100,000 for military contracts), subcontracting leads, sales of surplus property, and foreign business opportunities. [3.A., **3.B.**, Figure 3.6]

▶ Prime Contract Awards Over $25,000 by State, County, Contractor, and Place, FY 1983 (ST25) (formerly P12), DoD, issued February 1984, microfiche containing approximately 1,300 pages, $60.00, DIOR.
> This report lists every prime contract award (transaction) made by the DoD in FY 1983. It has approximately 50 contractors listed on each page and is very useful. [**2.A.**, 2.C., 2.D., Figure 2.1, 3.B., 6.B]

Prime Contract Awards Over $25,000 by State, Place, and Contractor, FY 1983 (ST24) (formerly P11), DoD, issued February 1984, microfiche containing approximately 1,600 pages, $60.00, DIOR.
> This report contains the same information as ST25 above, but lists it according to city. [**2.B.**, 2.C., Figure 2.3]

▶ 100 Companies Receiving the Largest Dollar Volume of Prime Contract Awards, FY 1983 (P01), DoD, issued February 1984, 20 pages, $12.00, DIOR.
> Data include the name of the company and its subsidiaries, the company's rank, and the net value of the awards. The May issue of Aviation Week and Space Technology has almost the same information as this publication. [4.A., **4.B.**]

▶ Alphabetical Detail of DoD Prime Contractors Over $25,000, FY 1983 (ST18), DoD, issued February 1984, 33 microfiche containing about 8,000 pages, $45.00, DIOR.
> A tabular list of every prime contract award made by the DoD, arranged alphabetically by contractor and principal place (city) of performance, and showing a code for the weapons system, type of work, date of contract, contract number, awarding agency, and more. A wealth of information on prime contracts awards. Requires decoding manuals MN01, MN02, and MN04. [2.D., 3.A., **3.B.**, Figure 3.3, 3.D., 4.A.]

Geographic Detail of DoD Prime Contractors Over $25,000, FY 1983 (ST11), DoD, issued February 1984, microfiche, $60.00, DIOR.
> The same information as ST18 above listed in the same format, but arranged by state and city and then alphabetically by contractor. [3.B]

Prime Contract Awards over $25,000 by Major Systems, Work Performed and Awarding Department, FY 1983 (ST08), DoD, issued February 1984, microfiche, $60.00, DIOR.
> A listing of awards for major systems by contractor and FSC and showing the state where work was performed (but not city!), and the awarding Department. [3.B.]

Prime Contract Awards over $25,000 by Federal Supply Classification (FSC) and Service Codes (SVC), FY 1983 (ST06), DoD, issued February 1984, microfiche, $65.00, DIOR.
> Contains the FSC code, contractor name, state of performance (but not city!), awarding Department, and net value of the awards. [3.B.]

Also see the Atlas/State Data Abstract for the United States, FY 1983 (L03) listed under Military Bases and Personnel.

Research, Development, Testing, and Evaluation (RDT&E) Contracts

500 Contractors Receiving the Largest Dollar Volume of Prime Contract Awards for RDT&E, FY 1983 (P02), DoD, issued February 1984, 32 pages, $18.00, DIOR.
   Provides information on firms receiving contracts for Research, Development, Test, and Evaluation (RDT&E).

Educational and Nonprofit Institutions Receiving Prime Contract Awards for RDT&E, FY 1983 (P04), DoD, issued February 1984, 15 pages, $12.00, DIOR.

Federal Funds for Research and Development, Fiscal Years 1982, 1983, and 1984, Detailed Statistical Tables, Volume xxxii, NSF83-319, issued Winter 1984, 190 pages, free (?) from National Science Foundation, Washington, DC 20550.
   This report has 135 tables of information on Federal R&D expenditures listed in various ways by broad categories for the agency, type of performer, and field of science. It also has the percent and total amount of R&D expenditures to each state for these years.

The National Science Foundation also has many other reports on research and development and scientists and engineers. But the data is usually aggregated on a national level. Write to the NSF at the address above for a list of publications.

Purchasing Offices (POs)

▶Selling to the Military, DoD, issued in 1983, 144 pages, $6.00, GPO.
   This report has a wealth of information on the military contracting agencies including addresses, phone numbers, and a short (but readable) description of their activities and procurement requirements. It also has a list of Federal Supply Classification (FSC) codes and what they mean and a glossary of acronyms and abbreviations. [3.A., **3.C.**, 3.E., Figure 3.9]

Code Translation Manuals

▶Defense Acquisition Management Data System (DAMDS) Code Translation Manual (MN04), DoD, issued ?, 16 pages, $12.00, DIOR.
   Very useful. See the description in the text. [3.A., 3.B., **Figure 3.4**]

▶DoD Procurement Coding Manual, Volume I: Commodities and Services (MN02), DoD, issued ?, 100 pages, $22.00, DIOR.
   Very useful. See the description in the text. [**3.B.**, 3.C., 3.D., Figure 3.5]

▶List of DoD Purchasing Offices (PO) (MN01), DoD, issued ?, 30 pages, $18.00, DIOR.
   Each office is identified with its PO number and address. [3.C.]

Subcontracts

Geographic Distribution of Subcontract Awards, Fiscal Year 1979, DoD, issued ?, 66 pages, $?, DIOR.
   This was the only year this report was published before the program to collect the information was cancelled. For each state it lists how much money was subcontracted out to firms in other states and how much was subcontracted out from firms in other states to firms in the state. Because it was the first year firms were required to report this information, only about 36.5% of the total that should have been was actually reported. [**2.E.**]

Procurement Activities and Costs

The following reports are prepared annually. Ask for the most recent version.

Program Acquisition Costs by Weapon System: DoD Budget FY 1983, DoD, issued February 1982, S/N PB82-160045, 171 pages, $10.00, NTIS.
> This report contains 171 tables, one for each weapon system. Each table has a short description of the weapon, contractor, mission, quantity procured, and amount spent to date.

RDT&E Program (R-1), FY 1983, DoD, issued February 1982, S/N PB82-160060, 145 pages, $6.00, NTIS.
> This report has 7 charts and 9 tables showing RDT&E funding, component, mission category, performance and defense programs.

Procurement Program (P-1), FY 1983, DoD, February 1982, S/N PB82-160078, 137 pages, $9.00, NTIS.

References on Military Bases and Personnel

Atlas/State Data Abstract for the United States, FY 1983 (L03), DoD, issued February 1984, 175 pages, $35.00, DIOR.
> Contains information on major military installations and also includes several summary tables on personnel, payrolls, and prime contract awards and a statistical data abstract for each state. The statistical abstracts contain information on total personnel and expenditures by military service and other defense activities. We haven't seen this report, but it looks like it would be very good. [5.A.]

Distribution of Personnel by State and by Selected Locations FY 1983, (M02), DoD, issued February 1984, 95 pages, $22.00, DIOR.
> Data on the number and operating location of DoD active duty military and direct hire civilian personnel in each of the 50 states. Detailed data are also provided in a separate table for major installations and selected cities in each state. This one also looks good, but we haven't seen it yet. [5.A.]

References on Weapons

Nuclear Weapons Databook, Vol. 1: U.S. Nuclear Forces and Capabilities, by Thomas B. Cochran, Thomas B., William M. Arkin, and Milton M. Honig, Ballinger Publishers, 1984, 329 pages, $19.95 paperback.
> This book is a comprehensive summary of the nuclear weapons and their delivery systems currently available or under development by the U.S. It opens with a short history of the development of the U.S. weapons stockpile and a primer on the basic types of weapons and their construction. Then it presents the distribution of weapons to the various branches of the armed services and where they are based. But the focus of the book is on hardware. The function, yield, weight, dimensions, development, history, etc. of more than two dozen types of warheads are presented. Technical and comparative data, including prime and subcontractors, on most delivery systems (including the MX, Trident II, and cruise missiles) are summarized in a comprehensible form. All branches of the service are included with descriptions of nuclear-capable ships, aircraft, artillery, and even nuclear commando demolition devices. This book presents an immense amount of information in an easily accessible and digestable form, making clear, for example, the differences that make the Pershing II a considerably more formidable weapon than the Pershing 1a. It also provides extensive references.

Arsenal of Democracy: American Weapons Available for Export, by Tom Gervasi, Grove Press, 1977, 240 pages, $8.00.
> This book is primarily a catalog of weapons produced in the U.S. and available for export up to 1977. Consequently it covers many but not all U.S. combat and support aircraft, helicopters, tanks and armored vehicles, naval vessels, guided missiles, infantry weapons, mortars, machine guns, bombs, torpedoes, mines, grenades, and artillery. Because not all weapons are exported, this book is not a complete guide to U.S. weaponry. Coverage concentrates on aircraft, helicopters, and land weapons. A substantial number of guided missiles are included, but naval vessels are almost entirely absent. The book gives descriptive technical information for each weapon, and emphasizes the history of foreign sales of the weapons and the effect of these sales on U.S. defense policy and production. While much of the technical information is presented in tabular form, the accompanying prose histories are easily understandable. They reveal the astonishing level of technology used in the weapons, the performance track-records of the weapons, and their history of cost-overruns.
>
> The strong point of the book is its commentary on the weapons, U.S. defense policy, and U.S. arms deals with foreign governments. However, aside from naming the principle contractor, it gives no information on other contractors or production locations. [3.A.]

Arsenal of Democracy II: American Military Power in the 1980s and the Origins of the New Cold War, by Tom Gervasi, Grove Press, New York, 1981, 298 pages, $11.00.
> About two-thirds of this book is an updated version of the book above. Most of the remaining third of the book is an extremely interesting and informative account of world events in the 1977-81 period, how these events have affected the world military and political balance, how U.S. defense policy has evolved in response, and the motives or pretexts for Reagan administration policies. Added since the 1977 work is a 14-page compilation of American arms transfers to foreign groups since 1978. This book shares the strengths and weaknesses of the earlier volume; the analyses and descriptions are very strong, but there is little information relating the weapons to producers and production sites.

The U.S. War Machine: An Illustrated Encyclopedia of American Military Equipment and Strategy, by James E. Dornan, Jr., consultant, Crown Publishers, New York, 1978, 271 pages, $18.00.
> Written by 14 contributors drawn from U.S. academia, government, military, and industry, this book is primarily a catalog of U.S. weapons of all types. Technical descriptions of the weapons and their development and production histories are given, along with color photos of the weapons in action. For each weapon, the principal contractor is given, and sometimes the weapon's production site. For air and land weapons, Arsenal of Democracy II is superior, but this book is preferable for guided missiles and naval weapons.
>
> Almost half the book contains essays by the various authors on military topics, for example, the U.S. concept of national security, the history of the U.S. nuclear "triad."

Polman, Norman, The Ships and Aircraft of the U.S. Fleet, Naval Institute Press.
> Includes some information on electronic systems and which ship or submarine they are used on. Invaluable to determine which ships/subs do or don't carry nuclear weapons.

Also see the Jane's series of books (Jane's All the World Aircraft, etc. and Section 3.D.]

General Publications on the Military

Military Spending

Military Expansion, Economic Decline, 1983, by Robert W. DeGrasse, Council on Economic Priorities, 240 pages, $11.95 + $2.85 postage.

Defense Spending and the Economy, Y10.2:D36/6, Congressional Budget Office, issued February 1983, S/N 052-070-05817-0, 90 pages, $5.50, GPO.
    This is an interesting report explaining the effects military spending may or may not have on the economy. It contains 13 charts and 22 tables.

National Defense, by James Fallows, Vintage Books, 1981, 205 pages, $5.00.
    This book by the Washington correspondent for The Atlantic Monthly analyzes the shortcomings of defense policy and points out the technical, bureaucratic, and psychological sources of these shortcomings. [3.D.]

The Effect of Increased Military Spending in California, Office of Economic Policy, Planning, and Research, Department of Economic and Business Development, State of California, issued May 19, 1982, 70 pages, free ?.
    This report is an excellent example of how the regional impact of military spending can be assessed. The report concludes that if the Reagan administration program of defense budget increases and non-defense cutbacks is enacted, California will be a net loser of jobs despite the creation of as many as 670,000 defense-related jobs in the state. These changes will affect industries, occupations, and regions in the state unequally. It is unlikely that the state will be able to attract all the skilled personnel for the military jobs without competing directly with the civilian electronics industry in California. The competition for personnel will bid wages up, adversely affecting the civilian industry's competitive abilities in world markets.

    The report is explicit about the methods and sources it uses to obtain these conclusions. Among the information it determines for the state are such things as military expenditure receipts, the shipments and employment of defense-oriented industries, receipts from prime and subcontracts, the outlook for increased military spending, distribution of the increase by sector, employment growth in various sectors due to the increase, estimated spending cuts for California, consequent job losses, employment bottlenecks, and prospects for dealing with labor shortages. This report is highly recommended. [6.B.]

Guide to the Military Budget, Fiscal Year 1985, SANE, 8 pages, $0.25 each or 100 for $15.

Military Industry

The Defense Industry, by Jacques S. Gansler, MIT Press, Cambridge, Mass., 1980, 346 pages, $20.00 ($10.00 in paperback).
    Written by a 25-year veteran of DoD, ITT, Raytheon, and other companies, this book analyzes the defense industry from a free-market viewpoint and concludes that the industry does not operate by free-market principles, is economically inefficient, and is unable to respond to national needs promptly. The book examines the history and structure of the defense industry, R&D, industrial mobilization capacity, the problems faced by subcontractors, the dependence of the defense industry on foreign sales and foreign suppliers, and the defense industries of other nations. It is a fascinating source of facts and anecdotal information, but is a poor guide to sources of information for the general public. It has 10 pages of bibliography and some footnotes. [4.B., 5.F., Appendix 2]

The Nuclear Weapons Industry, by Kenneth A. Bertsch and Linda S. Shaw, IRRC, 1984, 405 pages, $22.00 for individuals, $45 for corporations and non-profits.

Conversion to Civilian Production

Economic Conversion: Revitalizing the American Economy, Suzanne Gordon and David McFadden, eds., 1984, Ballinger Books, Boston.
    Most recent book covering the conversion issue and activities in depth.

"Making Peace Work: Jobs, Conversion, and the Economy," Nuclear Times, Vol. 1, No. 6, April 1983.
    Issue devoted to military economics and conversion with a listing of groups working on conversion.

Buyout: A Guide for Workers Facing Plant Closings, by Julia Parzen, Catherine Squire, and Michael Kieschnick, Office of Economic Policy Planning and Research, State of California, December 1982.
    Prepared to help guide workers interested in worker buyouts as a response to plant closings. [9.C.]

Profits Without Production, by Seymour Melman, Alfred A. Knopf, New York, 1983.
    Melman's most recent book, linking military economy, conversion, and industrial policy.

Barriers to Conversion from Military to Civilian Industry, by Seymour Melman, prepared for the United Nations Center, Ad Hoc Group of Governmental Experts on the Relationship Between Disarmament and Development, 1980.
    Report on the comparative problems of military industry conversion in several nations with market, planned, and developing economics.

The Permanent War Economy, by Seymour Melman, Simon and Schuster, New York, 1974.
    An important sourcebook for understanding the military economy and conversion.

"The Political Economy of Arms Reduction," by Lloyd J. Dumas, ed., 1982, AAAS Selected Symposium 80, American Association for the Advancement of Science, Washington, DC.
    Up-to-date review of the military economy and conversion issues with contributions from major writers in the field.

Creating Solar Jobs: Options for Military Workers and Communities, 72 pages, by DeGrasse, Bernstein, McFadden, Schutt, Shiras, and Street, the Center for Economic Conversion (CEC), November 1978, $4.00.

"Industrial Conversion: Beating Swords into Plowshares," by Joel S. Yudken, Business and Society Review, Spring 1984.
    Brief overview of conversion issues and current status of the conversion movement.

Defense Dependency in Connecticut, Economic Conversion Task Force of the Connecticut Freeze Campaign.

"Converting an Industry," by Geoffrey Sea, Plowshare Press, January-February 1984, Center for Economic Conversion.
    About the efforts of the Oil, Chemical, and Atomic Workers' union-led Atomic Reclamation and Conversion Project to do site conversion of nuclear reprocessing facilities in three states.

"A New Course for Shipbuilding," by Elizabeth Sherman, Plowshare Press, January-February 1984, Center for Economic Conversion.
    On South Shore Conversion Committee's conversion efforts at the General Dynamics Quincy Shipyards.

"Getting Together at McDonnell Douglas," by Joel S. Yudken, Plowshare Press, March-April 1984, Center for Economic Conversion.
    On CEC's McDonnell Douglas Project.

Let's Rebuild America, International Association of Machinists and Aerospace Workers, Washington, DC., 1983.
    Presents the Machinists "Rebuilding America Act" and program for economic and industrial revitalization.

Summary of Completed Military Base Economic Adjustment Projects: 1961-1981, 20 Years of Civilian Reuse, November 1981, 28 pages, free, OEA.
    This report has one table describing the 100 or so military closures in the last 20 years, the number of jobs lost and created by the new activities at the base, and the number of years it took for the transition.

Communities in Transition, Defense Office of Economic Adjustment, Washington, DC, 1977.
    Several examples of community adjustments to base and military facility closures.

A more extensive bibliography is available from the Center for Economic Conversion.

Contracting

The Iron Triangle: The Politics of Defense Contracting, by Gordon Adams, Council on Economic Priorities, 1981, 470 pages, $?.

Misguided Expenditure, by David Gold, Christopher Paine, and Gail Shields, Council on Economic Priorities, $?.

Nuclear Weapons Freeze

The Freeze Economy, by Dave McFadden and Jim Lake, Center for Economic Conversion (CEC), 1983, 48 pages, $2.50.

The Economic Consequences of a Nuclear Weapons Freeze, by William Hartung, Council on Economic Priorities, May 1984, 120 pages, $?.

Local Studies

Our Own Worst Enemy: The Impact of Military Production on the Upper South, by Tom Schlesinger, Highlander Center, 1983, 285 pages, $10.00 + postage.

Production for Destruction: Military Spending in New York State, by Tom Webster and Beth Cohen DeGrasse, New York Public Interest Research Center, 1980, 80 pages, $2.50.

Projected Impact of a Freeze on Connecticut, 1983, by Kevin Bean, Kevin Cassidy, and Marta Daniels, Connecticut Freeze Campaign, 18 pages, free ?.

Jobs, Security, and Arms in Connecticut: A Study of the Impact of Military Spending on the State, by Marta Daniels, Connecticut Freeze Campaign, January 1980, 64 pages, $2.50.

Down the Federal Drain: The Impact of Military Spending on Mendocino County, by Don Lipmanson and David Colfax, Mendocino County Jobs With Peace Coalition, 1983, 8 pages, $2.00.

The Pentagon Tilt, 1983, $5.00 and The Unprotected Flank, 1980, $3.00, Northeast-Midwest Institute, 218 D Street, SE, Washington, DC 20003 (202) 544-5200.
    These two volumes show the distribution of DoD spending in the country and the bias against the Northeast and Midwest regions in favor of the Sunbelt regions.

Towards a Boston Peace Budget, Jobs with Peace National Network, 60 pages, $5.00.

Boston Peace Budget, Jobs with Peace National Network, 16 pages, $5/dozen.

Sandia Labs: A Report, New Mexico Peace Conversion Project, 20 pages, May 1983, free ?.

Reaganomics, the Military, & New Mexico, New Mexico Peace Conversion Project, 16 pages, January 1983, free ?.

Other

The Puzzle Palace: A Report on NSA, America's Most Secret Agency, by James Bamford, Houghton Mifflin Company, 1982, 465 pages.
> A detailed investigation of the National Security Agency. [3.C.]

The Role of Defense in Santa Clara County's Economy, SRI International for the President's Economic Adjustment Committee, Office of the Assistant Secretary of Defense, (Manpower, Reserve Affairs, and Logistics), The Pentagon, Washington, DC 20301, August 1980, 80 pages, free.
> This was a study done partly at the urging of CEC. SRI concludes that military spending is good for Santa Clara County and it provides a lot of employment. They also conclude that the spending is spread out between enough weapons systems and contractors so any particular cutback will not hurt the area. The methodology is not very clear and we disagree with the conclusions, but it gives you some idea of how an impact assessment might be done.

Planning and Forecasting in the Defense Industries, J.A. Stockfisch, ed., Wadsworth Publishing Company, Belmont, CA, 1962.
> This (old) book has many interesting chapters that discuss the problems, imperatives, and techniques of planning in the defense industries. It probably has historical, theoretical, and methodological value for understanding military economics and corporate planning. It is most likely to be available in college or university libraries, and may still be in stock at the publisher.

"Arms Control Impact Statements," available yearly from the Arms Control and Disarmament Agency.
> Similar to the DoD Appropriations Hearings in general descriptions of new weapon systems and their functions.

Dictionary of Military and Associated Terms, JCS Pub.1, Joint Chiefs of Staff, Washington, DC, 20301, 377 pages, free ?.
> Mostly a dictionary of terms on military strategy and doctrine, but also covers some technical terms. [List of Abbreviations]

How to Get It -- A Guide to Defense-Related Information Resources, Institute for Defense Analysis, Technical Information Services Office, 400 Army-Navy Drive, Arlington, VA 22202, prepared for Defense Technical Information Center, Cameron Station, Alexandria, VA 22314 (202) 274-6434, revised January 1982, 531 pages, $?.
> Lists a lot of government documents prepared internally by various agencies and tells if you can get them, what your clearance level must be, etc.

References on Industry

General Information on Industry

Directory of Companies Required to File Annual Reports with the Securities and Exchange Commission, Alphabetically and by Industry Groups, 1983, SE1.27:983, Securities and Exchange Commission, issued April 30, 1982, 390 pages, $?, GPO.
> An alphabetical listing of these Corporations and their addresses and phone numbers. Also contains an index by 3-digit SIC code. [4.D.]

Quarterly Financial Report (QFR) for Manufacturing, Mining and Trade Corporations, C3.267:(year, number), Bureau of the Census, issued quarterly, S/N 018-000-80001-2, 165 pages, $19.00/year, GPO.

Issued about 2 months after the close of the quarter. Average financial data by 2-digit SIC codes derived from corporations' income statements and balance sheets. This data is presented in the form of an income statement and balance sheet plus selected profit ratios, etc. for the last 5 quarters. Useful for comparing the profit margin, etc. for a specific company with the industry average.

1980 OBERS BEA Regional Projections, Economic Activity in the United States, by State, Economic Area, SMSA, and State Portions of the Areas, Historical and Projected -- 1969-2030, Volume 3, Standard Metropolitan Statistical Areas, C59.17:980/v.3, Bureau of Economic Analysis, issued July 1981, S/N 003-010-00092-9, 290 pages, $8.00, GPO.

This report lists the employment by private industry (2-digit SIC code breakdown) and government (federal civilian, federal military, and state and local) for each SMSA in the country for 1969, 1978 and projections for the next 50 years. [5.A.]

Also see 1983 U.S. Industrial Outlook for 250 Industries with Projections for 1987 listed under Input-Output Models of the Economy.

Statistics on Product Shipments, etc. by Industry

Annual Survey of Manufactures, 1981, Value of Product Shipments, C3.24/9:M81(AS)-2, Census Bureau, issued May 1983, 36 pages, $2.75, DUSD.

This report lists the value of product shipments for the last 5 years for 5-digit SIC industries.

Census of Manufactures, 1977, Volume III, Geographic Area Statistics, C3.24:977/v.3, Census Bureau, issued August 1981, 2 volumes, S/N 003-024-03159-7 and 003-024-03160-4, $22.00 each, GPO.

This data is only now available for 1977. In addition to lots of other information, it contains, for each SMSA, a breakdown for the largest SIC industries of the number of establishments, number of employees, value added by manufacture, value of shipments, cost of materials, etc. [7.C.]

Annual Survey of Manufactures, 1981, Statistics for Industry Groups and Industries (Including Supplemental Labor Costs), C3.24/9:M81(AS)-1, Census Bureau, issued April 1983, $3.50, DUSD.

This contains the same information as the document above, but only nationwide data is recorded and only for 1980 and 1981.

1977 Census of Manufacturers, Industry Series, Ordnance and Accessories, N.E.C., C3.24/4MC77-I-34E, Census Bureau, issued July 1980, $?, DUSD ?.

Information on SIC industries 3482, 3483, 3484, 3489.

The Current Industrial Reports Series (C3.158) lists the quantity of shipments and value of shipments by 7-digit SIC product code for the last few months, quarters, and/or years. One report in this series is especially useful to us:

▶Shipments to Federal Government Agencies, 1981, C3.158:MA175(81)-1, Census Bureau, issued December 1982, 48 pages, $4.00, DUSD.

This annual report was formerly called Shipments of Defense-Oriented Industries. It lists the total employment, value added, value shipments, and government shipments (broken down by agency) for 92 military-related 4-digit SIC industries. It also has the same information for each SMSA. The 1982 edition includes the information in Manufacturing Activity in Government Establishments listed below. [1.D., 5 Intro, 5.A., 5.B., 5.C., Figures 5.1 and 5.3]

The other reports in the series are not all that useful, but can give you an idea of the kinds of things produced. Some that might interest you are:

Selected Instruments and Related Products, 1980, C3.158:MA38B(80)-1, Census Bureau, issued January 1983, 24 pages, $2.25, DUSD.

Selected Electronics and Associated Products, Including Telephone and Telegraph Apparatus, 1981, C3.158:MA36N(81)-1, Census Bureau, 36 pages, $2.75, DUSD.

Backlog of Orders for Aerospace Companies, Annual Summary, 1981, C3.158:MQ-37D(81)-5, Census Bureau, issued December 1982, 12 pages, $1.50, DUSD.

Complete Aircraft and Aircraft Engines, Annual Summary for 1982, C3.158:M37G(82)-13, Census Bureau, issued July 1983, 16 pages, $1.50, DUSD.

Government-Owned Facilities

Manufacturing Activity in Government Establishments, 1982, C3.24/12:MC82-S-2, Census Bureau, issued August 1983, S/N 003-024-05625-9, 32 pages, $3.75, GPO.
     For Government-Owned Government-Operated (GOGO) facilities nationwide this report shows the number of employees, costs, value of shipments, and value added by 3-digit SIC industry and by SMSA. It also lists the cost of fuel and electricity used by these facilities by 3-digit SIC industry and by SMSA. [4.F., 5.A.]

U.S. Army Industrial Reserve Plant/Maintenance Facilities Report, Department of the Army, January 1980.
     CEP has a copy of this report. It lists good information on the operator of Army GOCOs, its land area, and the weapons manufactured. There are similar books for the Navy and probably the Air Force too. [4.F.]

Imports and Exports

United States Exports, Domestic Merchandise, SIC-Based Products by World Areas, 1981, FT 610, C3.164:610/981, Foreign Trade Division, Census Bureau, S/N 003-024-04112-0, issued April 1982 ?, $11.00, GPO.
     This lists the amount of shipments of products, listed by 5-digit SIC product codes, to each country in the world. Unfortunately, military products are only reported for the world as a whole.

U.S. Commodity Exports and Imports as Related to Output 1977 and 1976, C3.229:17, Census Bureau, issued August 1982, 350 pages, $8.00, DUSD.
     Information on the quantity and value of imports and exports listed by 5-digit SIC product code.

Input-Output Models of the Economy

Defense Economic Impact Modeling System: A New Concept in Economic Forecasting for Defense Expenditures, 20 pages, free, from Office of the Under Secretary of Defense for Research and Engineering, Defense Industrial Resources Support Office (DIRSO), Two Skyline Place, Suite 1406, 5203 Leesburg Pike, Falls Church, Virginia 22041, (202) 756-2310.
     This report describes the DEIMS and explains the type of data output you can obtain from DIRSO. [5.C., Figures 5.4 and 5.5]

1983 U.S. Industrial Outlook for 250 Industries with Projections for 1987, C62.17:983, Bureau of Industrial Economics, issued January 1983, S/N 003-008-00188-2, $11.00, GPO.
     Mostly this report contains a listing of the number of units sold and their value for 250 industries with a description of the current status of the industry and

projections for the future. This 1983 issue, however, contains an article in the preface called "Defense Spending: A Growth Market for Industry" by David Henry which lists the defense share of output in 1979, 1982, and projections for 1987 of 58 4-digit SIC industries. [5.C.]

Sectoral Implications of Defense Expenditures, Bureau of Industrial Economics, issued August 1982, 20 pages, free, BIE.
 This is a background paper describing the methodology and results of a study on the input/output flow of military production in the economy. This model is similar to the DEIMS, but covers fewer industrial sectors. Some of the results of this model are also described in the report above. [5.C.]

Input/Output Structure of the United States Economy, 1972, C56.109/a:In 7/972, Bureau of Economic Analysis, issued 1979, 72 pages, free, BEA.
 A reprint of the articles in Survey of Current Business, C59.11, February 1979 and April 1979.
 An explanation and the results of the summary (85-industry groups) input-output model of the economy. It also lists other publications describing the 400-industry I-O model. [5.C.]

The Aerospace Industry

NASA Annual Procurement Report, FY 1982, NAS1.30:982-2, issued 1983, NASA, 52 pages, free from NASA, Office of Procurement (Code HM-1), Washington, DC 20546
Presents data on all contract awards over $10,000 including the name, place, and amount of awards to the top 100 business firms and the top 100 educational and nonprofit institutions. Also contains summary data on the NASA budget. [2.F.]

"Analysis of NASA's FY 1983 Budget Request for Research and Development to Determine the Amount that Supports DoD's Programs," MASAD-82-33, General Accounting Office, issued April 26, 1982, GAO, free.
 This report shows that 20.5% of NASA's R&D budget is for military work. [2.F.]

Aerospace Facts and Figures, by the Aerospace Industries Association of America, Inc., 1725 DeSales Street, NW, Washington, DC 20036, $9.95.
 This report includes a listing of the 60 largest NASA contractors and the total amount of their contract awards as well as other general information on the aerospace industry. Some of this is taken from the NASA Annual Procurement Report. [2.F.]

Space and Aeronautics Activities in FY 1984, DoD, $?, from Naval Publications and Forms Center (NFPC), 5801 Tabor Avenue, Philadelphia, PA 19120, (215) 697-3321.

Reports on Particular Companies

 Many of the Resource Centers have prepared reports on individual companies. See the Resource Center section for more on this.

Statistical References on Employment

County Business Patterns: Employment and Payrolls, Number and Employment Size of Establishments by Detailed Industry, California, 1981, C3.204:81-6, Census Bureau, issued May 1983, S/N 003-024-04953-8, $6.00 for California, GPO.
 A copy of this report is available for each state and the entire United States for each year. The -6 in the call number stands for California (the fifth state alphabetically -- The U.S. as a whole is -1). Cost, stock number, and issue date varies from state to state.

This report lists the number of employees, annual payroll and number of establishments in each size class for 4-digit SIC industries for each county in the state and the state as a whole. [5.B., 5.C., Figures 5.2 and 5.4, 7.C.]

Labor Force Statistics Derived form the Current Population Survey: A Databook, Volume 1, L2.3:2096/v.1, Bureau of Labor Statistics, issued September 1982, S/N 029-001-02721-4, 805 pages, $14.00, GPO.
Besides lots of other information, this report contains nationwide data on the number of people employed in each detailed occupation and 4-digit SIC industry and median salaries of wage and salary workers. Not all that useful.

Employment and Earnings, L2.41/2:(volume number), Bureau of Labor Statistics, S/N 029-001-80002-9, about 170 pages, $31/year, GPO.
Monthly report of U.S. employment, unemployment, hours, earnings, and labor turnover and some industry data at the 4-digit SIC level. [7.C.]

Supplement to Employment and Earnings, States and Areas, Data for 1977-81, L2.3:1370-16, Bureau of Labor Statistics, issued in September 1982, S/N 029-001-02723-1, 322 pages, $9.00, GPO.
Lists the number of employees, and salary of production or nonsupervisory workers by the largest 2- and 3-digit SIC industries for each SMSA. Not all that useful.

Occupational Employment in Manufacturing Industries, L2.3:2133, Bureau of Labor Statistics, issued September 1982, S/N 029-001-02724-9, 96 pages, $5.50, GPO.
A listing of the number of people employed nationwide in each job classification by 2-digit SIC industry. Not all that useful.

Handbook of Labor Statistics, L2.3/5:2175, prepared by Bureau of Labor Statistics, issued December 1983, 480 pages, $?, GPO.
Detailed statistics on the nationwide labor force.

Also see the publications of Employment Research Associates.

(California References)

Reference Book for Labor Market Information, Employment Development Department (EDD), Central California Labor Market Information Group, 1525 South Broadway, Room 232, Los Angeles, CA 90015, (213) 744-2514, April 1981, 36 pages, free.
Lists all the documents published by the EDD on the labor market.

Occupational Employment in Manufacturing Industries: San Jose SMSA, 1977, EDD, Employment Data and Research Division, December 1979, 54 pages, free.
For each large 2- or 3-digit SIC industry in Santa Clara County (San Jose SMSA), this lists the estimated employment by job classification. [5.D.]

Annual Planning Information: San Jose SMSA, 1983-84, EDD Employment Data and Research, Coastal Area Labor Market Information Group, for more information contact Ricka Pirani, 297 W. Hedding, San Jose, CA 95110, (408) 277-1722, May 1983, 105 pages, free.
This document reports the outlook for industry in Santa Clara County and lists job classifications with a good outlook for entry-level employment. It also has a lot of statistical information on race, sex, and ethnic origin by occupation from the 1980 census. [5.D.]

Projections of Employment by Industry and Occupation, 1980-1985, San Jose SMSA, EDD Employment Data and Research, Coastal Area Labor Market Information Group, for more information contact Ricka Pirani, 297 W. Hedding, San Jose, CA 95110, (408) 277-1722, 105 pages, May 1983, free.
This report shows the number of people employed in 1980 and projected for 1985 for 375 occupations by each of 9 major industry divisions. The EDD has this same

information in a computer file for 2-digit SIC codes, which is still not very detailed, but may be of use. This data is available on request. [5.D.]

California Labor Market Bulletin and Statistical Supplement, EDD, Employment Data and Research Division, Economic Analysis Group, 800 Capitol Mall, Sacramento, CA 95814, monthly, free.
>These reports shows monthly employment trends in California by SMSA and 2-digit SIC code.

Other Statistical References

General Statistical References

Statistical Abstract of the United States, 1984, C3.134:984, Census Bureau, issued December 1983, 1,016 pages, paperback $11.00 ?, GPO.
>This is an excellent resource book containing 1,500 tables, each with a reference to the source. Most of the data is for the nation as a whole. It also contains a Guide to Sources which tells you about various publications prepared by the Census Bureau and other agencies. [1.D., 5 Intro, 5.E.]

State and Metropolitan Area Data Book, 1982, A Statistical Abstract Supplement, C3.134/5:982, Census Bureau, issued August 1982, S/N 003-024-04932-5, 701 p., $15.00, GPO.
>Contains summary statistical information for SMSAs and central cities on area, population, households, births and deaths, health, education, welfare, crime, housing, employment, establishments, and income. This book is useful for broad statistical information, but it doesn't have most of the information you would like. Much of that information is available from the detailed census taken every 10 years.

County and City Data Book, 1983, A Statistical Abstract Supplement: Regions, Division, States, Counties, Metropolitan Areas, Cities, C3.134/2:C 83/2/983, Census Bureau, issued November 1983, 966 pages, $21.00 ?, GPO.
>Similar to the above document.

1980 Census of Population and Housing, Summary Characteristics for Governmental Units and Standard Metropolitan Statistical Areas -- California, C3.223/23:980, PHC80-3-6, issued October 1982, 60 pages, $?, GPO.
>Lists population by sex and race, number of households, type of housing, civilian labor force, and number and percent unemployed people for the state, SMSAs, counties, and cities. This is the detailed data derived from the major census taken every 10 years. [7.C.]

Also see the other documents reporting the results of the 1980 Census on age, sex, etc. of the workforce.

Federal Procurement Data System Standard Report, quarterly, issued about 5 months after the quarter ends, Office of Management and Budget (OMB), 140 pages, free from Federal Procurement Data Center, 4040 N. Fairfax Drive, Suite 900, Arlington, VA 22003, (703) 235-1326.
>This report lists the total amount of procurement awards (contract actions) for each of 60 Federal government agencies (including the DoD, DoE, NASA, etc.). Currently the DoD represents about 65% of the total awards. For each quarter this report lists the Top 100 Federal Contractors, the total amounts of R&D and supplies and equipment by category, and the total amount going to each state. The information is available for individual counties and in other formats through the FPDS system. [2.H.]

Geographic Distribution of Federal Funds in California: A Report of the Federal Government's Impact by State, County, and Large City, Fiscal Year 1980, CSA1.10:C12/980, Community Services Agency, issued May 1981, NTIS S/N FIXS-80-05, $6.50, NTIS.

> This report is available for each state and a summary for the U.S. The NTIS S/N is listed for California.
> This report lists by county and large city all the federal funds spent by each agency and program within that agency. This report is very useful, but was unfortunately discontinued when the Reagan administration came into office and so 1980 is the last available issue. [2.G., Figure 2.12, 6.B.]

California Statistical Abstract, 1983, Department of Finance, Population Research Unit, 1025 P Street, Room 325, Sacramento, CA 95814, (916) 322-4651, 230 pages, $5.00.

> Similar to the U.S. Statistical Abstract, this document has numerous tables concerning California. [7.C.]

State of the State, American Federation of State, County, and Municipal Employees (AFSCME), 1625 L Street, NW, Washington, DC 20036, (202) 429-1000, January 1984, about 175 pages, free.

> This report lists the cuts in Federal aid grants to state and local governments for the last 3 years. For each state and for the nation it reports the amount of cuts for 172 individual Federal aid programs grouped into 39 categories (social services mostly). These 172 programs account for 90% of all Federal aid to state and local governments.

Facts and Figures on Government Finance, Tax Foundation, Inc., One Thomas Circle, NW, Washington, DC 20005, 365 pages, $20 + $1 postage.

> This publication contains 283 tables of information on government taxation, expenditures, and debt on the federal, state, and local level. A good reference, but not particularly useful for our purposes. [6.B.]

Classifications of Industries and Occupations

Standard Industrial Classification (SIC) Manual, 1972, PrEx2.6/2 In27/972, S/N 041-001-00066-6, 650 pages, $?, GPO.

> Titles and descriptions of industries at the 4-digit SIC level with a numeric and alphabetic index.

Dictionary of Occupational Titles (DOT), 1977, L37.302.0, U.S. Department of Labor, Employment and Training Administration, S/N 029-013-00079-3, 1,372 pages, $?, GPO.

> A listing of 20,000 occupations by a 9-digit DOT code with a detailed description of the job. The 9-digit code includes three digits identifying an occupational group, three digits describing the worker's functions, and a 3-digit item number. DOT also includes a glossary, alphabetical index of occupational titles, and occupations arranged by industry designation. [9.B.]

Standard Occupational Classification (SOC) Manual, 1980, U.S. Department of Commerce, Office of Federal Statistical Policy and Standards, C1.8/3.0c1/980, 550 pages, $?, GPO.

> A listing of occupations by SOC code and DOT code.

Research Guides

Researching the Military

▶Research Guide to Current Military and Strategic Affairs, by William M. Arkin, Institute for Policy Studies, 1901 Que Street, NW, Washington, DC 20009, (202) 234-9382, 1981, 232 pages, $8.00.

> This book is a guide to sources of information on worldwide military and strategic

affairs. More than 1,000 reference sources and 600 periodicals are given. The book lists research guides, bibliographies, indices, abstracts, publications, almanacs, and factbooks dealing with the following topics and organizations: worldwide military forces and regional power, military expenditures and trade, current events and personalities, international relations; U.S. government organizations, Congressional hearings and committee proceedings, Congressional Agencies such as the General Accounting Office (GAO); Freedom of Information Act and officers; Executive branch activities such as executive orders, reviews of presidential activity; CIA activities, State Department foreign policy and posture; Defense Department policies, agencies, doctrine, technical information; defense policy and posture, U.S.-Soviet military balance, the defense budget, the military-industrial complex, military personnel; the local impact of military presence and spending; overseas military bases, commitments, and aid; worldwide armed forces and weapons, worldwide defense issues; Soviet and Warsaw Pact issues, events, foreign policy and forces; Western Europe and NATO defense issues; arms control and disarmament, international organizations and law. This book contains an immense amount of information, but it is somewhat difficult to wade through.

▶How to Research Your Local Military Contractor, by Schlessinger, Gaventa, and Merrifield, Highlander Center, 1983, 16 pages, $2.00.

▶Uncovering the Nuclear Industry: A Research Guide, by Eric Segal, Mobilization for Survival, 1984, 8 pages, $2.

"How to Research Your Local War Industry," NARMIC, February 1983, 4 pages, $0.50.

"How to Read Defense Contract Listings," 10 pages, free, NARMIC.

NACLA Research Methodology Guide, $1.50 + $0.50 postage and handling, from North American Congress on Latin America, 151 West 19th Street, 9th Floor, New York, NY 10011, (212) 989-8890.

 This booklet has a comprehensive section on how to do research on the military and police, describing government, industry, business, and other sources, often listing several ways to get a given kind of information. Somewhat out of date, but a good general guide.

 The DoD collects all kinds of data for internal use which they are reluctant to give out for fear you will take it and sell it to other people or they will be forced to use their limited resources distributing it. However, they will gladly give the information to state government agencies or Congresspeople who have a need for it in their work. You can try asking for it directly, but if that fails, try enlisting the help of these people.

 It would be nice if the government collected good information on local military installations and industry. Ask your Congressmember to have the government prepare and disseminate this information.

Researching Corporations [4.E.]

Open the Books: How to Research a Corporation, the Midwest Academy, 600 W. Fullerton, Chicago, IL 60614.

Manual of Corporate Investigation, Food and Beverage Trades Department, AFL-CIO, 815 16th Street, NW, Washington, DC 20006.

How to Find Information about Companies, Washington Researchers, 181 15th Street, NW, Washington, DC 20006, $75.

Business Information Sources, by Lorna Daniels. [4.E.]

Doing Other Research

The Reporter's Handbook: An Investigator's Guide to Documents and Techniques, by John Ullman and Steve Honeyman, St. Martin's Press, 1983.
> A terrific new book that helps readers learn how to think as investigators and analysts. It has a solid corporate research section and contains much, much more that can be tailored to military-industrial complex research for beginners.

The Court Index and Other Treasure Troves, by Will Collette, The Institute/TRAIN, 413 8th Street, SE, Washington, DC 20003.

Research for Action: A Guidebook to Public Records Investigation for Community Activists, by Don Villarejo, California Institute for Rural Studies, P.O. Box 530, Davis, CA 95616, 112 pages, $7.50.

Other General Publications

Budget of the United States Government, FY 1985, PrEx2.8:985, Office of Management and Budget, February 1984, S/N 041-001-00270-7, 650 pages, $12, GPO.
Appendix, S/N 041-001-00271-5, $19, GPO.
> This is a good source of information on the current year's total budget amounts by large program and by major department as well as the President's proposed budget for the next fiscal year.

Catalog of Federal Domestic Assistance, PrEx2.20:982-1, Office of Management and Budget (OMB), issued June 1982, S/N 041-001-81001-3, about 1,000 pages for each edition, $30/year, GPO.
> Lists, indexes, and explains in detail all the federal programs which award money to individuals, companies, and state and local governments. [6.B.]

Almanac of California Government & Politics 1983-84, May 1983, 194 pages, $5.25 (includes tax), California Journal, 1714 Capitol Avenue, Sacramento, CA 95814.

SEVERAL USEFUL TRADE MAGAZINES

Aviation Week and Space Technology (AW&ST)
McGraw Hill Building
1221 Avenue of the Americas
New York, NY 10020
(212) 997-1221

Subscriptions to:

P.O. Box 432
Hightstown, NJ 08520

AW&ST is published weekly and has 130,000 paid subscribers. It costs $45.00/year for qualified subscribers (management, engineers, and scientists in aviation, aerospace, military, etc.) and $58.00 for nonqualified. The ads in AW&ST are for just about every kind of electronic and aerospace product imaginable, often described in amazingly militaristic terms. Each issue has an advertiser's index at the end, a good place to look for the products of obscure subcontractors.

Each March, AW&ST publishes an Aerospace Forecast & Inventory Issue. Articles cover the outlook for various aerospace systems. Much of the issue is devoted to specification charts for Soviet, United States, and international commercial and military products in the categories of aircraft, helicopters, hovercraft, remotely piloted vehicles (RPVs) and drones, spacecraft, launch vehicles, research rockets, missiles, gas turbines, and reciprocating engines. Each chart lists the primary mission, name, model designation, manufacturer, popular name, dimensions, performance, and other remarks.

Every December AW&ST publishes a Marketing Directory Issue. In 1982 it included 6,500 companies in 2,000 product categories. Most of the listings are of small companies selling off-the-shelf military specification (or not) products to larger contractors. Listed for each company is its name, address, phone number, and marketing or sales representative.

Every April or May AW&ST publishes the Department of Defense List of the Top 100 Contractors for the fiscal year. It lists the rank, company name and all the company's subsidiaries, the amount of prime military contracts over $25,000 for the company and each subsidiary, and the percentage of the U.S. total that amount represents. This is essentially the same information as listed in the DoD report 100 Companies Receiving the Largest Dollar Volume of Prime Contract Awards, (P01).

[also see Sections 2.E., 3.A., 3.B., 3.D., 4.A., and 4.B.]

Defense Electronics
EW Communications, Inc.
1170 East Meadow Drive
Palo Alto, CA 94303
(415) 494-2800

Every February, Defense Electronics publishes a Marketing Directory and Buyers' Guide. The marketing directory lists companies alphabetically, giving their main office, address, and product line. Some companies list their separate divisions.

In the September 1983 issue of <u>Defense Electronics</u> (page 48) is a list of the top 60 defense electronics contractors, their sales of defense electronics (hardware only), total sales, and defense electronics as a percent of total sales. The accompanying article reports that defense electronics sales were $32 billion in 1982 with annual increases of 14.1% over the next 5 years (compared to about 7 percent for the overall military budget. We discovered that a surprising 29.5% of the sales of SRI International (formerly Stanford Research Institute) is for defense electronics. [3.C.]

Other similar publications to look for are <u>Military Electronics</u>, <u>Journal of Electronic Defense</u>, and <u>Electronic News</u>. [2.E., 3.B]

Sales and Marketing Management

<u>Sales and Marketing Management</u> magazine is aimed at salespeople. Besides the articles on "how to sell products" and "new products to sell," S&MM tries to identify potential sales markets. The DoD, prime military contractors, and military sub-contractors are all potential buyers of materials and services and hence are markets. So are all the people who work for these companies.

Every six months, <u>Sales and Marketing Management</u> publishes their "U.S. Metropolitan Area Projections." This basically tells how rich various areas of the country are and how likely the people there are to buy things. But it also provides information similar to Census Bureau data on such things as the number of Blacks and total retail sales of six different types of products. It also lists by SMSA the population, the number of households, total "disposable personal income," and total retail sales. The last such issue was October 31, 1983 with data for calendar year 1982.

Each year <u>Sales and Marketing Management</u> also publishes the results of a survey of Industrial and Commercial Buying Power done by Economic Information Systems (EIS). The information is for the previous calendar year (scooping the Census Bureau's Census of Manufactures by several years). This issue lists and ranks in order all the counties with 1,000 or more employees for each 4-digit SIC detailed industry. For each industry and county is listed the number of establishments, the number of large establishments (100 or more employees), total employment, total shipments, the percent of U.S. output that county produces, and the percent of the county's output that the large establishments produce. At the end of the listings is the U.S. total for that industry.

Also in this issue (the last was April 25, 1983) is a list of the Top 50 Counties in Manufacturing Activity (representing about one third of the total shipments) and the 50 Biggest Manufacturing Industries (producing about half the total shipments). Overall, there is a lot of information easily accessible in any good library.

[also see Sections 4.A., 5.B., and 7.C.]

<u>Wall Street Journal</u> [2.E., 3.B., 4.E.]

Resource Centers

There are several peace and social action organizations that can help you with your research. Most have limited staff time and may require you to pay for their services, but they are invaluable resources.

Center for Economic Conversion (CEC)
formerly the Mid-Peninsula Conversion Project (MPCP)
222C View Street
Mountain View, Calif 94041
(415) 968-8798
Joel Yudken, Michael Closson, Tim Stroshane, Randy Schutt

CEC was founded in 1975 to promote the conversion of military industry in Santa Clara Valley (Silicon Valley) to socially useful production. CEC has much expertise in analyzing military contractors (especially in the electronics industry) and working with coalitions of the religious community, unions, sympathetic technical people, and peace organizations. They can provide help in conversion efforts as well as in researching military contractors.

CEC has been working with the United Auto Workers and the California State Office of Business and Industrial Development to develop a plan for alternative production at the McDonnell Douglas Corporation (MDC) plant in Long Beach, California. [9.C.]

CEC publishes the Plowshare Press ("beating their swords into plowshares") bi-monthly ($20/year; back issues $0.25 each). This 8-page newspaper has articles on conversion efforts in Northern California and the rest of the country and it now also includes SANE's Conversion Planner. [10.A.]

The Freeze Economy, 1983, edited by Dave McFadden and Jim Wake for the Nuclear Weapons Freeze Campaign, 48 pages, $2.50.
> This is a short, but excellent guide to working on the Bi-Lateral Nuclear Weapons Freeze from an economic perspective. It includes a discussion of the economic and unemployment effects of a nuclear weapons freeze, a guide to organizing on these issues, and an extensive list of resources. It has a list of the principal contractors for each of the weapons affected by a Freeze. [2.F., 5.C., 8.C.]

Creating Solar Jobs: Options for Military Workers and Communities, by DeGrasse, Bernstein, McFadden, Schutt, Shiras, and Street, November 1978, 72 pages, $4.00.
> This report discusses production of solar equipment as an alternative to military production and evaluates the ease with which workers at Lockheed Missiles and Space could convert to solar equipment production. It also discusses the need for alternative energy development, military conversion, and favorable government

programs for financing new industry and the peril of large corporate takeover of the emerging solar energy business. [9.B., Figure 9.1]

Pacific Studies Center
222B View Street
Mountain View, CA 94041
(415) 969-1545
Lenny Siegel

     PSC, the Center for Economic Conversion's neighbor/sister organization, maintains a library of information on high-technology electronics, business in the Santa Clara Valley (Silicon Valley), the political economy of Asia and the Pacific, and U.S. foreign and military policy. Founded in 1969, PSC has 140 file drawers of clippings from newspapers, trade journals, and alternative magazines pertaining to these areas. PSC also has a good collection of Congressional Armed Services and Appropriations Committees Hearings since 1970.

     Use of the library is free (donations are gladly welcomed) and it is open to the public from 10-6 weekdays. PSC researchers will search through their files and copy pertinent materials for you for $7.50/hour and up (sliding scale), plus the cost of copying and postage.

Data Center
464 19th Street
Oakland, CA 94612
(415) 835-4692
Tom Fenton

     The Data Center in downtown Oakland is an excellent resource for research on companies. The center, associated with Information Services on Latin America (ISLA), was set up as a library and research service for activists, journalists, and students. They have a very comprehensive set of 300 file drawers of clippings on over 6,000 companies, as well as on industries, labor, people-in-the-news, countries, and organizations extending back 15 years. The clippings are taken from 400 business, news, and alternative magazines including 12 major newspapers (New York Times, Washington Post, Los Angeles Times, Wall Street Journal, San Francisco Chronicle, Oakland Tribune, San Jose Mercury, Miami Herald, Christian Science Monitor, Financial Times of London, Journal of Commerce, and the Manchester Guardian/Le Monde (weekly)). They also have a historical collection, much of it donated by other organizations which folded. Their military files include military expert Michael Klare's personal files extending back 10 years. They have a staff of 12 as well as many volunteers. They are open from 1-5 Monday through Thursday and late on Wednesdays to 9 PM.

     For a $20 individual membership or a day-use donation you can look through any of these files and other library resources. For those who cannot come to Oakland, the staff will go through the files and copy pertinent articles for you at a cost of about $15-25/hour depending on your resources. For $50-100 you can get a good overview of materials on a particular company or topic. A complete Corporate Profile containing news clippings on a corporation's history, geographic operations, finances, and relations with labor, consumers, and government cost $350 (less for activist groups). The Data Center also serves as a clipping service, copying articles on a particular topic for you as they come in. The Center tries to accommodate your information needs (and financial constraints) so call them to discuss what they have and for estimates of the time and cost to get it to you. [9.B.]

NARMIC (National Action/Research on the Military Industrial Complex)
1501 Cherry Street
Philadelphia, Pennsylvania 19102
(215) 241-7175
Tom Conrad

NARMIC, a project of the American Friends Service Committee (AFSC), was established in 1969 to provide action-oriented research on the U.S. military establishment to social change organizations. NARMIC has extensive resources on all aspects of the military industrial complex including defense industry publications, government reports, and files on more than 600 companies. They have various factsheets on human rights and disarmament issues and 6 maps comprising "The Military Industrial Atlas of the United States."

NARMIC can provide information, including dollar amount and purpose, on DoD contracts by company or county. They can also provide specific detailed information on missiles, aircraft, research & development, army sales, ordnance, electronics/communications, and the companies that work on these products.

NARMIC also has the Technical Abstract Bulletin (TAB) listing of classified military documents published by DTIC through 1982 (see Section 3.E.). And they have experience making requests under the Freedom of Information Act (FOIA) and can advise and consult with you on this process.

"How to Research Your Local War Industry," 4 pages, $0.50, February 1983. [3.A.]

"How to Read Defense Contract Listings," 10 pages.
> This lists the main DoD Purchasing Agencies and lists all the Federal Supply Classification (FSC) codes and what they mean. [3.C.]

Council on Economic Priorities (CEP)
84 Fifth Avenue
New York, NY 10011
(212) 691-8550
Bill Hartung

The Economic Consequences of a Nuclear Weapons Freeze, by William Hartung, May 1984, 120 pages, $?.
> This book examines the way the national economy would be affected by the immediate implementation of a bi-lateral freeze on the testing, production, and deployment of nuclear weapons. The author estimates the number of defense jobs lost (350,000), the amount of military expenditures saved ($95 billion over 5 years), the skills level of displaced workers (predominantly white-collar and skilled tradespeople), the number of new jobs created by a Freeze (more than 350,000), the potential uses of the military money saved (social programs, public works, alternative energy, etc.), and the potential benefit to the economy of the diversion of talented labor into the civilian sector. Examples of preparatory conversion planning are presented, such as the Defense Economic Adjustment Act before Congress, Connecticut's Defense Readjustment Act of 1980, the Washington State Proposal, the International Association of Machinists' Rebuilding America Act, the activities of the Center for Economic Conversion in Silicon Valley, and others. While the book's emphasis is more national than local, the methods and assumptions used by the author to make his estimates are clearly explained and sources of relevant information are given. [2.F., 8.C., 9 Intro]

Military Expansion, Economic Decline, by Robert W. DeGrasse, Jr., 1983, 237 pages, $11.95 + $2.85 postage ?.
> This book studies the effect of military spending on economic growth by comparing economic statistics from 17 non-communist industrial nations during the post World War II period. The first part of the book finds that defense spending is the largest federal mechanism for buying durable goods. It distributes money unequally to the

various regions of the country, and is a relatively poor way of creating jobs, particularly blue-collar jobs. The statistical comparisons show that nations with high military spending have low investment and productivity growth. On the other hand, labor costs, demographics, and high non-military governmental spending did not strongly affect the productivity and growth of the 17 nations. The military, through direct employment and R&D funding, diverts substantial technologically talented workers away from work beneficial to the civilian economy. Civilian "spin-offs" from military development are uncommon, and military funding policies often fail to stimulate desired technological advances. The large federal budget deficits caused by the Reagan arms buildup are likely either to boost the inflation rate or interest rates, depending on federal monetary policy. In addition, diversion of industrial facilities and skilled workers to defense industries will cause production bottlenecks and manpower shortages, further depressing the economy.

The book is clear and well-written. The methods used to obtain the results are explained well, with numerous footnotes, graphs, and references given. Although concerned with the entire U.S. economy, the methodology can probably be applied to more local studies. [5.F.]

The Iron Triangle: The Politics of Defense Contracting, by Gordon Adams, 1981, 485 pages, $?.

This book studies the political power of the defense industry, with emphasis on the activities of eight major defense contractors: Boeing, General Dynamics, Grumman, McDonnell Douglas, Northrop, Rockwell International, and United Technologies, during the 1970-1979 period. Information is given about each company's Washington, D.C. lobbying activities, political action committees, contributions to key legislators, and efforts to mount grass-roots campaigns on behalf of their defense contracts. The book shows that the companies have access to Department of Defense (DoD) and NASA policy-making through the movement of personnel between government and public employment. All eight companies help formulate defense projects through their participation on DoD and NASA advisory committees. The companies maintain close relationships with each other and with financial institutions through interlocking boards of directors.

Although the book provides a wealth of information on the 8 companies, it devotes only four pages to describing its research methods and general sources. But numerous footnotes provide extensive sources of information for particular details, and the book has 13 pages of bibliography. Of specific interest might be the lists of each company's principal defense/space contracting operations, giving locations of plants and their products. [Appendix 2]

Misguided Expenditure, by David Gold, Chistopher Paine, and Gail Shields, 1981, 220 pages, $?.
An excellent report on the MX missile and its contractors.

"Top 100 Military Contractors," CEP Newsletter, annually.
Published each year, this lists the top 100 military contractors, their rank, prime contract amount, and percent of sales represented by military contracts for the last three years. [4.A., 10.A.]

Institute on the Military and the Economy
225 Lafayette Street, Room 205
New York, NY 10012
(212) 219-0694
David Gold, Christine D'Onofrio

The Institute is a nonprofit research, education, and consulting organization whose work focuses on the economic impacts of military spending and military policy. It conducts studies for other organizations, on such topics as the likely economic impacts of large cuts in military spending and the impact of the Reagan buildup on U.S. manufacturing industries, and conducts its own research, on the economics of basing cruise missiles in New York Harbor and the impact of Reagan administration military and budget policies on women. A current Institute focus is on industrial policy and peace conversion. Institute staff members have written articles for newspapers, magazines, and books in addition to the Institute's own Occasional Papers and Fact Sheets.

Committee for a Sane Nuclear Policy (SANE)
Ben Spock Center for Peace
711 G Street, S.E.
Washington, DC 20003
(202) 546-7100
Ed Glennon

SANE publishes resources on the military budget and nuclear weapons and sends legislative alerts and background information to its grassroots lobbying network (which you can join). SANE can also provide updates on the status of conversion legislation in Congress.

Guide to the Military Budget, Fiscal Year 1985, 8 pages, $0.25 each or 100 for $15.
This little gem briefly summarizes the military budget; explains the flawed "Soviet threat" rationale for increased spending and poses legitimate national security alternatives; describes the major weapon programs, the budget request for each one in FY 1985, and the real purposes they serve; and concludes with a section on how to reduce military spending. [3.D.]

Highlander Research and Education Center
Rte. 3, Box 370
New Market, TN 37820
(615) 933-3443
Tom Schlesinger

Founded in 1932, Highlander has worked with the Southern labor, civil rights, and Appalachian movements. It has published research in environmental, occupational health, and land use issues.

The Center recently completed the two publications listed below. They have expertise and files of information on the military contractors of the Appalachian region. Because of their work on the Oak Ridge National Lab, they have great knowledge of government-owned contractor-operated (GOCO) facilities.

Our Own Worst Enemy: The Impact of Military Production on the Upper South, by Tom Schlesinger, 1983, 265 pages, $10.00 + postage.
This book is a fascinating and highly readable account of the pervasive influence of military spending on the economies of 8 states of the Upper South, with emphasis on Tennessee. The book demonstrates how national security policy decisions in peace and war times have affected the industrial growth of the area and the activities of the Tennessee Valley Authority (TVA), determined which mines operated and the style of mining, affected workers' health and safety and their participation in unions, and affected small businesses in "company towns" such as Oak Ridge, Tennessee.

How to Research Your Local Military Contractor, by Schlesinger, Gaventa, and Merrifield, 1983, 16 pages, $2.00.
An excellent guide showing how to determine the commodity purchased with each contract, its destination, price, and other factors. Some information is given on how to research the contractor, including the contractor's health and safety performance, land ownership and usage, tax payments, environmental record, and labor

performance, land ownership and usage, tax payments, environmental record, and labor relations. A brief section describes how to use the Freedom of Information Act to get information. [4.E., 6.B.]

New York Public Interest Research Center (NYPIRC)
9 Murray Street
New York, NY 10007
(212) 349-6460
David Schorr

The disarmament project at NYPIRC has analyzed military production in New York State. Their publication, listed below, is an excellent example of a military dependency study for New York State and includes a short methodology section.

Production for Destruction: Military Spending in New York State, by Tom Webster and Beth Cohen DeGrasse, 1983, 80 pages, $2.50.
    [3.A., Figure 3.2, 4.A., Figure 4.2, 8.C., 10.A.]

Investor Responsibility Research Center, Inc. (IRRC)
1319 F Street, NW, Suite 900
Washington, DC 20004
(202) 833-3727
Kenneth Bertsch, Linda Shaw

The Investor Responsibility Research Center was founded in 1972 as an independent, not-for-profit corporation to conduct research and publish impartial reports on contemporary social and public policy issues and the impact of those issues on major corporations and institutional investors. IRRC's work is financed primarily by annual subscription fees paid by more than 170 investing institutions.

IRRC publishes reports on shareholder resolutions that appear in corporation's proxy statements, some of which concern the company's military contracts. These reports provide background on details of each resolution and each corporation's response, and background and analysis of the issues raised. Although these reports primarily are prepared for IRRC's subscribers, individual copies of recent reports are available at $15 to $25 a copy. Write IRRC for a listing of these reports.

The Nuclear Weapons Industry, by Kenneth A. Bertsch and Linda S. Shaw, 1984, 405 pages, $22.00 for individuals, $45 for corporations and non-profits. .
    This book is an excellent general reference on the nuclear weapons industry, U.S. nuclear policy, nuclear weapons systems, arms control, corporate influence in defense policy, the economics of defense spending and of a nuclear weapons freeze, and the possibilities for conversion conversion of defense industries to non-defense applications. It gives short, well-written, and informative expositions on a wide range of topics relating to the nuclear weapons industry, and it presents the arguments of both pro- and anti-nuclear groups on these topics.

    Though it profiles the 26 largest nuclear-weapons related contractors, it is not specifically written to help the local activist determine the impact of military spending in his or her community. It sporadically tells where the 26 companies perform various types of work and says nothing about companies numbered 27 and higher. However, as a single volume covering much of the material found in The Iron Triangle and The Nuclear Weapons Databook, it is recommended. It covers events up to Summer, 1983.

    The bulk of the book is devoted to profiling the 26 leading corporations participating in the manufacture of nuclear weapons and their delivery systems. The companies profiled are

Allied (Bendix)	General Tire and Rubber	Rockwell
AT&T	(Aerojet General)	Singer
Avco	Honeywell	TRW
Boeing	Litton	Tenneco (Newport News
Dupont	Lockheed	Shipbuilding Co.)
EG&G	Martin Marietta	UNC (formerly United
GTE	McDonnell-Douglas	Nuclear Technologies)
General Dynamics	Monsanto	Union Carbide
General Electric	Northrop	United Technologies
	Raytheon	Westinghouse

For each company, it gives various historical information on sales, the volume of defense business, the company's defense dependence, its defense contract backlog, R&D, proportion of employees and facilities allocated to defense work, the particular weapons systems being produced, the company's PAC and lobbying efforts, its exchange of personnel with the government, its contingency plans in case of defense cuts, and its efforts toward diversification and conversion.

An appendix describes nuclear weapons systems produced by these companies, covering not only the primary delivery systems such as aircraft, missiles, submarines, etc., but also important subsystems such as electronic countermeasure systems, fire control systems, radar, sonar, satellite communications systems, anti-satellite weapons, blue-green lasers, optical trackers, etc. Other parts of the book give brief but highly informative discussions of U.S. strategic policy, arms control efforts, the impact of military spending on the economy, the effect of a weapons Freeze or arms limitation agreement on the economy, and the possibility of conversion. [2.F.]

Interfaith Center on Corporate Responsibility (ICCR)
475 Riverside Drive, Room 566
New York, NY 10115-0050
(212) 870-2293

ICCR, founded in 1971, is an organization of church and religious institutional investors concerned about the social impact of corporations and the application of social criteria to investments. Members currently include representatives of 17 Protestant denominations and more than 200 Roman Catholic communities. ICCR assists its members by facilitating exchange of views and sharing of research and information in an attempt to produce a more effective use of investments to support the social policy and program objectives of the participating agencies; developing common strategies; and conducting research on issues of common concern relating to policies and practices of U.S. corporations. Current issues include: nuclear weapons production, space warfare, South Africa, Latin America, racism and sexism in employment, alternative investment, infant formula, world marketing of drugs, and hazardous wastes. Publication: The Corporate Examiner, $25. Staff is able to provide some assistance to individuals or organizations doing research on corporations.

Mobilization for Survival (MfS)
853 Broadway, Room #2109
New York, NY 10003
(212) 533-0008

MfS is a national, multi-issue coalition of local peace and justice organizations working for nuclear disarmament, non-intervention, safe energy, and social and economic justice. MfS provides resources and organizing assistance on integrating human needs concerns with efforts to oppose nuclear weapons and military intervention abroad.

MfS's Nuclear Free Zone campaign provides an opportunity for groups to challenge local nuclear facilities and institutions, while raising alternative uses of community resources for local needs. In addition, MfS can provide assistance in raising conversion and human needs concerns in nonviolent direct action and other challenges to local weapons facilities.

Toward a Nuclear Free Free Future, 1984, 44 pages, $5.
A comprehensive organizer's guide to designing a local Nuclear Free Zone campaign. This guide includes suggestions for assessing community needs, using community organizing techniques, and working together with human needs and labor organizations, while challenging local resource priorities, production facilities, and investment practices.

Uncovering the Nuclear Industry: A Research Guide, by Eric Segal, 1984, 8 pages, $2.
This guide will help you find out which corporations, research centers, and other institutions hold nuclear contracts in your community. [3.B.]

Jobs with Peace National Network
76 Summer Street
Boston, MA 02110
(617) 338-5783

2460 16th Street, Room B-10
San Francisco, CA 94103
(415) 558-8615

Jobs with Peace (JwP) is a nationwide campaign which advocates a major shift in national priorities -- away from military spending and programs of foreign military intervention, and into the rebuilding of socially productive industries and programs in housing, health and human services, education, and transportation.

Jobs with Peace has many resources for activists trying to get a Jobs with Peace resolution passed in their community or to focus attention on the impact that military spending has on their community.

Towards a Boston Peace Budget, 60 pages, $5.00.
An excellent report detailing the advantages of civilian over military spending and its effects on Boston. The report includes some discussion of methodology and a list of sources of information. This report is an ideal guide for preparing a Peace Budget for your city.

Boston Peace Budget, 16 pages, $5/dozen.
A popularly written and attractively illustrated pamphlet version of the above. [**6.B.** Figure 6.3]

They also have other resources including guidelines on how to prepare a Jobs with Peace Budget, a model 1984 budget, and a labor slide show and labor organizing kit designed to help bring economic conversion issues to union members.

[See also Section 6.B.]

Employment Research Associates
474 Hollister Bldg.
Lansing, MI 48933
(517) 485-7655
Marion Anderson, James Anderson

Converting the Work Force: Where the Jobs Would Be, by Marion Anderson, 1980, 20 pages, $3.00.
A study showing the effect of moving $10 billion out of military procurement and into

fishing vessel construction, professional services, and education. This analysis is based on an input-output model of the economy. [Figure 9.1]

The Empty Porkbarrel: Unemployment and the Pentagon Budget, 1982 Edition, by Marion Anderson, 16 pages, $2.00.
    This study shows that increased military spending results in a net loss of jobs in the country. It calculates the number of jobs lost by state and major sector of the economy.

Bankrupting America: The Tax Burden and Expenditures of the Pentagon by Congressional District, by James Anderson, 1982, 16 pages, $2.00. [6.B., Figure 6.1]

Bankrupting American Cities, by James Anderson, 1982, 12 pages, $2.00. [6.B., Figure 6.2]

The Price of the Pentagon: The Industrial and Commercial Impact of the 1981 Military Budget, 1982, 16 pages, $2.00.

Neither Jobs Nor Security: Women's Unemployment and the Pentagon Budget, by Marion Anderson, 1982, 20 pages, $2.00

The Impact of Military Spending on the Machinists Union, by Marion Anderson, 20 pages, $2.00.

Economic Conversion Task Force of the Connecticut Freeze Campaign
11 Rings End Road
Darien, CT 06820
(203) 655-0114, 655-1456
Reverend Kevin Bean

    This group focuses on the economic aspects of the arms race in Connecticut, the most defense-dependent state. They have investigated weapons systems contracts in the State and conversion at the State level. They have directed their work, including outreach to labor, on General Dynamics/Electric Boat Division, United Technologies and subsidiaries, and smaller firms.

Projected Impact of a Freeze on Connecticut, by Kevin Bean, Kevin Cassidy, and Marta Daniels, April 5, 1983, 18 pages, free ?.
    A detailed analysis of the impact a Freeze would have on Connecticut DoD contracts by weapon system. This is an excellent guide to preparing such a report for your area. [3.A., 10.A.]

Jobs, Security, and Arms in Connecticut: A Study of the Impact of Military Spending on the State, by Marta Daniels, January 1980, 64 pages, $2.50.
    A very detailed discussion and analysis of the arms industry in Connecticut, including foreign military sales and economic conversion. This is an excellent guide for preparing this kind of detailed report for your area.

Cruise Missile Conversion Project (CMCP)
730 Bathurst St.
Toronto, Ontario M5S 2R4
CANADA
(416) 532-6720
Tom Joyce

    CMCP was organized in early 1980 to stop the production of the Cruise missile inertial navigational system at Litton Systems Ltd. (Canada) and to promote conversion. The group has extensive files on the economic effects of a military economy and the conversion process. It has active experience in attempting to build a coalition in support of conversion among the community, trade unions, the churches, and Litton workers and management. CMCP tries, particularly, to relate these questions to the Canadian economic context and the increasing military production there.

CMCP publishes a Jobs with Peace newsletter geared mainly toward and distributed to organized labor. It has articles on the effects of militarism on the economy, reports on conversion efforts worldwide, and reports on peace initiatives in the union movement in Canada. CMCP is also a resource base on Litton Industries and has published a booklet on this corporation: Arms Maker, Union Buster.

Bay State Center for Economic Conversion (BSCforEC)
639 Massachusetts Avenue, Room 316
Cambridge, MA 02139
(617) 497-0605
Lessie Klein, Susan Allein, Louise Bruyn

BSCforEC has prepared a detailed and very excellent questionnaire for recording important information about a company. They can also send you a very useful packet of information ($3) with one page on each of these topics:

-- Suggested Sources of Information to Answer the Questionnaire
-- How to Use Corporate Reference Guides
-- Suggestions for Approaching Unions
-- Sample FOIA Request for Contracts
-- List of Awarding Agencies
-- Partial List of Items Affected by a Nuclear Weapons Freeze

[See also Section 4.A.]

Mendocino County Jobs With Peace Coalition
P.O. Box 395
Navarro, CA 95463
(707) 895-2043 or 895-3241,

Down the Federal Drain: The Impact of Military Spending on Mendocino County, by Don Lipmanson and David Colfax, 1983, 8 pages, $2.00.

[**6.B.**, Figure 6.4]

Pacific Northwest Research Center (PNWRC)
University Station
Box 3708
Eugene, Oregon 97403
Stephen Johnson

Pacific Northwest Research Center was formed in 1971 to research and distribute information on political, military, economic, environmental, and social issues affecting the Pacific Northwest. They maintain a library on these issues which includes files on all the military contractors in the Northwest and on a variety of military topics. They publish a newsletter called Northwest Bulletin.

Boeing Arms the Corporate Empire, December 1974.

Rockwell International... Where Business Gets Down to the Science of War, October 1975.

Zirconium Hazards and Nuclear Profits: A Report on Teledyne Wah Chang Albany, 1979.

Defense Budget Project
Center on Budget and Policy Priorities
236 Massachusetts Avenue, NE, Suite 305
Washington, DC 20002
(202) 544-0591
Gordon Adams

Center for Defense Information (CDI)
303 Capitol Gallery West
600 Maryland Avenue, SW
Washington, DC 20024
(202) 484-9490

CDI publishes the Defense Monitor, a monthly analysis of military issues.

Corporate Data Exchange
Room 707
198 Broadway
New York, NY 10038

[9.B.]

New Mexico Peace Conversion Project
3211 Silver, SE
Albuquerque, NM 87106
(505) 268-9557
Dorie Bunting

Sandia Labs: A Report, 20 pages, May 1983, free ?.
A good summary of the work performed at this nuclear weapons lab and the impact it has on the local economy. It has a list of research sources used.

Reaganomics, the Military, & New Mexico, 16 pages, January 1983, free ?.
Discusses the impact of increased military spending and cutbacks in other Federal spending in New Mexico.

Snake River Alliance
P.O. Box 1731
Boise, ID 83701
(208) 344-9161

Focuses on the DoE's Idaho National Engineering Laboratory (INEL) that reprocesses used fuel rods from government nuclear reactors.

AFSC's Rocky Flats Disarmament/Conversion Project
1660 Lafayette Street
Denver, CO 80218
(303) 832-4508

Focuses on the DoE's Rocky Flats Nuclear Weapons Plant that manufacturers the plutonium triggers for all U.S. nuclear weapons.

South Shore Conversion Committee
c/o Quincy Community Action Organization
1495 Hancock St. (Rear)
4th Floor
Quincy, MA 02169

[Figure 9.1]

St. Louis Economic Conversion Project
438 North Skinker Blvd.
St. Louis, MO 63130
(314) 721-3421
Mary Ann McGivern

[9.B., Figure 9.2]

Oak Ridge Peace Conversion Group
Knoxville United Ministries
1538 Highland Avenue
Knoxville, TN 37916

Washington State Conversion Project
225 North 70th
Seattle, Washington 98103
(206) 784-8436

Santa Barbara Peace Resource Center
331 North Milpas Street #F
Santa Barbara, CA 93103
(805) 965-8583
Greg Cross

List of Abbreviations

Peace and Social Action Organizations

AFSC   American Friends Service Committee (Quaker service organization)
BSCforEC   Bay State Center for Economic Conversion
CEC   Center for Economic Conversion (formerly the Mid-Peninsula Conversion Project)
CEP   Center for Economic Priorities
IRRC   Investor Responsibility Research Center
JwP   Jobs with Peace
MfS   Mobilization for Survival
MPCP   Mid-Peninsula Conversion Project (now CEC)
NARMIC   National Action/Research on the Military Industrial Complex
NYPIRC   New York Public Interest Research Center
PSC   Pacific Studies Center

Government Organizations

DoD   Department of Defense
DoE   Department of Energy
DSA   Defense Supply Agency
DTIC   Defense Technical Information Center
GPO   Government Printing Office
NASA   National Aeronautics and Space Administration
NSA   National Security Agency
NTIS   National Technical Information Service
USA   U.S. Army
USAF   U.S. Air Force
USN   U.S. Navy

Also see the list of agencies at the beginning of the References section.

Other Organizations

DMS   Defense Marketing Service
GDP   Government Data Publications

Abbreviations Frequently Used in Contract Descriptions

AAP   Army Ammunition Plant
ACFT   Aircraft
ADP   Automatic Data Processing (computers)
ADV   Advanced

AFB	Air Force Base
AI	Artificial Intelligence (smart computers)
AMT	Amount
AN	Code for electronic equipment (see Figure 3.8)
AP	Armor Piercing
APERS	Anti-personnel
APPL	Applicable or Applied
ASSY	Assembly
AT	Anti-tank
AUTO	Automotive
BALL MSL	Ballistic Missile (goes into outer space and returns to Earth)
BD	Base Detonating (refers to fuzes)
C-E	Communications Equipment
CHG	Charge
CKT	Circuit
COMM	Command (Command Center)
COMM-EQUIP	Communications Equipment
COMP	Composition
CPFF	Cost Plus Fixed Fee (refers to contracts)
CSG	unknown
CTG	Cartridge
CTR	Center
CY	Calendar Year
DEF	Defense
DIV	Division (refers to agency or company)
DS	Discard Sabot (refers to projectiles)
EA	Each
ECM	Electronic Countermeasures (jamming, etc.)
ENG DEV	Engineering Development
EST	Estimated
EW	Electronic Warfare (detection, jamming, etc.)
EXPL	Exploratory
FAC	Facility
FFPC	Firm Fixed Price Contract
FLCH	Flechette (anti-personnel weapon projectiles)
FSD	Full-Scale Development
FMS	Foreign Military Sale
FY	Fiscal Year (October 1 to September 30)
GFE	Government Furnished Equipment
GOCO	Government Owned, Contractor Operated
GOGO	Government Owned, Government Operated
GP	General Purpose (refers to bombs)
GREN	Grenade
HC	Hexachlorethane-Zinc Smoke Mixture
HE	High Explosive
HEAT	High Explosive Anti-Tank
HEDP	High Explosive, Dual Purpose
HEI	High Explosive-Incendiary
HEP	High Explosive-Plastic
HF	High Frequency radio
HQ	Headquarters
HV	Hypervelocity

ILLUM	Illuminating
IN	Inch
INCORP	Incorporate or incorporating
LB	Pound
LCHR	Launcher
LOG	Logistics
M&S	Management and Support
MAT	Materials
MGMT	Management
MIL	Military
MIL SPEC	Military Specification (meets stringent specifications set by DoD)
MM	Millimeter
MOD	Modification (refers to weapons or to contracts)
MPTS	Metal Parts
MSL	Missile
MT	Mechanical Time (refers to fuzes)
NAS	Naval Air Station
O&M	Operation and maintenance
OEM	Original Equipment Manufacturer (component manufacturer)
PD	Point Detonating (refers to fuzes)
PI	Point Initiating (refers to fuzes)
PO	Modification (refers to contracts)
PROJ	Projectile
PRX	Proximity (refers to fuzes)
PWP	Plasticized White Phosphorus (smoke and incendiary agent)
QTY	Quantity
R&D	Research and Development
RDT&E	Research, Development, Testing, and Evaluation
READ	Readiness
REP	Representative
RES	Research
RKT	Rocket
RPV	Remotely Piloted Vehicle (drone)
SD	Self-Destroy
SER	Series
SMK	Smoke
SP	Self-Propelled
SPEC	Specification or Special
SQ	Superquick (refers to fuzes)
SVCS	Services
S/N	Serial number
SYS	System
-T	With Tracer ("HE-T" = High Explosive with Tracer)
TAC	Tactical
TGT	Target
TNG	Training
TP	Target Practice
TTD	Total to Date (refers to contract amount)
TWT	Traveling Wave Tube (an electronic device used in radar, etc.)
VT	Proximity (refers to fuzes)

W/   With
W/O   Without
WP   White Phosphorus (smoke and incendiary agent)

Other Abbreviations

CBD   Commerce Business Daily
FOIA   Freedom of Information Act
FSC   Federal Supply Classification code
SMSA   Standard Metropolitan Statistical Area

Also see <u>Dictionary</u> <u>of</u> <u>Miltary</u> <u>and</u> <u>Associated</u> <u>Terms</u>. To learn what other abbreviations or acronyms mean, contact NARMIC.

Glossary

Fire Control   Equipment (usually electronic) to control the firing of weapons (especially on aircraft)

Appendices

APPENDIX 1: STANDARD REFERENCES ON COMPANIES

Most libraries have at least one of the following standard business references and business libraries probably have most of them. Your library may have a special resource written for your area (like Rich's Guide described below).

The Million Dollar Directory 1983
     Dun's Marketing Service
     Dun & Bradstreet Corp.
     Published in January 1983

This resource lists 115,000 U.S. businesses with net worth greater than $500,000 in three volumes totalling about 15,000 pages.

Vol. 1:   43,000 businesses with net worth greater than $1,670,000
Vol. 2:   36,000 with net worth between $847,000 and $1,670,000
Vol. 3:   36,000 with net worth between $500,000 and $847,000

Each volume has:

-- A master index to all 3 volumes and to America's Corporate Families, Dun's Industrial
     Guide, and Dun's Business Rankings.
-- Listings of businesses alphabetically.
-- Listings of businesses geographically (by state, city, and alphabetically with the
     address and SIC codes.
-- Listings of businesses by 4-digit SIC codes (each company may be listed under six
different codes).

Each of the listings in the alphabetical section includes the name, incorporation state if incorporated, whether the listing is of a subsidiary of a larger company, address, phone, sales to the nearest million dollars, total employees, stock exchange ticker symbol and exchanges on which it is traded, subsidiary names and principal products, division names, SIC codes of principal business listed in order of importance, description of principal activities/products, principal bank, accounting firm, legal counsel, officers and their titles, and directors or trustees.

This directory is quite comprehensive, covering most companies of interest and giving most of the information you would be interested in.

Here is a typical listing:

```
ROLM CORP (CA)
 4900 Old Ironsides Dr, Santa Clara, CA 95050
 Tel (408) 988-2900   Sales 300 MM   Emp 5174
 Tkr Sym  RM   Exch NYS
 MILSPEC COMPUTER DIV
 TELECOMMUNICATIONS DIV
 SIC 3573   Mnfr Electronic Computing Equipment
 Bk  Bank of America, Sunnyvale
 Accts  Arthur Andersen & Co.
*M Kenneth Oshman          Pr
*Leo J Chamberlain         Ex VP
*Robert B Maxfield         Ex VP
 James Kasson              VP Mgr
 Walter Lowenstein Jr      VP
 Richard Moley             VP Mgr
 Dennis Paboojian          VP Mgr
 Wayne J Mehl              VP Mgr
 Anthony V Carollo Jr      VP Mgr
 Robert K Dahl             Chief Fin Ofcr
*Michael H Morris          Sec
 O Stanfield               Tr
 Ed Van Bronkhorst         C Lester Hogan
 Robert Noyce              Jack L Melchor
```

Rolm had sales of $300 million in 1982 from its two divisions: the Military Specification Division (produces equipment that meets military specifications) and the Telecommunications Division. Its chief business is manufacturing electronic computing equipment. The board of directors comprises those people with a * by their name and those people listed at the end.

Standard and Poor's Register of Corporations, Directors, and Executives 1983
        Standard & Poor's Corporation
        Published in January 1983

    This resource lists about 10-15,000 U.S. businesses in about the same format as the Million Dollar Directory.

Vol. 1: Corporate Listings   2,486 pages (about 10-15,000 listings)
Vol. 2: Directors & Executives 1,428 pages
Vol. 3: Indexes   1,016 pages

-- The Corporation Listings have name, address, phone, corporate officers, accounting firm, primary bank and law firm, total sales, number of employees, stock exchanges where listed, directors, products, and SIC codes.
-- The Directors & Executives Listings have the name, birthdate, birthplace, education, occupation, employer, employer address, home address, and affiliations (corporations, universities, and associations for which the person is a member, director, partner, officer, etc.).
-- The Indexes list by 4-digit SIC code, state/major city and region of the state, cross-references of subsidiaries, divisions, and affiliated businesses listed in Volume 1.

California Manufacturers Register 1983
        Sponsored by the California Manufacturers Association
        Published by Times Mirror Press (LA Times)

    This resource has essentially the same information for each company as the Million

Dollar Directory except sales are given in ranges and it lists the date the company was established, sales office addresses, and whether the company is an importer or exporter.

Firms are listed in absolute alphabetical order followed by their subsidiaries with the same kind of information then listed for the subsidiaries.

This resource doesn't seem nearly as useful as the Million Dollar Directory since it has less information and the information doesn't seem as reliable.

Registers like this are also available for many other states. For example, Times Mirror Press publishes registers for Colorado, Oregon, Idaho, Arizona, and Washington. Each costs between $50 and $100 depending on the size of the state. Commerce Register, Inc. prepares State Directories of Manufacturers for each of the New England states, New York, New Jersey, and Pennsylvania for $40 - $80 depending on the size of the state.

Most state governments also produce industrial directories, listing even the small companies within the state. These usually list the companies by county and will sometimes indicate whether a firm is controlled locally or from the outside.

Moody's Industrial Manual
        Moody's Investors Service
        A Subsidiary of Dun & Bradstreet

This reference lists about 1,500 - 2,000 companies in two volumes totalling about 6,000 pages.

The companies are listed in four categories depending on how much the company has paid to be listed:

Complete Coverage	$3,500
Full Measure Coverage	$2,500
Comprehensive Coverage	$1,000
Standard Coverage	$ 0

Most of the data has been taken from annual reports filed with the Securities and Exchange Commission and is put into a standard format for the use of investors. Each company description takes 1/2 to 6 pages and includes a stock summary, a history of acquisitions, mergers, etc., subsidiaries (the percent ownership of each by the parent), a summary of plant property, officers, directors, auditors, number of stockholders, number of employees, executive office address & phone, and then detailed statements for the last several years for income, balance sheets, and financial & operating data. This last table includes several ratios indicating the profitability of the company:

        Percent net income (profit) to total assets.
        Percent net income (profit) to net worth (stockholders' equity).
        Total income (before income taxes) as a percent of gross sales.
        Net income (after taxes) as a percent of gross sales.

Corporation Descriptions
        Standard & Poor's Corporation

This directory also costs a fee ($400 - $800) to be listed. It lists most of the financial data from the annual report and the stock exchange for the last 2 or 3 years with a brief corporate description and long listings of stock and bond offerings and sales.

Moody's Handbook of Common Stocks

This handbook is issued 4 times per year and has a total of 900 stocks with one described on each 5" x 9" page. Each description has capsule stock information, Moody's one line comment on its prospects, a summary of stock prices, capitalization, earnings, and dividends, then a short company background description, recent financial developments, and prospects.

It then lists statistics for the last 10 years including gross revenues, percent operating profit margin (before tax), percent return on equity, and net income (after tax) amount. The description also includes the incorporation date and place, principal office address and phone, number of stockholders, stock held by institutions (investment companies, insurance companies, banks, and college endowment funds), and officers.

Ward's Directory of 55,000 Largest U.S. Corporations, 1981
Baldwin H. Ward Publications

This resource has 982 pages of listings for 47,000 private companies and 8,000 public corporations including the top 25,000 U.S. manufacturers. The last issue we found in our local libraries was for 1981.

The directory entries are all one-line long in tablular form divided into several sections:

-- An alphabetical listing of all 55,000 companies with address and chief executive officer(s), sales volume, number of employees, number of plants, major 4-digit SIC code, and codes indicating whether the company is a subsidiary of another (though no indication of which company it is a subsidiary), division, affiliate, joint venture, or private company.
-- A listing in Zip Code order with most of the same information.
-- A listing ranked within 3-digit SIC codes by sales size with most of the same information (and the total sales in each SIC category.
-- A listing of the 8,000 publicly-held corporations ranked by sales size within 3-digit SIC codes and listed with 30 fields of financial data taken from the annual report and 10-K forms including sales and after-tax profit as a percentage of sales and shareholder's equity.

Thomas Register of American Manufacturers -- Company Profiles (Volumes 10 and 11)
Thomas Register

These two volumes out of the 17 volume set (2,500 pages in all) has listings of 115,000 U.S. companies in alphabetical order with address, phone, asset range, company executives, location of sales offices, distributers, plants, service/engineering offices, and for some large conglomerates (who pay extra for the listing no doubt) a "complete profile of their subsidiaries and divisions and entire product lines."

Rich's Complete Guide to Santa Clara County's Silicon Valley
Rich's Enterprises

This guide ($45) contains 150 very detailed maps with 1,100 company locations cross-indexed with name, address, phone (by building), number of employees, and major product/service. You can also get 8 wall maps covering the same information, each 38" x 48" for $10 - $15 each.

The organizations listed in the Resource Center section may also be able to give you more information on companies from the newspaper clippings in their files.

Sources on Corporate Families

<u>America's</u> <u>Corporate</u> <u>Families</u> / <u>The</u> <u>Billion</u> <u>Dollar</u> <u>Directory</u> <u>1983</u>
     Dun's Marketing Service

     This resource lists 2,522 ultimate parent companies and over 28,000 subsidiary
companies with 29 million employees and $2.7 trillion of sales.

     To be listed, the parent company must have:

          Sales of $50 million
          10 or more locations
          Net worth of $500,000
          Controlling interest in one or more subsidiaries

     This directory has the following:

-- A roster of America's Corporate Families in alphabetical order.
-- An index of all division and subsidiary business names listed alphabetically and cross
     referenced to ultimate parent companies.
-- An alphabetical list of each parent company with the same information as is listed in
     the <u>Million</u> <u>Dollar</u> <u>Directory</u> followed by every division listed alphabetically with
     name, address, telephone, number of employees, SIC codes, divisional line of
     business, and chief executive. This is followed by all the subsidiaries listed by
     its level within the corporate family (some companies are subsidiaries of companies
     which are in turn subsidiaries of other companies), the same information as for the
     divisions, plus total sales.
-- An alphabetical listing of every parent and subsidiary by state and city.
-- An alphabetical listing of every parent and subsidiary by SIC code.

<u>Directory</u> <u>of</u> <u>Corporate</u> <u>Affiliations</u> <u>1983</u> -- "<u>Who</u> <u>Owns</u> <u>Whom</u>"
     National Register Publishing Co. Inc.
     A Macmillan, Inc. Company
     (prints the Advertiser Red Book)

     This resource lists about 3,500 parents and 20,000 affiliates and divisions. It
lists information similar to that in the <u>Million</u> <u>Dollar</u> <u>Directory</u>, but for many fewer
companies. It also lists divisions, subsidiaries, plants, and foreign subsidiaries with
the percentage of ownership by the parent. It has a cross-reference index of divisions,
subsidiaries, and affiliates, a geographic index by state/city, and a 2-digit SIC index
which is not very useful.

     [Also see Sections 4.B., 4.D., and 4.E.]

APPENDIX 2: WHY COMPANIES LIKE MILITARY CONTRACTS

In many ways, contracts from the Department of Defense for military work are very easy and lucrative. Below are listed several of the specific aspects of military contracts which make them attractive, especially to large corporations.

-- Cost-plus contracts guarantee that the company cannot lose. With a **cost-plus contract**, the contractor is paid for all the costs it incurs plus a profit based on a percentage of this cost. Most contracts are not cost-plus, but those that are can be very lucrative.

-- Typically the profit margin looks low for military companies, usually only a few percent. But this is because the profit rate is usually listed as a percent of sales. Since the government often supplies much of the machinery and facilities to a company to do the work, their investment is very low, so their profit as a percent of investment is very high. This can be seen in the profit as a percent of stockholder equity figures. Essentially all the company must do is hire the workers and write the proposals to the government. There is no risk to the company itself.

-- Risk to the company is very low. Contracts can be cancelled at any time, but (1) they usually are not, (2) it is usually possible to get follow-on contracts without much effort, (3) if a contract is cancelled the company can simply lay off the people working on the contract -- the equipment and facilities are often supplied by the government so if it is idled it is no big loss, and (4) contracts sometimes have a "cancellation fee" clause which commits the DoD to pay a termination penalty fee if it terminates the contract early.

-- If the company meets the specifications that the government has specified in the contract, then it gets the money -- even if the device doesn't work very well, or it is not what is needed, or if the specifications are bizarre.

-- The government pays for research and development work, but the ownership of the technology developed and knowledge of production techniques can frequently be transferred to the company's commercial business.

-- Contracts are frequently for long-term runs. Once awarded a development contract, the contractor usually can be assured of a 5- to 10-year development program, then 5 years of production, and then additional years of support and maintenance work. The military service which issued the contract then develops an allegiance to the company and is likely to award the contract for the next generation weapon system to the company.

-- Since military spending often expands when the rest of the economy is doing badly, military contracts provide a counter-cyclical balance to the company's civilian business.

-- The DoD pays on a monthly basis, providing a steady, secure cash flow.

-- Large military contractors frequently are operating in an oligopolistic market with many contracts only bid on by one company. The largest 8 firms in almost every sector of the defense procurement business garner more than 50% of the the value of contracts in that sector. The Top 25 firms get about 40% of all prime contracts and the Top 100 get about 75%. This means that these companies can often charge the DoD a much higher amount than if they were operating in a competitive free market.

-- Foreign military sales are frequently **sole-source** (only one company bids for the contract) which means they can make very high profits.

-- Selling to the Pentagon is in many ways easier than selling to numerous commercial customers since all the company's sales efforts can be directed to this one customer. Company personnel can serve on Pentagon advisory committees that make recommendations on what weapons to purchase. Company Political Action Committees (PACs) can give money to friendly Congressmembers to encourage them to fund the company's weapons. And the company's Washington lobbying office can promote the company's product and also promote increased military spending in general (by proclaiming a growing military threat from the Russians) so there is more business for the company and its competitors. (See the Iron Triangle by CEP for more on these practices.)

"History shows that whenever a company has been in bad shape and about to go out of the defense business, it has received the next award -- through a combination of desire, low bids, political reasons, and a good proposal effort." [Gansler, The Defense Industry, p. 49]

Determining a Company's Profit Rate from the Statement of Income

In a company's Annual Report and 10-K Report is usually a table called Selected Financial Data that lists various types of information for the previous 3 or 5 years. Most of the important financial information may be obtained from this table or from the more detailed tables that follow in these reports.

Below is a description of financial data and how it is used to calculate "the bottom line" (profitability).

Statement of Income

	Net Sales and Contract Revenues	(or Net Revenues)
(minus)	Cost of Sales	(or Cost of Production, Salaries, etc.)
(equals)	Gross Profit	(or Gross Margin or Gross Income)
(minus)	Engineering & Product Development Expenses	
(minus)	Selling Costs	(or Marketing Costs: Advertising, Salespersons Salaries, Depreciation of Sales Offices, Equipment, Etc.)
(minus)	General and Administrative Expenses	(Office Rent, Office Supplies, Management Salaries, Depreciation of Office Equipment)
(minus)	Interest Expense	(Interest on Bank Loans, Etc.)
(plus)	Interest Income	(Interest from Working Funds Held in a Bank or Money Market Fund)
(minus)	Other Expenses	(Losses on Sales of Equipment, Fire Losses, Etc.)
(equals)	Income Before Income Taxes	
(minus)	Provision for Income Taxes *	
(equals)	**Net Income**	(Profit)

* Note: The amount listed as Provision for Income Taxes may not actually be paid to the IRS. Because of accelerated depreciation of equipment and facilities and tax benefits (loopholes) for research and development, investment, stock option plans, foreign sales, etc., the amount paid may actually be less than listed. The actual Net Income (Profit) the company realizes is correspondingly higher. Accounting games like this make it very difficult to figure out how much profit a company really has made.

Profitability of a company is frequently measured in several ways:

-- Before Taxes.

-- After Taxes. As noted above, the ability of the company to make use of various tax benefits and the accounting department to report earnings in creative ways can greatly cut the amount of taxes actually paid to the IRS. After Tax profitability is thus not really the profit after payment of taxes, but the nominal rate if taxes had been paid at the rate that might be expected.

-- As a Percentage of (Net) Sales. Net Income divided by Net Sales x 100 = After Tax Profit as a Percentage of Sales

-- As a Percentage of Stockholders' Equity. **Stockholders' Equity** is the value of all the stock (at the time it was issued) owned by all the stockholders. Profit as a percent of this equity gives an indication of the amount of money each stockholder receives as a percent of the money they have invested; the increase in the value of the stock, however, is not considered.

-- As a Percentage of Total Capital Investment. **Total Capital Investment** is equal to Stockholders' Equity plus Long-Term Debt (loans from banks, etc.). This is the total amount of money invested and loaned to the company to buy the all the company's facilities, machinery, etc. (total capital).

[Also see Section 4.C.]

APPENDIX 3: CONGRESSIONAL HEARINGS

There are three basic sets of hearings of interest: hearings on (1) the DoD budget, (2) the weapons portion of the Department of Energy, and (3) military construction. For each of these categories there are hearings published from four different committees listed below. The easiest way to get them is to send a written request, along with mailing labels with your organization's address, to each of the committees in the spring. Hearings are generally held from February through May and published by mid- to late-summer. It is important to ask for each category of hearings separately if you want all of them, since the first (the DoD budget) is more frequently requested than the other two.

Senate Appropriations Committee
Russell Senate Office Building
Room 132
Washington, DC   20510
(202) 224-2726

Senate Armed Service Committee
Russell Senate Office Building
Room 212
Washington, DC   20510
(202) 224-2127

House Appropriations Committee
Capitol Building
Room H-218
Washington, DC   20515
(202) 225-2771

House Armed Services Committee
Rayburn House Office Building
Room 2120
Washington, DC   20515
(202) 225-4151

[Also see sections 3.B., 3.D., and 4.F.]